YOU CAN FIND MORE TIME
FOR YOURSELF EVERY DAY

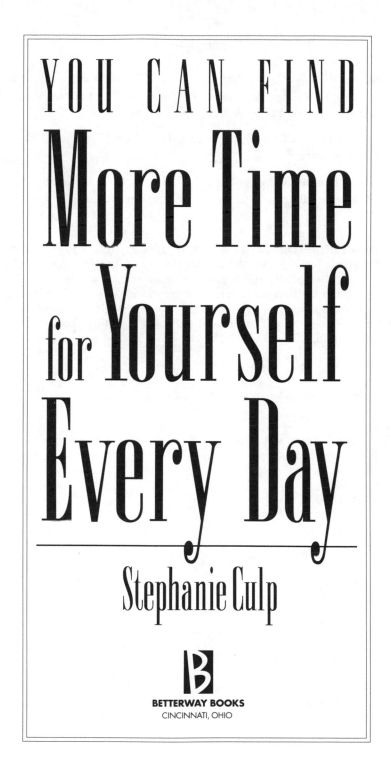

YOU CAN FIND
More Time
for Yourself
Every Day

Stephanie Culp

BETTERWAY BOOKS
CINCINNATI, OHIO

Permissions

LeBoeuf, Michael, *Working Smart*, published 1980 by Warner Books by arrangement with McGraw-Hill Book Company. Used by permission of Michael LeBoeuf represented by Arthur Pine Associates.

Mackenzie, Alec, *The Time Trap*, published 1990 by Amacom. Used by permission of Amacom.

Taylor, Harold, *Time Worp*, published 1993 by Harold L. Taylor, Harold Taylor Time Consultants, Inc. Used by permission of Harold Taylor.

98 97 96 95 94   5 4 3 2 1

Library of Congress Cataloging in Publication Data

Culp, Stephanie.
    You can find more time for yourself every day : a seven step plan that can change your life / by Stephanie Culp. — 1st ed.
        p.   cm.
    Includes index.
    ISBN 1-55870-358-6
    1. Time management. I. Title.
HD69.T54C86   1994
640'.43 — dc20   94-18456
                                                                      CIP

Edited by Beth Franks
Designed by Sandy Conopeotis
Cover illustration by Thomas Post

Quantity Discounts Available
This and other Betterway Books are available at a discount when purchased in bulk. Schools, organizations, corporations and others interested in purchasing bulk quantities of this book should contact the SPECIAL SALES DEPARTMENT of F&W Publications at 1-800-289-0963 (8 A.M.-5 P.M. Eastern Time) or write to this department at 1507 Dana Avenue, Cincinnati, OH 45207.

Acknowledgments

There's a great deal to be said in support of sticking with a winning team; luckily, Writer's Digest provides that for me. Bill Brohaugh does a good job of getting things started, and Mert Ransdell is great at making me think I got what I wanted. Hugh Gildea cheerfully makes himself available to my calls, and handles critical paperwork with much appreciated dispatch. My editor, freelancer Beth Franks, goes above and beyond the call of duty in every sense of the word. The book benefits from her many talents—from her flair for organization, to her creativity and common sense. And I benefit from her remarkable ability to put up with me.

Here in Wisconsin, I've been fortunate to add Diane Johnson to the team. Along with bringing me up to speed by turning my typed copy into computerized copy, she provided invaluable input and proofreading services that made life much easier for us all.

And while Jim Reed is no longer on the team, Fritz and Boca Culp still serve up a great deal of daily love and support on the home front.

Thank you all!

SEVEN STEPS TO FINDING TIME FOR YOURSELF EVERY DAY

PART I
Finding Time: The Plan

UNDERSTAND THE VALUE OF YOUR TIME AND
THE IMPORTANCE OF BALANCE IN YOUR LIFE

CHAPTER 1
The Value of Your Time   11
What's Your Time Really Worth? / $125,000 per Day / Where Does the
Time Go? / Time Wasters by the Dozens / Is It Worth It? / Balancing
Your Life / Facing Up to Change

DECIDE WHAT YOU WANT OUT OF LIFE — AND GO FOR IT

CHAPTER 2
The Power of Purpose   21
Your Personal Mission Statement / Turning Dreams Into Reality /
Strategies for Success

PRIORITIZE AND PLAN REGULARLY

CHAPTER 3
Prioritize and Plan Regularly   31
Establishing Your Priorities / Deciding What to Do / Prioritizing
Relationships / Learn to Say No / Planning Techniques That Work /
Efficient vs. Effective

CHAPTER 4

Converting Your To-Do List Into Projects   43

The Master List / Turning Unfinished Business Into Projects / Project
Planning From Start to Finish / Organizing Your To-Do List

CHAPTER 5

Managing Your Schedule Successfully   50

Using a Calendar or Planner Book / Plan Your Schedule by Scheduling
Your Plan / Getting Out the Door on Time / Early Risers Benefit / Strive
for Balance / Why We Do Too Much, and How to Stop / Special
Scheduling Situations / Finding Quality Family Time / Finding Time for
Romance / Putting Out Fires / Avoiding Crisis Management / Making
and Keeping Appointments / Coping With the Day That Gets Away /
Reducing Waiting Time

PART II

Overcoming Everyday Obstacles

CHAPTER 6

Pushing Past Procrastination   71

How We Procrastinate / Excuses, Excuses / Why We Procrastinate /
Great Escapes / Overcoming Procrastination / The Price of
Procrastination

CHAPTER 7

Eliminating Perfectionism   80

Why People Are Perfectionists / Time-Consuming Habits of
Perfectionists / Letting Go of Perfectionism

CHAPTER 8

Making Decisions   84

Are You Indecisive? / Why We Avoid Making Decisions / Overcoming
Indecision / Decide to Decide

CHAPTER 9

Learning to Delegate 90

Why We Refuse to Delegate / Ten Good Reasons to Delegate /
Delegating Dos and Don'ts / Delegating at Work / If You Are
Delegating / If You Are Being Delegated To / Delegating at Home /
The Household Chore List / Where to Find Help

CHAPTER 10

Eliminating Interruptions 103

Why We Allow Interruptions / Overcoming Interruptions / The Drop-in
Visitor at Work / The Telephone / Successful Telephone Screening / The
Interruption Circle / Self-Interruptions / Children

CHAPTER 11

Making Meetings Count 116

The Purpose of Meetings / Why We Have So Many Useless Meetings /
Making the Most of Meetings / If You Are Arranging the Meeting / If You
Are Attending the Meeting / Going Out for a Meeting

CHAPTER 12

Working Wisely 125

Why People Work Too Much / Time-Wasting Habits of the
Workaholic / What's Wrong With Working a Lot? / Overcoming
Workaholic Tendencies / Improve Procedures

PART III
Getting Organized

❻

SIMPLIFY AND STREAMLINE YOUR LIFE BY GETTING ORGANIZED

CHAPTER 13

Conquering Clutter 133

Excuses for Clutter / The Dollar and Time Cost of Clutter / Getting
Organized — Where to Start / Deciding to Dump / A Place for
Everything / Letting Go of Clutter / Getting Organized in Eight
Weekends / Don't Let Clutter in the Door / Do It Now / Taking It
With You

CHAPTER 14

Conquering the Paper Pile-Up 145

Paper Personalities / Bad Habits / Getting Organized — Where to Start /
Four-Step Paper Sorting System / Keeping Up With Your Reading /
Setting Up a File / Deciding to Dump / Organizing Your Desk / Letting
Go of Paper / Desktop Baskets / Controlling Paper / Streamline the
Paper in Your Life

CHAPTER 15

Giving Yourself the Electronic Edge 162

Computers / The Downside of Computers / Computer Dos and Don'ts /
E-Mail / Taking an Honest Look at Other Electronic Wonders

PART IV

Finding Time in Bits and Pieces

LOOK FOR WAYS TO SAVE TIME IN BITS AND PIECES

14 Telephone Time-Savers 175

11 TV Time-Savers 178

10 Commuting Time-Savers 181

41 Travel Time-Savers 184

21 Housework & Kitchen Time-Savers 193

16 Shopping Time-Savers 198

22 Holiday Time-Savers 201

INDEX 207

Introduction

As if you could kill time without injuring eternity.
—Henry David Thoreau

I f I only had more time . . ."

This universal refrain is uttered by somebody every day. Think about it. Did *you* have enough time yesterday to get everything done? What about last weekend? Come to think of it, what about *this* weekend? Will you be able to enjoy yourself, or will you spend most of that time doing chores and running errands? Do you get frustrated because you never have enough time to do what you really want to do?

Sooner or later, almost everyone falls prey to the daily rat race. Lurching from one chore or crisis to another, too many people find themselves exhausted at the end of the day, with little or no energy left to do what they really want to do. Long- and short-term goals—personal and professional—are all but abandoned in the wake of daily obligations. This depressing pattern can result in the treadmill blues for everyone from working couples with children to single people working hard to carve out a successful career.

If you are like most people, your number-one desire today is to find more time for yourself without taking an economic hit. You'd like to enjoy life a little. Perhaps you've started thinking about cutting back a bit . . . maybe you secretly dream of a life that is simpler and more secure with more time for friends and family, not to mention yourself. If this sounds like you, you're not alone. Today, millions of people are taking a new look at what is important in their lives. And finding more time for themselves is at the top of the list.

I JUST DON'T HAVE ENOUGH TIME

There are, of course, reasons why everyone runs out of time all the time. While we all know that time flies when you're having fun, these days, most of us are finding that time flies even when we're *not* having fun. These may be some of the reasons you don't have enough time for yourself:

- You agreed to go someplace that you really didn't want to go.
- You put off doing something until it became a crisis situation.
- You spend almost all of your time working, giving short shrift to your

1

personal needs, and family and friends.

- You set a goal so unrealistic that you gave up after a few weeks.
- You gave up planning your life some time ago — since so much happens, it's impossible to plan anything in advance.
- You don't take extra time to figure out your priorities since *everything* seems like a priority.
- You say yes when you'd rather say no, and you wind up hopelessly overcommitted.
- You spend time with people you don't even like anymore.
- Your house or office is chaotic because you don't have time to get organized.
- You know you could get twice as much done every day if it weren't for all the interruptions.
- You have to do everything yourself, because nobody can do things as well as you.
- You tend to put off making decisions, and end up putting papers in piles "just for now."
- You're always in meetings and can't control how much time they take.
- You've got stacks of material that you absolutely *must* read, but you never have the time.
- You don't set deadlines for getting things done because, actually, you like the pressure of doing things at the last minute.
- You think scheduling and planning take all of the spontaneity out of life, and refuse to schedule because you think it's for dullards.
- You hang on to everything because you "might need it someday"; consequently, you can never find anything when you *do* need it.
- You waste a lot of time waiting in lines and reception rooms and lose hours commuting every day.
- You never have time for yourself because you are too busy helping others.

Excuses Take Over

The truth is, reasons are often just excuses for bad habits. Bad habits tend to multiply, and before you know it, you feel like a hapless, helpless victim of circumstances every day. Then you find yourself saying things like:

- "I'm way too busy for that."
- "It's not my fault."
- "I'm too creative for that clock-watching stuff."
- "Organized people are just a bunch of nitpickers. I don't want to be like that."

- "I'll get around to it as soon as I can."
- "It's been another one of *those* days."
- "I meant to do it, but the day got away from me."
- "Planning is boring and wastes time."
- "I couldn't help it; traffic was murder."
- "I overslept."
- "I lost it."
- "I had to do something else instead."
- "I forgot."
- "Nobody else can do it but me, and I don't have time to do it now."
- "I can't do everything, can I?"
- "Who am I, Superman?"
- "Give me a break, I'm swamped."
- "Who has time for that stuff? Not me."

When you find yourself saying these things, it's a sure bet that not only do you not have time for yourself, you don't even have enough time to get the necessary things done in a normal day or week.

CHANGING HABITS

An honest look at how you (and others) spend your time means examining any bad habits you may have unwittingly adopted. By replacing these poor habits with good ones, you will have more time for yourself every day to do with as you see fit. Studies show that it takes twenty-one days to change a bad habit into a new, and hopefully better, habit. Put a new habit into place for only twenty-one days, and chances are, you will have banished the old habit for good.

Exchanging habits need not be difficult. But you will need a fair amount of willpower and resolve. That, along with some new skills that can be learned, will make changing habits relatively simple and painless. To replace bad habits with good ones, you must do the following:

- Face up to bad habits. Admit that you need to change.
- Research your options. Based on your particular needs, select the new, good habits that you intend to use to replace the old ones.
- Commit yourself to your new habit. If you tend to pile papers, stop yourself every time you find yourself about to put another piece of paper in a pile "just for now."
- Be enthusiastic about the new habit.
- Don't let fear of change get in the way and tempt you back into the old ways of doing things.
- Don't make excuses; put the new habits to work for you immediately.

- Don't try to change everything at once. Change some of the worst habits first; once that's been done, tackle another bad habit.
- Operate with the new habit religiously; eventually you'll do it the new way all the time without a second thought.
- Don't give up. When you see yourself falling back on old ways, consider it a temporary lapse. Tomorrow is a new day; you can start over then.
- Remember, all it takes to get started is a burst of motivation. Follow that with a commitment of only twenty-one days, and you will likely find yourself with a new habit that can keep you going down whatever path you have selected.

This Book Can Help You

If you really want to change to find more time for yourself every day, this book can help you. You'll discover the real value of your time, so you can take an objective look at how that time is spent. You'll discover how implementing a seven-step strategy can give you the basic tools you need to plan effectively to find more time for yourself. And, you'll read hundreds of ways to replace time-consuming habits with timesaving ones. Then select your favorite ideas from a smorgasbord of techniques that are guaranteed to give you more time on a daily basis.

If you are committed to changing your life in a meaningful way, read the entire book from start to finish. Make notes and establish a personal plan for saving and finding time for yourself. Then, keep the book handy so that when you run up against a new time waster, you can refer to the book for advice.

Success Is Up to You

In this age of instant gratification, some of you may be tempted to flip through the book and read only the sections that seem most pertinent to your situation. With this in mind, I have duplicated a few tips in some of the sections. I don't want you to miss out entirely just because you don't have time to read the entire book. But I don't really recommend the flip-through approach. Reading the entire book will not only provide the information you need to make immediate changes, it will also give you the opportunity to plan long-term changes in your life. This will not only save you time every day, it will help you get what you want out of life—today, tomorrow and well into the future.

Only you can make this book work for you. Your success in finding more time for yourself and eliminating the frustration, guilt and anxiety that go along with the time-starved rat race is entirely up to you. It can be as simple as resolving to put one timesaving idea into practice each week.

If you want a balanced life with more time for yourself, you can have it. Read this book, then go for it. And know that my personal wishes for your success go with you.

Seven Steps to Finding More Time for Yourself Every Day

UNDERSTAND THE VALUE OF YOUR TIME AND THE IMPORTANCE OF BALANCE IN YOUR LIFE

Your time is valuable; each moment, once spent, is gone forever. Remember that, and make it a point to lead a balanced life that includes time for all of the really important people and activities in your life.

DECIDE WHAT YOU WANT OUT OF LIFE— AND GO FOR IT

The biggest decisions you can make are those that concern what you really want to do and have in life. Set both short- and long-term goals, and make it a point to incorporate those goals into your action plan on a regular basis.

PRIORITIZE AND PLAN REGULARLY

Not everyone and everything is equally important. Pay more attention to prioritizing the people and activities in your life, and then plan accordingly. Make prioritizing and planning a daily ritual so that each of those days has maximum value for you.

ORGANIZE PROJECTS AND MANAGE YOUR SCHEDULE EFFECTIVELY

Everyone has the same twenty-four hours each day to spend; those who do it successfully do so by organizing projects logically and managing their schedule realistically. Learn how to master project management and scheduling skills, and you'll spend your time successfully as well.

WORK ON OVERCOMING EVERYDAY OBSTACLES

Everyday, time-consuming obstacles are often the result of poor habits. Those habits can easily be eliminated or replaced with better methods that can equal more time for you every day. Resolve now to change the habits that are holding you back and replace them with habits that will move you forward.

SIMPLIFY AND STREAMLINE YOUR LIFE BY GETTING ORGANIZED

Whether it's the piles of paper in your office or the clutter in your home, getting organized is a major time-saver. Eliminate what you don't need, organize the things that you must keep, and put some simple systems into place to keep things from getting out of control in the future.

LOOK FOR WAYS TO SAVE TIME IN BITS AND PIECES

Time saved in small increments adds up to more time for yourself. Take a look at how you do things every day and streamline how you get things done by saving time in bits and pieces. Then spend that time on yourself.

THOMAS PRIST

PART ONE

Finding Time: The Plan

Don't waste precious planet time.
   —Oprah Winfrey

F inding time for yourself involves changing the way you think about time and what you do with the time you have. In order to make that change, you need a healthy dose of commitment. Making changes in your life is easier if you take it one step at a time. Of the seven steps in this book, perhaps the most important are the first four, which will give you the master plan that guarantees you can have more time for yourself every day. The four steps that will go into your master plan are:

Step 1   Understand the Value of Your Time and the Importance of Balance in Your Life

Step 2   Decide What You Want Out of Life—and Go For It

Step 3   Prioritize and Plan Regularly

Step 4   Organize Projects and Manage Your Schedule Effectively

Putting these steps in place in your life requires some thought and action on your part so that you can make the plan uniquely yours and so that you can reap maximum benefits from that plan.

Once you have mastered the four steps that go into the plan for finding more time for yourself, you will want to increase that time for yourself by implementing the final three steps:

Step 5   Work on Overcoming Everyday Obstacles

Step 6   Simplify and Streamline Your Life by Getting Organized

Step 7   Look for Ways to Save Time in Bits and Pieces

As the old saying goes, there's no time like the present, so why not start putting the Seven Steps into your life today. Each step that you thoughtfully incorporate into your life will bring you the success you seek in finding more time for yourself every day.

1

Understand

the Value of Your Time

and

the Importance of

Balance in Your Life

Your time is valuable; each moment, once

spent, is gone forever. Remember that, and

make it a point to lead a balanced life that

includes time for all of the important

people and activities in your life.

CHAPTER ONE

The Value of Your Time

Many people assume that they can probably find many ways to save time. This is an incorrect assumption for it is only when you focus on spending time that you begin to use your time effectively.
—Merrill Douglass

While you are scrambling just to keep up, other people are finding enough time to do not only what they have to do, but also what they want to do. Their lives are balanced, and they control how they spend their time. And they are working with the same amount of available time that you are: twenty-four hours each day, 365 days a year. If you asked these people what their secret is, they probably couldn't give you a simple answer. But one thing is clear: They are acutely aware of the value of time as a resource, and use it with that value firmly fixed in their minds. Alec Mackenzie, author of *The Time Trap* (Amacom), describes time as a unique resource that "cannot be accumulated like money or stockpiled like raw materials. We are forced to spend it, whether we choose to or not, and at a fixed rate of 60 seconds every minute. It cannot be turned on and off like a machine or replaced like a man. It is irretrievable."

Each moment, once spent, is gone forever. But today, the actual dollar value can often be applied to so many of the hours of the day. Before you can begin to change habits and regain control of your time and your life, it's important to truly understand the value of your time so you can put everything else in perspective.

Understanding the real value of your time is the starting point to finding time for yourself every day. This chapter is the gateway to that information, and should help you not only put a price on your time, but also start moving toward the balanced lifestyle that results from understanding how to make good use of the time available.

WHAT'S YOUR TIME REALLY WORTH?

Most people have heard the phrase "time is money." Nevertheless, value all too often is assigned only vaguely to time spent working, and frequently not at all to other expenditures of time. Knowing the value of your time can be a key tool and a deciding factor in how to prioritize the use of the time available. Consider Bob, for example, a retail manager who makes $30,000 a year. He works fifty 40-hour weeks with two weeks' paid vacation each year. Each of Bob's hours at work is worth $15. If Bob wastes one hour per day for one year, it will cost the company he works for a total of $3,750. Louise works the same number of hours, but she's an executive at a computer firm, with a yearly salary of $150,000. Each of Louise's hours at work is worth $75. If Louise wastes one hour each day, she will cost her company a whopping $18,750 per year! And this doesn't include the value of a full benefit package that is paid for by both Bob's and Louise's employers.

What about placing a value on time that doesn't have a dollar value? Suppose you don't have a job that pays a salary, but you work all day anyway. The homemaker and parent works long, hard hours, but because society hasn't assigned a dollar amount to that work, those services are often taken for granted and grossly undervalued by others. To attempt to place a dollar value, let's look at the services provided.

He or she cooks two to three meals a day; cleans the house; babysits round the clock; provides taxi, errand and shopping services; does the laundry and irons clothes; makes appointments with doctors, repair people, etc.; and entertains (parties for children, dinners for friends and associates).

And those are only some of the services provided. From decorating to sewing to paying bills, the homemaker keeps everything and everybody in the family organized. Even if you could place a dollar value on the combination of those services, it's almost impossible to figure against the number of hours worked. The homemaker often is the first person up in the morning and the last one to bed at night. You can attempt to place a dollar value on the job by trying to figure the total cost of all the different services being provided. It would take these professionals—all working part-time—to fill the shoes of one homemaker:

Babysitter	Party Planner
Bookkeeper	Secretary/Receptionist
Caterer	Shopping and Errand Service
Chef	Taxi Driver
Housekeeper or	
Cleaning Crew	

By examining the current rates charged by these professionals, you could conceivably arrive at a per-hour value placed on the homemaker's time. Since fees change, and since it is difficult to pinpoint the number of hours worked, it's impossible to figure the rates of all those services and apply them to the average homemaker and parent. But it's clear the homemaker is worth a bundle.

Take a pencil and figure out what your time is worth. Determine your hourly dollar value based on your gross salary and the number of hours you work. Then the next time you are tempted to fritter away an hour fussing with the batteries in the pencil sharpener or some other such nonsense, stop and think about how much that time is worth. If you're not spending your time doing a task that is at least equal to the dollar value of your hourly time, it's probably a task you shouldn't be doing at all. And the next time you find yourself procrastinating or wasting time in some other way, be honest with yourself. Your time is worth money—whether you are wasting that time or making good use of it.

$125,000 PER DAY

If you're having trouble determining the value of your time and making choices based on the value, you might want to study the example of Houston Oilers tackle David Williams. Mr. Williams chose to miss a game to be with his wife during the birth of their child. His employer, the Houston Oilers, promptly assessed him a fine of $125,000. Mr. Williams is unrepentant, and the Houston Oilers stand by their action. That makes for one very expensive baby. Clearly David Williams decided that being with his wife and newborn was worth more than money.

WHERE DOES THE TIME GO?

Once you've figured out—or decided—what your time is worth, you need to take a look at how you're spending it. The most common way to do this is to keep a time log for a week or two. Essentially, this involves writing down just about everything you do, noting how much time you spent doing any one thing. If you spend fifteen minutes on the phone with your mother, write it down. If you spend twenty minutes daydreaming, write it down. If you spend one hour in the sales meeting, note that, and if you spend thirty minutes preparing the sales figures for the boss write that down as well. A few hours on your time log might look like this:

    9:00- 9:15   Kibitzed with Ken in the coffee room
    9:15- 9:30   Talked with Mom on the phone
    9:30-10:30   Sales Meeting

10:30-11:00   Worked on Sales Figures Report
11:00-11:20   Daydreaming
11:20-12:00   Returned phone calls

Generally, after keeping a time log for a couple of weeks, it becomes glaringly apparent that you are wasting time in several different ways. You may also see a pattern where other people are wasting your time (which you allow), and—if you're honest—you'll even see where you have been guilty of wasting others' time. In fact, there are lots of ways to waste valuable time. Be alert for some of the following time wasters in your life.

Time Wasters by the Dozens
- Unexpected drop-in visitors
- Meetings that have no objective or are spontaneous (unscheduled)
- Disorganization
- Overinvolvement
- Office trivia
- Uncooperative people (including yourself)
- Procrastination
- Watching too much TV
- Gossip
- Constant crisis management
- Lollygagging in bed (when you should be getting up)
- Acute perfectionism
- Worrying
- Nagging
- Indecision
- Needlessly feeling guilty
- Busywork
- Junk mail
- Daydreaming
- Bureaucrats
- Interruptions
- Duplicate efforts
- Professionals who make you wait
- Regretting what wasn't done ("If only I had . . .")
- Resisting change ("Yes, but we can't do that . . .")
- Computer games (when you should be doing computer work)
- Reading unnecessary journals and magazines
- Minutiae
- Avoiding issues and problems

- Doing everything yourself instead of delegating
- Unnecessary telephone calls

Most people resist keeping a time log, even though two weeks' worth of it invariably highlights wasted time that could easily be turned into *saved* time. So if you really want to find some time for yourself, inventory your time with the log and keep your eyes peeled for time wasters as you go along.

Never lose sight of what you're worth per hour. While you're filling your time log with notations like, "Stopped at the cleaners and drug store — 1 hour," remember what that hour cost you. Why didn't you hire the kid down the street for a few dollars to do this? If you had, you'd have had one hour for yourself. If you resist hiring people to help you out, ask yourself if how you're spending your time really makes sense.

Is It Worth It?

- Is it worth $20 to me to have Saturday all to myself to spend however I wish, or would I rather do all the yard work myself and be exhausted?
- Is it worth $10 a week for me to drop all the shirts off at the professional launderers, or would I rather spend three hours each week doing them myself? Is my time really worth only $3.33 per hour? For $40 a month, I could have an entire day (twelve hours) back for myself.
- Is it better use of my time to spend all day Saturday cleaning house or to spend it with the kids doing something fun? If I hired a housekeeper to come in only two Saturdays each month, would it be worth the $50 per month to me to have those two Saturdays back (or $25 per Saturday)?
- If I work all day, is it fair that I then come home and work all night getting dinner, cleaning up, and getting the kids ready for bed? Could I insist that at least one or two nights a week I don't have to do these things, because my spouse will take over? If he or she refuses, is it worth it to me to take the family out to eat or order take-out food once or twice a week so that I can have an extra two hours each week (or one full eight-hour day per month)?
- Is it worth it to buy things from catalogs and order over the phone, even if it means paying shipping charges? Or would I rather spend all day Saturday and a half tank of gas in the car running all over town to shop?
- Is it worth running to three different supermarkets all over town to save money on certain items, or should I save two hours of my time and spend $20 more at only one supermarket?
- Would I be willing to make less money at work by working fewer hours so that I can have more time for myself and my family?
- Besides being a friend and family member, there is nothing that I do

that someone else can't do. Therefore, is it worth it to me to insist on painting the entire house myself if it means I will have no time for my family and friends for the next nine weekends?

BALANCING YOUR LIFE

Taking a good, hard look at the dollar value of your time as well as how you currently spend that time often reveals that your life lacks balance. How much of your time is devoted to work every week? How much to family and friends? How much for personal pursuits and health and fitness? And what about the spiritual side of your life? Are you so busy you've fallen back on a hastily uttered prayer or meditation in the face of a crisis?

Most people can benefit from putting more balance into their lives in the following areas: friends and family, health and fitness, home, personal self-development, professional/career, and spiritual.

Obviously, the category of professional/career will take up a major portion of most people's lives, but it's still important to also make room for friends and family, health and fitness, spiritual needs, your home, and personal self-development on a regular basis. Along with illuminating time wasters, your time log should help you realize where your life is out of balance. If you never pay attention to your own health and fitness, now is the time to vow to schedule three 20-minute walks or exercise sessions into your week. If you have let your spiritual needs slip by the wayside, perhaps ten minutes a day in quiet meditation or spiritual reading will put that back into your life in a meaningful way.

Facing Up to Change

Review your time log several times until you have recognized not only what you are doing wrong, but what you can do right. Ask yourself these questions when analyzing how you spend your time:

- Is my life balanced? If not, what do I need to incorporate into my life so that it's more balanced?
- Do I allow needless interruptions to take up large amounts of my time?
- How many telephone calls do I really need to take, and how many do I really need to make?
- Have I done a good job of delegating? If not, where could I save more time for myself by doing just that?
- What activities can I eliminate to save more time for myself?
- What areas of my life need to be streamlined to facilitate how I use my time?
- Do I have too much paper, reading material, and clutter in my life?

- Did I always handle my priorities first, or do I allow myself to be distracted from what's really important?
- Am I working with outdated systems or equipment that waste time or result in duplicated efforts?
- What can I change so that I can have more time for myself every day?

Analyzing the value of your time, and looking at how you currently spend or waste that time, is the eye-opener that prepares you for doing what needs to be done to find more time for yourself every day. If you're convinced that you can't possibly make room for the six key areas that add up to a balanced lifestyle, try making small changes at first.

Friends and Family: If you never have time for friends and family make it a point to spend Thursday evenings on a "date" with your spouse or significant other. Order tickets to an event once every six weeks and take a friend with you. If you have children, plan three hours every Saturday to spend with them doing something fun—no matter what. If you can't do it every week, do it every other week, but make it a commitment that you stick to.

Health and Fitness: You should exercise at least thirty minutes three times a week. Take a walk after dinner. Get up thirty minutes earlier so you can exercise. Don't circle the mall parking lot looking for the parking space closest to the door; park far away and walk. Take the stairs instead of the elevator. Gradually build up the time you spend until you have a healthy habit of exercising every week.

Home: Get the house in order, even if it takes the next four weekends to catch up. Clean and organize everything, and then put some simple systems in place so that you can maintain an organized and serene house that serves as a peaceful haven to you and your family.

Personal Self-Development: Make an appointment at least once every six weeks to do something for your own development and personal maintenance. Get new glasses. Sign up for a class that you are interested in. Set aside thirty minutes each day to read things you want, but aren't required, to read.

Professional/Career: If you find yourself working all the time, cut back slowly. Refuse to work on Sundays, no matter what. Or refuse to work past 5:00 P.M. on Fridays. Or commit to working on Saturday morning only, leaving the afternoon free for other things.

Spiritual: Whatever your beliefs, devote time to them regularly. If you don't go to church or synagogue, spend five minutes a day reading a meaningful meditation. Then try to live that meditation during the day.

Author Sandra Felton perhaps summed it up best when she said, "Some of us try to live to the fullest by gathering too many things, doing too many activities, having too many commitments. . . . We can balance our lives by continuing the choices we make which cause us to live this way." If you have a hard time deciding how to put a value on your time or put balance back into your life, remember that a balanced lifestyle is more rewarding and usually lasts longer than one that is not. Live your life with that in mind, and then learn to make each moment count.

DECIDE WHAT YOU WANT

OUT OF LIFE—

AND GO FOR IT

THE BIGGEST DECISIONS YOU CAN MAKE ARE THOSE THAT CONCERN WHAT YOU REALLY WANT TO DO AND HAVE IN LIFE. SET BOTH SHORT- AND LONG-TERM GOALS, AND MAKE IT A POINT TO INCORPORATE THOSE GOALS INTO YOUR ACTION PLAN ON A REGULAR BASIS.

CHAPTER TWO

The Power of Purpose

Establishing priorities and using your time well aren't things you can pick up at Harvard Business School. If you want to make good use of your time, you've got to know what's important, and then give it all you've got.

—Lee Iaccoca

Almost everybody knows somebody who is successful in what they do. How often have you heard it said about such people that "that's what they always wanted." If this is someone who's reaped success professionally, it's easy to say that he was just "lucky," or that success came "easy" to him. If it's someone who reaped personal success, the tendency can be to attribute success to other cliches such as, "Well, she always did get whatever she wanted without trying."

And while you're busy looking at other successes—from the wealthy CEO to the happy wife and mother—you aren't doing anything substantial to achieve what they achieved: to devote time to getting what you want out of life. You don't have time, you tell yourself. You're not lucky. It's silly to hope for such things because they'll never happen. While you're having these less-than-pep talks with yourself, you are wasting time rather than spending it pursuing what you want out of life. Maybe the real reason is you don't know what you want.

Most people who achieve personal or professional success can point to exactly how they did it. Luck may have played a small role, but most successful people know what they want, and set goals to accomplish those things. Finally, they set aside enough time on a regular basis to work toward achieving their goals.

Now that you've completed Step 1, and know the value of time and importance of balance in your life, the next step is to give some serious thought to what you really want out of life.

It really is possible to have what you want—even if what you want is simply to have more time for yourself. This chapter takes you through the important steps necessary to deciding and working toward what you want out of life, and therefore, how to really spend your time for yourself.

YOUR PERSONAL MISSION STATEMENT

The idea that you can find more time for yourself every day seems simple enough. But, obviously, it can be much easier said than done. Maybe the main reason finding extra time is so difficult is that the purpose for that time is ill-defined. What is your purpose in life? What is your mission? Developing an answer to that question can mean the difference between success and failure in your efforts to find more quality time for yourself. A belief system rooted in a personal mission will propel you to achieve the goals that are grounded in a mission statement and results that are strictly goal driven. Charles Garfield, author of *Peak Performers* (Morrow), is careful to note the distinction:

> Every day, people with no particularly deep purpose achieve a lot of goals. They complete reports; make sales; ship orders; check off everything on their to-do lists. In the short run, those completions feel good. And they gradually fit together to make a trap. If, over time, the people checking off one goal after another do not see their work contributing to a larger pattern and an overall objective, they can develop the treadmill blues.

A logical starting point for finding more time for yourself is to determine your mission in life. Don't fall back on a vague idea or a fuzzy notion of your mission; think about it, and write it down. Your personal mission statement may be only a sentence or two, or it could be several paragraphs. Getting started can be difficult, so ask yourself this question: *"What would I want people to say about me if I died tomorrow?"*

Then picture everyone standing around your grave or at the wake. "Boy, Bob sure did play a mean game of golf—and he hated to lose, that's for sure." Or, "Nobody could make rhubarb pie as good as Phyllis, I'll say that." Or, "I really didn't know Dad too well. He was always working." There's nothing wrong with golfing, baking or working, of course. But surely you want your life to mean more than that when all is said and done. By working out what your mission is now—before it's too late—you can have, and use, time wisely every day. Charles Garfield defines *mission* this way:

> Mission is bound by no preconceived limitations. It inspires people to reach for what could be and to rise above their fears and preoccupations with what is. Mission starts with determining what you really care about and want to accomplish, and committing yourself to it. . . . aligns

personal ambition, job, and organization; preserves health and family; and is grounded in the peak performer's values — those basic qualities that used to be known, in less ambiguous times, as character.

Mission statements can cover all areas. Consider the following examples.

Erica C:

My mission is to find a loving person who shares my values and beliefs; and who will be my life mate and raise a family with me. I want to be a loving woman to friends and family, and to give something back to the community consistently. I want to be a good example of a loving wife and mother, trusted friend, and pillar of the community.

Jack S:

My mission is to achieve according to my highest potential in creative fields. I want to be a painter who creates pieces that are understood and appreciated by people not only now but long after I am gone. It is important to me to create works of beauty and feeling to share with as many people as possible.

Lucinda W:

I want to be a spokesperson for my people; I want to always serve as an example of the modern woman with the refinements of my cultural heritage. I want to help others of my race who are less fortunate than I am, and want to help make sure that the historical traditions of our culture are not lost.

George S:

My mission is to put my energies and money to use to benefit the human race. I want to be a loving husband and father and I want to be generous and kind to people that I do business with. I want to always be fair but firm, and I want to know that after I am gone I will be remembered for my integrity as well as my efforts.

Your mission statement will be uniquely yours, of course. Perhaps you are passionate about wildlife or the environment. Or maybe government service is your mission — maybe you feel the only way to help people is to ultimately be governor of your state. Or perhaps you just want to be a kind and honorable human being. Whatever. Give it some thought, and write your mission statement down. Then keep that statement with you. Put it in your wallet or next to your bed, or slip it in your calendar so you see it every day. If you really want to keep it in front of you, tape it to the bathroom mirror, and you'll be constantly reminded of your mission in life.

A few years from now, it's possible that you will revise or refine it. But for now your mission statement will be the arrow that points the way to action for you.

TURNING DREAMS INTO REALITY

If you want to turn your mission into action, the next step is to write down your goals. Setting goals is the first step to achieving them, obviously. And all kinds of goals can be considered. These are examples of goals that many people set at one time or another:

- Save more money
- Get a new job
- Buy a house
- Move to another state
- Buy a new car
- Get a promotion
- Make more money
- Get organized at home and at the office
- Spend more time with my family every week
- Own my own business within two years
- Write a book
- Take six months off and travel
- Meet someone I can fall in love with and marry
- Lose weight and get fit
- Learn Spanish
- Make friends with influential politicians
- Find more time for myself

This is not to suggest that any of those goals are necessarily your goals. Your goals will be specific to your dreams and ambitions and aligned with your personal mission in life. Use your mission statement as a touchstone. If you find yourself going off in several different directions, or, for example, if you find yourself setting goals just to have more material things — and those material things aren't bringing you the satisfaction you thought they would — review your mission statement. It will bring you back to what is really important in life so that you can set goals that will complement your mission and bring you a lifestyle that is rewarding in far more than the material sense. Goals are not the *same* as your mission, but they should not *get in the way of* your mission either. Goals should either complement or be aligned with your personal mission. Setting goals with this in mind will give you all the direction you need to get what you really want out of life.

But no matter what your dreams consist of, one of the first steps to achieving them is to write them down. If you don't write your goals down, they will stay in the dreamlike state of the "I wish" mantra. I wish I could go to Tahiti. I wish I could run for city council. I wish I could speak another language. I wish I had more money in the bank. I wish I had more time for myself.

If you really want something, and it aligns with your personal mission (or at least doesn't conflict with it), write it down. But don't do what Mary G. did. She wrote her goals down on paper, and then filed them. They didn't surface again until two years later when she was cleaning out her files. In the meantime, of course, her goals were no better than wishes that didn't come true.

So, write your goals down. Studies show that your chances of achieving your goals increase significantly if you just *write them down*!

Once you have written your goals down, review them to see if they are realistic and achievable and to determine whether you are willing to make the necessary sacrifices to accomplish those goals. A goal cannot succeed without three components:

1. *The goal must be realistic.* You may want to buy a new car, but if you are unemployed and have no money in the bank, this may not be a realistic goal. Make sure your goals are in line with your circumstances and potential.

2. *The goal must be achievable.* If you want to write a book, don't plan to do it in three weeks' time. It's simply not possible. Don't set goals that aren't attainable.

3. *You must be willing to make any necessary sacrifices.* If your goal is to lose weight and get fit, you will need to make some sacrifices. You will have to change some habits and attitudes and begin eating differently and less, and exercising more. If you're not willing to do that, you won't be successful. Make sure you're willing to make any necessary sacrifices before you commit to a goal.

Strategies for Success

Once you have settled on goals that fulfill those requirements and once you have written the goals down, you can start making plans to achieve those goals. These guidelines will help you keep on track.

Be consistent. Set goals that are consistent with your personal mission, as well as those you are close to. It can be counterproductive, for example, to have goals your spouse is totally opposed to. At work, of course, your goals should be in line with the company's mission statement and the company's expectations of you. On the other hand, don't get caught in the trap of constantly living your life by setting goals that others want for you. If your family wants you to settle down and work at the plant for the next twenty years, and you want to take a chance on your own business, don't automatically opt for the plant. Explore the options for a realistic run at owning a business, and if it looks achievable and you are willing to make the necessary sacrifice, then go for it.

Be specific about your goal. What, exactly, is it you want? Do you want to move? If so, where exactly do you want to live? Do you want to be an elected official? If so, precisely what office would you like to hold? At the same time, allow yourself some flexibility. Life brings changes, and like life, sometimes goals undergo change as well.

Commit yourself to attaining your goal. Don't just write it down and then adopt a wait-and-see attitude. Commitment leads to action, and action leads to success.

Always give each goal a deadline. A goal without a deadline is guaranteed to languish absentmindedly in the back of your thoughts forever. Create a realistic deadline so you have something to shoot for. If you want to start your own business, give yourself a deadline for researching the idea, raising the money, and taking the plunge. If you want to start a landscaping business, for example, give yourself three months to research the idea, and six months to raise the capital. Add three months to find a facility and stock the necessary supplies and equipment. You will be in business one year from today.

Divide and conquer. Break each goal down into manageable segments. Instead of thinking about how long it will take to save $500, think about saving only $10 each week. Before the year is out, you'll have the money in the bank.

Watch for roadblocks. List the obstacles that may stand in the way of achieving your goal. Be realistic about *all* obstacles, including your own tendency to procrastinate, for instance. Then map out a strategic plan on how to overcome those obstacles. (Part Two can help you overcome obstacles such as the inability to make decisions, the tendency to procrastinate, and other self-defeating roadblocks that we tend to put in our own way.)

Give your goals top priority. Turn your goals into personal projects. Then when others call you, wanting you to do something for them, tell them you are knee-deep in a project of your own. (For more specific suggestions on how to do this, see chapter three.)

Be enthusiastic. Enthusiasm is catching, and provides a much better cornerstone for success than does pessimism or a lackadaisical attitude.

Share your goal with others. If others know about your goal, their enthusiasm and energy can be a positive force that pushes you along toward success. And, when you let others know what you want, often people are able to help you when you least expect it. Be selective about who you share your goals with. Close friends and family can be your biggest boosters — and in turn you can cheer them on as well.

Have long-range goals as well as short-range goals. Where do you want your life to be five years from now? Start planning now and set a goal for yourself. But don't neglect short-term goals. You want a promotion this year, not five years from now.

Avoid setting too many goals at once. If you have a dozen goals, you'll be overwhelmed before you begin, and you won't be able to give each goal the attention it requires for successful accomplishment. Don't set any more than four or five goals at any one time. When one goal has been realized, add another one.

Avoid making all your goals materialistic. You may want a promotion or a new car. But you may want a loving relationship with someone whom you can spend the rest of your life with, too. Or, you may want to spend more time with your family each week. Balance your financial goals with goals for self-development, health and relationships.

Be careful what you wish for, you might get it. Occasionally we'll set a goal, and then as we move toward achieving it, realize we didn't want that particular thing after all. Review your goals regularly, and revise them when necessary — or eliminate them altogether and set new ones.

Affirm the positive. Use affirmations to help keep you on track. If you want to live in a more organized manner, every day tell yourself that through positive affirmations. Say, "I am an organized person who is in control of my surroundings and my life." In the meantime, work toward that goal by clearing the backlog of clutter and establishing simple systems so you *are* organized and in control every day.

Visualize success. Visualize yourself after you have achieved your goal. Visualize yourself every day as being thinner and more fit. Imagine yourself as the president of your own business.

Look for the silver lining. Always be alert to hidden opportunities. When an offer comes your way, before you turn it down, make sure it doesn't hold a hidden opportunity that would help you move closer to accomplishing your goals. At work, if the boss asks you to take on more work than anyone else, do that work, and do it well. Then point to it later as an example of why you are qualified for a promotion.

Give it time. Each week, schedule some activity that will help you achieve your goals. If you want to write a book but have a full-time job, work on your book idea for four hours each week. At the end of the month, you should have a proposal ready to send out to publishers.

Flock with birds of a feather. Associate with people who have goals similar to yours and who are high achievers. You'll benefit from the communication, association, and possibly even the networking. You can start a small group of like-minded people, or you can join an organization that already exists with people who have goals and interests similar to yours. Or, you can join a group as part of the process of achieving your goal. If you want to experience the great outdoors, for example, you might want to join a hiking club. Perhaps not everyone is there to commune with nature, but the process (hiking) is the same for everyone in the group.

Keep your eyes on the prize. Never lose sight of why you have set a goal in the first place. Keep that personal benefit firmly in mind during the time it takes to achieve that goal.

Establishing your own personal mission statement and setting goals will help you decide what you want to do, who you want to be, and what you want to acquire. It will give you the power of purpose, so that you can use your time to become who and what you want to be and to do what you want to do.

3

PRIORITIZE AND PLAN

REGULARLY

NOT EVERYONE AND EVERYTHING IS EQUALLY
IMPORTANT. PAY MORE ATTENTION TO
PRIORITIZING THE PEOPLE AND ACTIVITIES IN YOUR
LIFE, AND THEN PLAN ACCORDINGLY. MAKE
PRIORITIZING AND PLANNING A DAILY RITUAL SO
THAT EACH OF THOSE DAYS HAS MAXIMUM VALUE
FOR YOU.

CHAPTER THREE

Prioritize and Plan Regularly

Plan for the future, because that's where you are going to spend the rest of your life.
— Mark Twain

Prioritizing and planning are at the heart of successful time management and the ability to find time for yourself. If finding time for yourself is a priority and you plan for that priority, you can find more time for yourself. It's that simple. Yet, the concept of planning is often met with great resistance from otherwise sensible and intelligent people. "Well," they say, "that's all quite well and good, but I just don't have time to plan." Or, "Even the best laid plans go awry. Why plan, when anything could happen at any time (and usually does), throwing a monkey wrench into everything?"

These people dig their heels in and point to others as examples of why it's inadvisable to get into the prioritizing and planning habit. Citing compulsive overorganizers, clock watchers and nervous nitpickers, they explain away their failure to prioritize and plan. The result is that they have no control over their time; each day is virtually up for grabs. Whatever happens, happens. Often what happens eats up all the time available. People who endure these kinds of days find themselves chronically frustrated, resentful and annoyed.

But it isn't necessary to be compulsive or obsessive to plan and prioritize well. Some simple skills, along with a few daily habits, can help you regain control over your time so there's some left for you. This chapter will help you develop the habit of planning and prioritizing regularly so that you really can spend more time doing what you want to do.

ESTABLISHING YOUR PRIORITIES

Learning to prioritize on a daily as well as a long-term basis is the quickest route to getting what you want out of life. People generally prioritize haphazardly, and miss out on the benefits that result from a more thoughtful approach. Prioritizing, like planning, needs to be done faithfully and habitually. To learn to prioritize effectively, you'll need to give some studied attention to the people, events and obligations in your life so you can assign value accordingly. Only you can really determine who and what is important in your life. To do this, you'll need to be brutally honest with yourself so that you can prioritize on a daily, as well as long-term basis. To assess your current prioritizing skill, answer the following questions:

- Do you know what your purpose or mission in life is and do you prioritize with that in mind?
- Do you have realistic goals that you're working toward on a regular basis?
- Do you know how many projects you have taken on, and which ones are the most important?
- Do you have deadlines for your goals and projects?
- Do you plan your life by taking the time to schedule your day, week and month in advance, keeping your priorities in mind as you schedule?
- Do you review your priorities on a regular basis?
- Do you say no when you need to?
- Are you spending more time with people you care about and less time on social obligations that have no meaning for you?

Deciding What to Do

If you answered "yes" to most of those questions, prioritizing is probably not much of a problem for you. But, if you answered "no" to most of those questions, you need to pay more attention to prioritizing your life on a regular basis. If you have trouble prioritizing, remember that your priorities should relate to your mission and your goals as well as your obligations. And your obligations should be just that — don't turn something into an obligation that doesn't have to be one. For example, you needn't feel obligated to go to a party if, deep down, you'd rather spend time with a friend or family member. It's up to you to decide which is more *important*. This decision is always easier to make if you stop thinking that you must do things you don't really want to do. With that distinction in mind, these following techniques should help you put first things first.

Always write your priorities down. This helps ensure they don't get lost in the confusion of daily obligations. Review them on a short-term as well as on a long-term basis to keep yourself on track in a positive and productive manner.

Use a grading system. Make a list and mark everything in order of priority, as A, B or C. Do the As first, then the Bs. You can tend to the Cs much later. But don't fall into the trap of using this as an excuse not to make solid decisions or to delegate. It's tempting to mark dozens of items with a C, telling yourself they aren't really that important. Eventually, you'll have stacks and cartons of Cs, many of which will have died of old age. And what's left is still too much for you to handle. So don't give something a C just to postpone deciding, doing or delegating. First try to decide, delegate or eliminate the item altogether. Only when none of those actions are appropriate, does it make sense to give it a C priority in your life. To keep on top of the Cs, keep them in date order and work on them at least once a week.

Stay focused on your top priorities. Don't give in to low-priority tasks unless you have taken care of the more important priorities. Losing oneself in trivia, meaningless tasks or mindless TV viewing is merely a cover for that old bugaboo—procrastination.

Continually evaluate your priorities. Review your priorities once each week, and again on a monthly basis. You may find that some of them have changed, or that you are neglecting others. Take that review opportunity to reschedule your priorities as needed. An errand or the housework is not as important as visiting a friend in the hospital, completing a report for the boss, or spending time with your family.

Learn to work smarter rather than harder. Working hard means doing everything by yourself, perfectly. Working smart involves project planning, delegating tasks, taking advantage of new ways of doing things, accepting input from others and replacing perfectionism with standards of excellence. It's more effective to prioritize and use your time well than to simply work all the time.

Don't stoop to doing busywork just to seem active or productive. If you keep your goals and priorities in mind, you can always find useful things to do.

Stop letting information anxiety draw you away from your real priorities. You don't need to know everything, so don't waste time getting paranoid when you don't have the time to absorb all of the information that comes your way. Prioritize your reading and TV watching just like everything else in your life.

Don't let others sidetrack you. Don't forget the old adage, "first things first." You don't have to do everything for everybody. Later in the chapter you'll learn a variety of ways to say no to people and obligations that threaten to sidetrack you.

Know the difference between urgent and important. Important activities and people will relate to your mission, goals and unchangeable obligations, and as such have a long-term impact on your life. Urgent activities, on the other hand, often crop up unexpectedly and require immediate attention. It is critical to prioritize those people and things that are important to you, understanding that from time to time your priorities will have to be shifted to urgent matters. This shift in priorities is unavoidable, but care should be taken to get back on track as soon as possible so that you are giving proper priority to important aspects of your life, rather than spending most of your time on urgent matters, or putting out fires. (For more on putting out fires, see chapter five.)

PRIORITIZING RELATIONSHIPS

Relationships can be thought of in categories: friends, family, clients and colleagues. Within the categories, not everyone holds equal importance in your life — nor should they. You may find you need to focus on only the biggest clients to do a really good job for them. Or perhaps you have a friend or two who doesn't really fit your definition of friend any more. Decide who has priority, and either stop spending time with those who don't mean anything to you anymore, or cut down on the time you spend with them, so you can use your time where it counts.

Don't automatically shift your priorities for other people, and don't allow yourself to assign high priority to tasks that are the result of inappropriate requests or demands for your time and talent. Often people request your time and energy with very little thought to your priorities. (And why should they consider your priorities if you're not in the habit of doing it yourself?) So stick to your guns and your own priorities rather than taking care of things for other people that they should and could be doing for themselves.

Regularly clarify your priorities and those priorities that other people set for you (such as your boss). Be prepared to reset or revise those priorities from time to time as conditions in your life change unexpectedly.

Be prepared to reevaluate the relationships in your life — from that friend you've known since high school to that co-worker you feel obligated to socialize with on holidays. Perhaps you need to spend less time with the people who don't really matter so that you can spend more time with the people who do. This can be tricky, but it can also be one of the most beneficial aspects of prioritizing. Your neighbors, for example, might be a pain in the neck, and you'd love nothing more than to never speak to them again. Wonderful as that prospect sounds, it might not be practical; to-the-death feuds with neighbors have started over matters more trifling than a cold shoulder. So keep the lines of communication open, but reduce the number of contacts if you can (don't answer the doorbell every time it rings, for instance). This thinking applies to co-workers as well. Rather than socializing at holiday time, offer a gift and then dash off to your "in-laws." The friend from high school who still thinks like a sixteen-year-old, on the other hand, can be dropped. There is no nice way to drop someone. Telling friends you don't want them in your life is not nice. Keep phone calls brief ("I can't talk, I'm in the middle of something") and don't agree to get together anymore ("sorry, I'm tied up"). There is never any need to explain "middle of something" and "tied up."

Don't procrastinate when it comes to weeding out those people who take your time and give nothing in return, the people who drive you crazy every time you talk to them on the phone. If you're hanging up the phone and spending time complaining about how crazy the person is, it's time to let that person go. There are lots of people out there who agree with you more or less, who give as much as they take, and who aren't crazy, or won't drive you crazy. These are the friends worth spending your time on.

Friendships and relationships should be selected with great care. When they are treated with consideration and respect, they can last a lifetime. And a lifetime might not be long enough if time is used up with inconsequential people. If you find yourself neglecting people who matter to you—such as close friends—because you don't have the time, perhaps you need to reevaluate your priorities so that you put a little more balance in your life. You might have to force yourself to take the time to meet with these special people; one surefire way is to buy tickets to events for yourself and your friends well in advance and book it on your schedule, just as you would any other appointment.

If you can't find time to be with your family, try thinking of it this way: Nothing is quite so highly valued as love and parenthood. With that in mind, housework, yard work, and yes, even the football game, should probably take a back seat to the most important duty of all—being a loving, giving family member.

LEARN TO SAY NO

Perhaps one of the most important tools that is used to prioritize is the ability to say no when countless others would have you say yes to their demands on your time and talent. Learning to say no, when you have had years of experience saying yes (when you meant no), can be a traumatic lesson. But, it's a skill that needs to be mastered to prioritize effectively and have more time for yourself. Nowadays, it almost never comes as a surprise when someone asks you to agree to do something that will require your time, but benefit their interests. Consider the following "innocent" requests:

- "Will you serve on the PTA Committee this year? We really need you."
- "I sure could use a hand this Saturday fixing the roof. Whaddya say, will you help me out?"

- "Can you help me throw the going-away party for Jack over in accounting? He's getting married and leaving next month."
- "Mom, I really want to sign up for five extracurricular activities. You only have to drive me to four of them. C'mon, Mom, pleeeease!"
- "I'm moving next week. Can you help me pack over the weekend?"
- "Could you make that great specialty dessert you do for our alumni get-together next month? We expect about forty people."
- "I'm going away for a week. Would you mind walking my dog for me?"
- "Can you take my place in the car pool this week? I'm swamped."
- "Won't you take the minutes at the meeting for us? No one else here does it as well as you do."
- "I need a ride to the airport next Sunday morning. Can you take me? And, oh yeah, I need to be picked up next Friday night about ten."
- "I'm painting the house next week. C'mon over, I'll have some beer on hand."

Almost everyone says yes to something, when they would rather say no. Whatever the reason, this approach means that all too often "yes" pops out automatically in response to a request, and the result is yet again another burden or obligation to fulfill. Any time you might have set aside for yourself is now spent for the benefit of others. You kid yourself into thinking that you will have "more time later," so you can take more things on now. This thinking almost always proves fatal. Unless you drop something or complete something now, the new obligation you take on only adds to your time-consuming burdens. That extra time you expect never seems to materialize.

While helping others and contributing time and effort to good causes is a noble concept, if you find yourself taking on more than you can or want to handle, and start to feel like a time-starved martyr, you've gone too far. Chances are that when you shift into this volunteer/helper/do-everything-for-everybody-else mode, the pressure of being overcommitted may make it difficult to maintain the saintly attitude that's supposed to accompany all heroic good works performed by people such as yourself. You may even find that *crabby, cranky, resentful* and *sullen* are the more likely adjectives that describe how you secretly feel.

Saying yes when you'd rather say no is more than just a bad habit. There are actually reasons behind the verbal faux pas. Maybe we just want to be liked—or need to be needed. Perhaps we're flattered—it makes us feel important or powerful to be approached with a request, so of course we say yes. Maybe we are afraid we'll miss something. Some of us have been raised to think it's bad manners to say no. Or sometimes we're not really listening and an absentminded "yeah, sure" escapes our lips before we know what hit us. A lot of people feel guilty when they say no.

Why *No* Is an Acceptable Word

All of these reasons for saying yes can be retired by understanding and accepting that *no* is an acceptable part of your vocabulary. If you're still feeling squeamish about it, consider the following rationales:

- It isn't necessary to constantly say yes to be liked. But by always saying yes you may find yourself being used, which is very different from being liked.
- If you feel powerful when people come to you to take advantage of your willingness to say yes, you are operating under an illusion. It takes far more than saying yes to attain real power.
- Nowhere is it written that you must always say yes. It's not impolite to say no, you just need to say it politely.
- Not every request is equally important. Keep that in mind when people around you are making demands on your time, and prioritize and eliminate accordingly by saying no as needed.
- Feeling guilty is a total waste of time in every instance except one: when you are guilty. So unless you've committed a crime or violated ethical standards, saying yes because of guilty feelings is completely inappropriate.
- Once you've accepted that the word *no* can be regularly incorporated into your speech patterns, here are some specific ways to say *no* whenever you want to.

How to Say No

Leave nothing to the imagination. Listen closely to the request for your time. Ask for details. What *exactly* will you be expected to do, and how often? Don't settle for vague descriptions of your proposed obligations. Then think before you speak.

Stall. If you can't muster up the wherewithal to say no at the time of the request, say, "Let me think about that and get back to you." Wait a day or so, screw up your courage, call back and say no. If someone presses you for an immediate answer, immediately answer with a no; it is much easier to turn that no into a yes later (if you decide to) than to turn a hastily uttered yes into a no.

Say no nicely but firmly, without apology or undue explanation. If your thirteen-year-old wants you to take her to the mall, and you're not up to it, say no. Period. If your colleague asks you to serve on a fund-raising committee, say, "I really can't fit it in right now."

Use incompetence as an excuse. For example, if someone wants you to volunteer for something that involves a lot of paperwork, and paperwork is not your strong suit, say no. Then don't let the requestor back down and say "it really isn't that much" paperwork. There's always more paperwork than you think, and if they say there's even some paperwork, you can bet there's plenty. Simply say, "That's just not something I do."

Make your own plans top priority. Say no, followed by, "I'm booked at the moment." "I'm already overcommitted." If that doesn't work, say, "I'd love to help you, but I've already got five projects of my own to deal with." They will not offer to help you with your projects. More likely, they'll beat a hasty retreat.

Never say, "I don't have the time." People will inquire about your schedule in detail, and then proceed to help you find the time they need. You'll end up saying yes in spite of yourself.

Cut to the chase. Don't let people beat around the bush and manipulate you into offering your help. Cut to the heart of the hints by addressing the issue early in the conversation. Say, "I'm sorry to hear about this situation." Or, "I'm sorry you have that problem." Then go ahead and get it over with: "If you're asking me to help out, I'm afraid I can't do it now." If pressed, simply say, "I'm afraid I have to let it go at that for now." This method of saying no and sticking to it works particularly well with family members and close friends who have gotten in the habit of depending on you to spend far too much of your time helping them out with one thing and another.

Preface your no with flattery. Say things like, "I really admire your charity, but I can't commit any time right now," or, "I love having lunch with you, but I'm on a tight deadline, and can't make it this week." Or, "I'm really honored you asked me, but I can't do it."

Be selective. Invitations to social functions should be treated the same as other requests for your time. Don't get carried away with the flattery of being asked when deep down you know you'd rather be home with a good book. And don't say yes just because you're afraid you'll miss something. There will always be someone who can fill you in, and if it's really scandalous, you can read about it the next day in the newspapers. Say no when you really don't want to go, and whatever you do, don't feel compelled to provide an anthology of reasons to back up your no. Remember, it's social; it's not a requirement to attend.

Acknowledge opportunities — real and imagined. Often people making a request phrase it to sound like the opportunity of a lifetime. Most of the time it is no such thing. Other times, it's a bit of an opportunity, but not enough for you to drop everything. Say, "Thanks for offering me this opportunity, but I'm knee-deep in projects already and can't take on anything else right now." This puts those who have tried to manipulate you with the "opportunity" line in their place (they know full well it's not an opportunity for anyone but themselves), while it acknowledges and thanks those who may have presented a real opportunity.

Recognize good offers and ideas, but say no anyway. Good ideas and offers do come along now and then, but often they don't fit personal plans and priorities. Say, "Gee, that's a great idea (or offer), and I really wish I could take advantage of it. Unfortunately, I have other priorities that require my immediate attention. I know you'll do well. Good luck with your concept, however."

If you must say yes to something, consider a compromise or a trade-off. Say, "No, I won't do that, but I can do this," or bargain for a trade by saying, "I'll be happy to do that for you, if you'll do this for me." This method of saying no is tricky, since if you're not careful you'll find yourself being talked out of the compromise or trade-off, and before you know it, you'll be saying the dreaded yes to the entire request. Adopt this line of defense only as a last resort.

Be prepared for some indications of annoyance or displeasure—even perhaps some dramatic caterwauling—when you begin to reverse yourself and say no to those who have become accustomed to your automatic yes's in the past. In time, however, the shrieks will subside, and everyone will adjust their expectations accordingly—which will make it that much easier to issue more no's in the future. Each no that you utter—where you would have said yes in the past—buys you the freedom of more time for yourself to spend on what really matters to you.

So start today by giving your yes's only to those people and commitments that are truly meaningful and important in your life. Hand out nice no's to all the rest. You'll be amazed at the difference this will make in your life—and the amount of time you'll save.

WHAT'S HAPPENING TODAY

If you're a person who resists planning, chances are, your life is full of *happenings*. You find yourself saying things like, "I can't help what *happens*," or, "I don't know what *happened*; the day just got away from me," and, "Hey, don't look at me, I'm not responsible for what *happened*!" Or, "I have no idea what *happened* to those papers," or even, "I just *happened* to remember that I was supposed to call you last week." You may even ask, "How on earth did that *happen*?" or, "Why does this keep *happening* to me?" Then there's the old standby, "Accidents do *happen*!"

While many things do inevitably happen during the course of an average day, a lot of the problems, along with the unpleasant surprises, needn't always occur if you don't want them to. *Funk & Wagnall's Dictionary* defines *happen* this way: "to . . . seem to occur without prevision or voluntary and intelligent intention."

Plan, on the other hand, has a more upbeat definition in *Webster's*: "a means for achieving an end."

Obviously, better results can be achieved by planning. Consider the old adage, "fail to plan, plan to fail." People who don't plan, often fail (though not always). As a general rule, however, success doesn't just "happen." Pay attention to successful people, and nine times out of ten, they'll say they always wanted what they eventually achieved. They dreamed about it; they worked and planned for it. While some successes are a result of being in the right place at the right time, or pure luck, even those are often bolstered by the *plans* that moved a person to the right place at the right time in the first place.

Techniques That Work

To start planning or to plan your time better than you do now, keep these secrets of successful planning in mind.

Make your plans specific and realistic. Don't plan to do more than is realistically possible, but be specific about the plans you do make. If you want to learn Spanish, for instance, plan to listen to your language tapes for twenty minutes on Monday, Wednesday and Friday at 5:30 P.M. Study the grammar book on Tuesday and Thursday, and each week will put you closer to realizing your goal to speak Spanish.

Set deadlines both for starting and finishing what you plan to do. Lurching from day to day with no particular deadlines never produces much over the long haul. If you want to get a new job, start now and give yourself a deadline of twelve weeks from now to get that job. Then do the necessary research, send resumes, and make appointments that could lead to that change in employment.

Plan to do something every day that moves you closer to achieving a goal. This can be a small thing. For instance, if you need to save $500, save $2 each day in small change, and in eight months, you'll have the $500.

Also spend some part of each day going over your plans for the next day. Plan each week as well — at least one week in advance.

Take maximum advantage of your personal energetic prime time. Plan to tackle priorities during the time of day that you generally are most alert and most energetic. And make priorities the centerpiece of all your plans. (More on priorities in the next section.)

Set aside some time every week for important priorities that require blocks of working or creative time. If you don't plan this time in advance, you'll end up working on those priorities in bits and pieces of time, and ultimately, you may not do them justice or see them through to completion. If you're really serious about losing weight, set aside two to three hours each week to plan your menu for the coming week, shop for groceries, and prepare as much food in advance as possible. You can chop veggies and put them in food-storage bags in advance, which gives you something to grab when you're in a hurry or want a snack. And it makes it a cinch to throw together a healthy stir-fry dinner when you are so hungry you want something to eat immediately. Just that little bit of planning once a week can make all the difference between whether you stay on your diet or fall off it during the coming week.

Accept responsibility for your plans, and plan responsibly. Don't blame others for your problems. Instead, plan to solve those problems and prevent them from recurring. It's up to you to manage your own time effectively so that you can spend it the way that is the most meaningful to you. If you never have time for yourself, stop blaming outside forces for the problem.

Plan to create balance in your life. Plan time for work, play, friends and family, and yourself. If your professional life is more important than your personal life, make plans to devote more of your time to work. But allow at least some time for your personal life — even just a little. Some day down the road, you may regret giving your personal life short shrift now. And, it's important to remember at all times that a balanced lifestyle is more rewarding and usually lasts longer than an obsessive one.

EFFICIENT VS. EFFECTIVE

When you plan and prioritize, you want to be both effective and efficient. But don't confuse the two. Being efficient means doing a task or job right, and applies to the process of accomplishing something. Being effective, on the other hand, covers a much broader and more important view. Peter Drucker, author of *The Effective Executive* (Harper & Row), explains the difference this way: "Efficiency is concerned with doing things right. Effectiveness is doing the right things."

So remember that it doesn't matter how much time you spend doing things right if you aren't doing the right things.

Organize Projects and Manage Your Schedule Effectively

Everyone has the same twenty-four hours each day to spend; those who do it successfully do so by organizing projects logically and managing their schedule realistically. Learn how to master project management and scheduling skills, and you'll spend your time successfully as well.

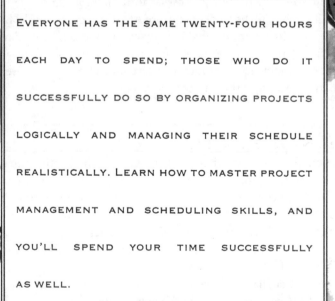

CHAPTER FOUR

Converting Your To-Do List Into Projects

*Have you ever noticed that on your last work day just before
going away on vacation, you get three days' work done?*
— Alec Mackenzie

One of the biggest obstacles to finding more time for yourself is that ongoing and apparently endless list of unfinished business — everything you *must* do plus everything you *should* do. There's usually no time left for things you *want* to do.

The last time you took a look at your to-do list, for instance, you nearly fainted from the impossibility of it all. And that didn't take into account all those half-finished projects — from paperwork to crafts projects — that are in holding patterns all over your home and office. Maybe you're so overwhelmed, you feel like the person who said, "God put me on earth to do certain things. Right now I'm so far behind, I may never die."

Don't give up. There are simple ways to organize your projects, to-do lists and schedule so you can get more done than you ever thought possible. You now understand the value of your time, and know what you want out of life. This, along with your newfound commitment to prioritize and plan, will make reviewing your endless to-do list far less threatening. You'll decide to let some things go, since they are not a priority in your life, or don't contribute to your goals. You'll delegate other things because, frankly, it isn't worth your time to deal with them.

The projects, unfinished business, and remaining things to do can be organized in a new way that allows you to plan your schedule effectively. This chapter will provide you with the framework you need to divide and organize projects and to keep a to-do list that doesn't overwhelm you. The second part of Step 4, scheduling, will be covered in chapter five.

THE MASTER LIST

To gain control over all the unfinished business in your life, the first step is to write it all down. Make a master list of everything you have to do and should do. Don't worry that the list will take up twenty pages (it probably won't), and don't worry about putting it in any order (for now). Just start writing, and don't stop until you can't think of another thing. Let's assume your list looks something like this:

- Pick up the cleaning
- Clean and organize all of the closets in the house
- Call the travel agent about the New York trip
- Buy a new suitcase
- Go to the dentist for a check-up
- Finish the marketing report for work
- Clean out the files in my office
- Put the fall plants in
- Take the dog to the vet for shots
- Take Linda shopping for her wedding dress
- Sell ten tickets for the Chamber fund-raiser
- Send photos of the kids to Mom
- Get season tickets to the opera
- Sew new button on the yellow silk blouse
- Lose twenty-five pounds before the high school reunion next year
- Clean and organize the rec room in the basement
- Prune the tree in the backyard
- Revise my resume
- Call a headhunter and get an appointment for a job interview
- Design a new brochure for the new product line at work
- Research prices for new computer equipment
- Sort the photos of Linda, label them, and put them into an album
- Join a gym and start working out
- Call Linda to catch up on the news
- Clean out my briefcase
- Call printers and get prices for the new brochure
- Organize my desk
- Call the caterer about finalizing the reception plans
- Send the deposit to the musicians
- Write the copy for the new brochure
- Call the photographer to confirm the date
- Get a new suit for the trip
- Call Mary and tell her my arrival date and time

You have a lot of unfinished business, no question about it. But rather than looking at the list as thirty-three things you have to do, think of it instead as a few projects along with a few things to do. Here's how it works.

TURNING UNFINISHED BUSINESS INTO PROJECTS

Obviously, you are in the middle of planning a wedding for your daughter—although thankfully, there isn't too much left to do. You have a major project or two due at work, but the project you'd really like to undertake is to find a new job. A week after the wedding, you're going on vacation, and from the looks of it, you'll need it. Because, among other things, the house will be full of guests before the wedding—some guests will be staying for several days. And the house is a wreck. All the closets are stuffed to bursting—there's no room for the guests' clothes. There's a rec room in the basement to gather in, but you've stored boxes of assorted memorabilia and outgrown clothes down there, and now you need that room for the guests' kids. The photos of Linda should be organized and put into an album for everyone to see at the reception. ("Wasn't she cute growing up?") Work is not much better. You've been so busy that there are piles of paper and files everywhere, and you can't find anything without at least a ten-minute search. No wonder you never have any time for yourself. You're up to your chin in unfinished business.

Let's look at your agonizingly long list and see what can be removed and transferred instead onto a Project page. It looks like you have these projects going on in your life right now:

- Plan the Wedding
- Get Organized at Home and at Work
- Find a New Job
- Take Trip to New York (Vacation)
- Fall Yard Work
- New Brochure
- Lose Twenty-Five Pounds

You assign priority according to the deadline imposed (such as the actual date of the wedding), and how important each project is for you. Then you schedule each task according to that priority and deadline. Working with those seven projects, you can move even more items off your unfinished business list.

Plan the Wedding
- Take Linda shopping for her wedding dress
- Call the caterer about finalizing the reception plans
- Sort all the photographs, label them, and put them in an album
- Send the musicians a deposit
- Call the photographer

Get Organized at Home and at Work
- Clean out all the closets in the house
- Reorganize and clean out the files at the office
- Clean out my briefcase
- Organize my desk
- Clean out the basement

Find a New Job
- Revise my resume
- Call a headhunter for an appointment

Take Trip to New York (Vacation)
- Call the travel agent
- Buy a new suitcase
- Buy a new suit
- Call Mary and let her know arrival time

Fall Yard Work
- Rake leaves and put the fall plants in
- Prune the tree out back

New Brochure
- Call printers and get prices
- Write copy

Lose Twenty-Five Pounds
- Join a gym and start working out

Now the list has dwindled substantially. Along with the seven projects, there are only ten things left to do on the unfinished business list. Some of these are *calls* and some of them are *errands*. By grouping those together they can be done at the same time.

Errands
- Take the dog to the vet for shots
- Pick up the cleaning

Calls
- Make calls to sell ten tickets for the Chamber fund-raiser
- Call Linda to catch up on the news
- Make calls to get preliminary price information on new computer
- Call and order season tickets to the opera

Now we have only a few things left *to do* on the unfinished business list.

To Do
- Go to the dentist for a check-up
- Send photos of the kids to Mom
- Sew new button on the yellow silk blouse
- Finish the marketing report at work

Now instead of thirty-three things to do, there are seven projects, two errands, and some calls to make. As you think of more things to do, add them to the appropriate project page, and when you are working on that project, tackle those things to do in order of importance. Your *Get Organized at Home and at Work* project, for example, is a big project, and probably can't be done all at once. In this case, you may want to clean out two closets in the guest rooms only, and tackle the basement rec room next, since the wedding guests will arrive in three weeks. You can clean out the other closets later. At work you may only have time to clean off the top of your desk this week; next week you can attack the desk drawers.

Project Planning From Start to Finish
Projects are an ongoing part of life, yet many people have a hard time getting through one project; others have a habit of starting several and completing none. Projects need to be planned and prioritized for successful completion. To get a grip on your project planning, try the following techniques.

Don't bite off more than you can chew. Stop agreeing to take on every project that comes down the pike. Take on only what you can comfortably accomplish or what you are absolutely obligated to do.

"What's in it for me?" Always assess the payback value of the projects you do. If completing a project holds no satisfaction or contributes nothing to your financial or emotional life, don't do it unless you have to.

Focus your energies on one thing at a time. Even though you might have several projects going at any given time, you need to be able to focus your energies for specific periods of uninterrupted time on only one of those projects. Spend an hour a day on the sales report, and an hour a week on your craft project, for example.

Go into seclusion. Make yourself unavailable if you have an important project that needs your full attention. Don't allow visitors, phone calls or other interruptions to disturb you while you spend the necessary time on the project.

Be innovative. Don't do things one way just because they've always been done that way. Look for the most expedient way to do things, even if those ways are new. Those new ways may mean making the best use of new equip-

ORGANIZING YOUR TO-DO LIST

Converting things to do into projects often starts with a long list of everything that needs to be accomplished. You then consolidate items from this list into projects, prioritize what needs to be done, and plan your day or week. Bear these tips in mind when working with your to-do list:

Use one list. Resist the temptation to write your to dos on several pieces of paper. If you do, you'll lose something for sure. Instead use a continuous list. A spiral notebook, a yellow legal notepad, or a section in your planner (if you carry one) are all good tools for keeping your to-do list in one place.

Consolidate information. Consolidate your to dos. If you have a lot of calls to make, devote a page to calls. Or you might have one page for all the errands you need to run.

Don't number the list. If you have twenty-five to-do items and number them as you think of them and write them down, you're likely to confuse priorities by automatically starting at the top and considering the first item your highest priority. Just scan the list and pick out the priorities on a daily basis.

Date the entries. Make a quick note of the date when you add something to your to-do list. Eventually, you may see some items that have been languishing for an unusually long time. You may finally decide to delegate those items or forget about doing them altogether, since you have other, more important things to do.

Out of sight, out of mind. Always have your to-do list near or with you. Don't put it in a drawer or file where you'll ignore it, lose it or forget it. You won't get anything done that way.

Refer to your list regularly. Refer to your to-do list throughout the day, so you can remind yourself what your priorities are. Mark off what you accomplish, and when necessary, use the to-do list as a tickler system and guide when you need to reschedule some of those things that you still need to do.

Don't rely on your memory. During the day, always write new to-do items on your list the minute you think of them. Trying to remember everything in your life *plus* that to-do list places an unnecessary burden on your memory bank. Why make things more difficult than they have to be? Write items down as soon as you think of them, and clear your head for more important thoughts. When you're out, if you don't want to (or for some reason can't) make notes to yourself about things to do when you get home or back to the office, simply call your answering machine and leave yourself a message. When you get back, you'll have your verbal reminder, and you can add the item to your to-do list.

Review and reprioritize your list every day. Review and prepare your to-do list on a daily basis. Star, highlight or somehow mark the priorities for that day, so important items aren't overlooked. But don't get caught up in meticulous rewriting of the list every day. It's too time-consuming and unnecessary. Besides, even if you didn't get everything done, it can be motivating to see all those things you *did* cross off because you accomplished them. So keep using the same list until everything is done or until it's in such bad shape that you can hardly read it. Consolidate and rewrite it at that time.

What's the worst that can happen? When reviewing your list of things to do, ask yourself what's the worst that will happen if you don't do something. If the consequences aren't dire, maybe you can eliminate it from your list of priorities or postpone it indefinitely when you put your energies into more important pursuits.

ment (such as computer or telecommunications innovations) or new ideas (which you might get from an outside consultant, for example.)

Always set deadlines for your projects. Let others know you are "on deadline" and don't let them distract you or keep you from meeting your self-imposed priority to devote time to the project.

Avoid nitpicking. Don't be obsessed by details. Tackle the major components of any project first. You can fine-tune the details later.

Finish strong. Finish what you start, and don't start what you can't finish. Apply this thinking to the projects you take on, and you can eliminate a lot of "undone project" agony before it has a chance to develop. If you don't start what you know—deep down in your heart—you won't finish, you won't have to look at all those half-finished projects all the time. You'll eliminate not only the clutter of unfinished projects, but the guilt as well.

Know when to quit. If you are pursuing a project that's patently pointless, cut your losses. If you never cook, there's no point in cataloging and indexing hundreds of recipes. If you aren't all that handy, why waste time labeling the pegboard for all the tools in the basement. Or, maybe you're in a research cycle—doing endless research for a project that absolutely no one (including yourself) is interested in. Give it up. Constantly tinkering with a project that is worthless generally means you are just procrastinating, which is obviously a waste of time.

CHAPTER FIVE

Managing Your
Schedule Successfully

There cannot be a crisis next week. My schedule is already full.
— Henry Kissinger

For too many people, the day begins in a veritable panic. Their feet hit the floor running, and it's like that all day long, until they fall into bed at night exhausted. "Is this all there is?" they ask. Overwhelmed with obligations, it becomes difficult, if not impossible, to imagine finding more time for anything, much less oneself. Of course, some people *do* have the time they need, and they are operating with the same twenty-four hours as everyone else. Even with the same obligations, why is it that some people seem to accomplish more and still have time left over, while others are constantly running, trying to catch up? The answer is that how we manage our time becomes a habit — and often as not, it's a bad habit.

Changing poor management habits includes taking a look at how you manage your time through scheduling. It takes some thought and a bit of skill to schedule days, weeks, months and years so that your time is managed successfully.

Using the right tools, planning in advance, prioritizing and staying flexible are all keys to streamlined scheduling. In this chapter, you'll discover dozens of ways to schedule effectively every day so that not only will you get things done, you'll have more time for yourself as well.

Managing your schedule starts with planning it in advance. With your goals and priorities firmly fixed in your mind, make it a habit to plan your schedule at least a week in advance. Mapping out what you have to do in your head can be an exercise in futility. You'll forget something you should have done and neglect something you wanted to do if you are relying only on memory. So, whether you are an executive at a busy firm or a mother supervising four kids and the house, the best tools for scheduling are a calendar and a pencil. The type of calendar you use depends on your lifestyle.

USING A CALENDAR OR PLANNER BOOK

The calendar you carry with you as part of a planner book and the calendar you use at work should always display a week rather than just a day. Planning your schedule one day at a time amounts to just trying to get through your to-do list each day. You need to look further into the future than today to find the time to schedule projects and goals as well.

When you purchase a personal planner with a calendar to carry with you, buy one that suits your lifestyle rather than opting for one that is the most elegant. If you have large handwriting, for example, you won't be happy with a tiny calendar/planner book. So consider the size of the pages and the room for your entries as an important factor in your decision regarding which planner to buy. Also keep portability in mind: Will it need to fit into your briefcase or your purse, or will you carry it separately?

If you buy a planner that features other sections such as Goals, Addresses, Expenses and so forth, don't feel that you have to keep the sections in the order that they are presented to you. If the Goals section is in the back of the book, move it to the front, where you'll be sure to see it regularly. You might want to customize other sections to include categories like Calls to Make, Shopping List, Menu Planning, Grocery List, Errands to Run. And don't get carried away with putting every phone number and address in your life in the Address section. You probably only need a few of those numbers when you're out and about, and there's no need to be hauling a virtual telephone directory around with you every day.

If you want to eliminate the address and phone number section of your planner, simply write or type the most important phone numbers on a card and have the card laminated. You can carry this card in your wallet or purse. While this may sound too simple for your complex needs, for a lot of people it is sufficient. After all, you don't need to carry every phone number when you are out, when you usually call the same few numbers most of the time anyway. If you don't have a number you need with you, most of the time you can call your home, the office or directory assistance to get the number.

If your planner book has removable pages, every six weeks or so remove some of the calendar pages for the previous weeks. You don't need to carry the last nine months around with you on a daily basis. Simply file the pages in chronological order for future tax and record-keeping purposes, and keep only the most recent past few weeks along with future weeks in your book.

Make sure that you have either a small notepad that you carry with you, or that your planner has a note section in it. Otherwise, you'll always be tempted to jot down names, phone numbers, directions, and other assorted notes on the calendar itself, leaving little room for adding appointments on the appropriate date. You can slip a pad of Post-It notes in your planner and use these to make notes for yourself during the day.

Some calendars are designed to encourage you to tear out and discard the pages once the day, week or month is over. Tearing the pages off is fine, but unless you know for certain that you will never need the information noted on those pages (such as for tax record back-up), don't throw them away. File them in chronological order in a drawer or box.

Use a pencil to make notations on your calendar. It makes it easier to change entries, and keeps the calendar looking neater and easier to read than if you use a pen and end up scratching out entries to add or change something you've scheduled.

Use a highlighter or a red pen to circle or highlight important dates. Checking to see what's on your calendar can become so automatic that it's easy to read right past something critical. Circling or highlighting important appointments or things to do helps guarantee that you won't overlook them.

Unless you never leave your home or office, it's a good idea to always carry a calendar with you, particularly if you are apt to run into people who ask you on the spot if you can do something on a future date. On the other hand, if you want to give yourself some thinking time before you commit to a future date, don't carry your calendar with you. That way, you can always say, "I don't know if I can make it. I'll have to check my calendar and get back to you later."

If you take your calendar with you as you leave the office, make sure you leave a record of your schedule behind. This is especially important if you have an assistant who regularly handles calls and scheduling for you when you are out. You can either have a second calendar on your desk that duplicates entries, or get into the habit of copying your calendar before you leave. Leave that copy with your assistant to work with in your absence.

When planning for the whole family, consider using a large monthly calendar that can be posted on a wall at home. Some of the calendars are paper, and others have a vinyl finish that allows you to write on them with a marker and remove the notations with a cloth, which makes changes easier to note. Once a week, on Saturday or Sunday, sit down with the family and go over the schedule so that everyone knows what's going on, and so that nobody misses getting picked up after an extracurricular activity. Planning in advance with the family and a calendar of this type can also discipline everyone to think ahead rather than waiting until the last minute to try to insist on being taken somewhere or picked up.

Once you have the right tools for scheduling, use them faithfully to plan a schedule that saves time and works for you.

Plan Your Schedule by Scheduling Your Plan

Plan each week's activities the week before, and plan each day's activities the day before. Get in the habit of checking your calendar first thing in the morning and again at the end of the day. Take a few minutes to plan the day in the morning, and another few minutes to plan the next day in the evening. If you need to reschedule some things on your calendar, do it then.

Every week or so, schedule time to work on your long-range goals—both personal and professional. Break goals into manageable short-range segments with deadlines. If achieving a goal is going to take you eighteen months, do something each month to work your way toward achieving that goal.

Always set deadlines, particularly for long projects. If the project is complicated, break it into segments, and set a deadline for each segment as you do with your goals. If you don't make setting deadlines a habit, you'll find yourself operating under Parkinson's Law: "Work expands to fill the time available for its completion." Schedule tasks, projects and goals according to priority *and* an established deadline.

On the other hand, don't underestimate the amount of time it will take to complete a project or task. Try to schedule the appropriate amount of time, then add a little extra. If you think it will take one hour, add thirty minutes for idiot time, since somewhere along the line, some idiot will probably screw things up so that the project takes longer to complete than originally estimated. Be realistic rather than idealistic about how much time you'll need to get things done.

Play it safe and schedule your most important projects and tasks for early in the week. This way, if something more urgent needs your attention, you still have the rest of the week to get back to your priorities.

Also remember that the best time of the day to get things done can be first thing in the morning before the rest of the world gets going. If you can get up ahead of the world (or the family), that's a perfect time to get some quiet work done. Getting to the office early can also make a big difference. Even if you don't get in early, you might want to schedule your most important projects for first thing in the morning before the phone starts ringing, and before you run up against the day's many obligations and interruptions.

The real secret is to match your energy level to your priorities and most important projects. If you're a morning person, do important projects then. If, however, you don't really come alive until 2:00 P.M., that's the time to tackle that critical task or project that requires your full attention and effort.

One of the biggest time wasters besides watching TV is the practice of constantly interrupting a good schedule to handle things that are necessary, but minor. The antidote to this problem is to schedule blocks of time for minutiae. Return telephone calls during the first or last hour of your work day, for instance. Handle routine clerical work right after lunch instead of constantly stopping to see what just landed in your in-box. Do all the grocery shopping on Saturday instead of trying to fit in three last-minute, harried trips to the store during the week.

Another way to head off trouble is to schedule maintenance appointments in advance. Have your car, your house, your pet, yourself and your family checked regularly. That way, any problems that are beginning to surface can be taken care of right away, before they blossom into major, schedule-busting, expensive ordeals.

Likewise schedule bill-paying dates by marking them on your calendar. Quarterly, once a year, or at the beginning of each month, note any major due dates for mortgage, health, house and car insurance. This way, large payments won't sneak up on you when you're least prepared to deal with them.

On the social front, when you receive invitations to events you want to attend — weddings, parties or gallery openings — write the date on your calendar as soon as you open the invitation. Then put the invitation itself into a special folder or in the back of the calendar book. When you're ready to attend the event, all the details such as the time and address can be pulled out for easy reference.

Schedule some things during off-peak hours and you'll save lots of time waiting in line. If you can, go to the movies during the week rather than on busy weekends (or go at the last minute and the line will have gone in already; your seat selection may not be great, but you won't have to wait). Do your grocery shopping in the very early morning or late at night (Saturday nights seem to be particularly good), and if you do your laundry at a commercial self-service laundry early mornings are always best, particularly Sunday. If you have to do something that involves the government (such as get a driver's license), try to do it when the rest of the world is doing something else. I got mine two days before Christmas. Total waiting time: 0.

At the beginning of each year, mark all birthdays, anniversaries and other important dates on your calendar in red so that you don't forget to honor them.

Getting out the Door on Time

Getting out the door in a calm, organized manner every day is one key to making the most of your time. A good morning helps make the day more pleasant and productive. These tips should help you kick start your day smoothly.

Get ready the night before. Decide what you are going to wear, and make sure it's presentable before you go to bed.

Straighten and pick up the house the night before. It's easier to wake up in serene surroundings, and you'll be able to get organized more easily in the morning if you aren't working your way past clutter at every step.

Don't stay up past your bedtime. You'll pay for it tomorrow when you won't want to get out of bed on time.

Get a good alarm clock and use it. Don't rely on your senses to wake up. But don't get a clock with a snooze button. It's an invitation to lollygag in bed. Put the clock across the room; when it goes off, you have to get up to turn it off.

Get up early. Get up thirty minutes before the rest of the family, and use that time as your own quiet time.

Make coffee in advance. If you are a morning coffee drinker, get a pot that you can set up the night before so that your coffee is ready when you get up in the morning. Make it a habit to prepare the coffee when you are cleaning up the kitchen after dinner.

Cut fussing time. Streamline the amount of time you spend on grooming by keeping it simple. Use a minimum amount of makeup (or none at all) and get a simple haircut that is easy to maintain.

Allocate bathroom time appropriately. If you have a large family—making it difficult for everyone to get into the bathroom in a timely manner in the morning—have everyone do some of their grooming in their bedrooms. Hair dryers, makeup and curling irons and the like can all be stored and used in the bedroom near a mirror. Everyone should use the bathroom for the basics— shower, shaving and brushing teeth—with all other grooming and dressing being done in their bedrooms.

Organize kids' gear in advance. If you have children, make sure their clothes, coats and mittens, and any papers that need to go back to school with them are organized and ready the night before. It's also helpful to set aside a specific time each day to sit down with your kids to go through the items they have brought home from school. Use that time to compliment finished work, sign permission slips, and review homework assignments. This will eliminate a last-minute search for important papers in the morning.

Don't rush. Give yourself ample time in the morning to wake up, get dressed, and mentally prepare for the day. Getting up at the last minute, or ten minutes past the last minute means you will start your day racing out the door, probably late again. This is a bad start. Leave on time and in an organized manner instead.

Put things near the door. Always keep your keys, briefcase and purse on a stand or hook near the door. Drop them there when you come in the door, and they'll be right there when you're ready to leave, saving you countless wasted minutes every day searching for them before you dash out the door.

If you want to get back in the door with fail-safe ease, color code your keys with rubber rings (available at hardware stores and locksmith shops) so you don't waste time fumbling with your keys.

EARLY RISERS BENEFIT

An informal employee survey at the telecommunications firm U.S. West discovered that more and more employees were starting their work days between 5:00 A.M. and 7:00 A.M. According to a report in *The Wall Street Journal*, the study found that there were definite benefits to the early start:

- One-third of the 156 early birds said they start early to avoid commuting hassles;
- Roughly 18 percent use the extra time they have late in the day to care for family members or do errands;
- About 18 percent use the early start to make sure systems are working before customers need them;
- 18 percent start early because they can get more done early in the morning before interruptions set in, and while the computer systems are free;
- One-tenth find the early morning beneficial in reaching clients in different time zones.

STRIVE FOR BALANCE

As you're scheduling each week, don't forget the importance of balance. Include time for work, play, family, friends and spiritual pursuits. And while you're at it be sure to schedule some time each week for yourself. Write the appointment in the calendar as you would any other. For example, on Wednesday night, you could note an appointment from 9:00 P.M. to 11:00 P.M. for reading. Then, unless it's an emergency, don't cancel that appointment. This gives you needed time for yourself, and provides a little reward of personal time to look forward to each week. Start with this small two-hour gift for yourself, and gradually increase it so that you are scheduling time for yourself on other days as well. These appointments with yourself will be easy to keep once you make it a habit to plan and prioritize and use your time well all of the time.

Schedule your weekend just as you schedule time during the week. Make plans for exercise, relaxation, and friends and family. You may also have to schedule shopping and chores, but delegate as much as possible and leave work completely behind you for the weekend. A relaxing weekend rejuvenates you physically and mentally for the upcoming week.

If you have a hard time keeping up with household chores, schedule time to do the housework, laundry, yard work and paperwork on a regular basis. Try scheduling laundry by doing a load or two twice a week rather than waiting until there are no clean towels in the house, and everyone is out of underwear. It's better to spend an hour or two twice a week than all day every other week with laundry, and having an ample supply of clean linens and laundry at all times makes for a smoother, happier household.

Then again, maybe some other able-bodied member of your household should be handling the laundry. Don't automatically schedule things to do without asking yourself if someone else could do it for you. Delegate, delegate, delegate. (If you need more help with the delegating process, refer to chapter nine.)

Similarly, don't fill in all the blank space on your calendar. Always try to leave some time for personal spontaneity in your life. Flexibility is important, because disasters as well as delights crop up, and you want to have time to handle either one.

Be realistic about how much time you can give to volunteer efforts. Resist the urge to become a super volunteer. Determine in advance how many hours or days a month you can give to volunteer work, schedule that time, and don't be afraid to let people know that you're already booked. Unless you have unlimited time to spare on your schedule, say no to pleas from others that you help out with "just one more project."

You might also want to make it a point to schedule one day every few weeks as a catch-up day. Don't make any appointments or schedule anything else to do. Just work on catching up on unfinished tasks and projects.

Why We Do Too Much, and How to Stop

All the best laid plans and schedules can fly right out the window if you constantly try to do too much. Taking something on doesn't mean you can accomplish it. So why try to do too much? According to Alec Mackenzie, author of *The Time Trap* (Amacom), reasons include:

The need to achieve, which leads us to take on more than we should.
Insecurity, which keeps us striving to prove our worth.
Failure to delegate authority, or lack of delegation skills.
Unrealistic time estimates, resulting in planning too much for the time available.
Not knowing how to say no, and a desire to please.
Lack of personal organizational skills; the piles on your desk seem to grow geometrically when you're working on too many projects.

Perfectionism, which leads us to unnecessary repetition and foolish investment in detail.

Mackenzie recommends these ideas to help you stop trying to do too much:

Stop telling yourself you work best under pressure; *nobody* works best under pressure.

Resist the urge to step in and take over because others are not doing their job; their work is their responsibility, not yours.

Don't assume that everything has to be done; learn to discriminate low-priority work . . . and ignore it whenever possible.

Ask yourself if part of the problem is lack of organizational skills.

Stop trying to make everything perfect; some things are simply not worth the extra effort.

Special Scheduling Situations

If you are involved in a charitable event, consider setting up a separate calendar with deadlines for each segment of the project leading up to the event. This can make it easier for everyone on the committee to coordinate efforts on the charity's behalf, and at the same time keep their own commitments scheduled on a separate personal calendar.

Likewise, when you travel, take a typed, detailed itinerary to back up your calendar notes. Most calendars don't have enough space to write all of the necessary details on each day of the trip (such as hotel information, car rental information, directions to meeting sites or sightseeing tour information).

Make your travel plans as far in advance as possible. It makes scheduling easier, and often you'll get better prices as well. Try to schedule an open day before you leave and another open day after you return. The day before will be needed for packing and tying up loose ends and will give you a little breathing room so you aren't racing out the door to catch the plane on travel day. You'll need the day after to reorient yourself and try to catch up on what's happened in your absence.

When others around you have chronic bad scheduling habits, you have two choices: You can either leave them behind (when, for example, they can't get ready on time) or adjust your scheduling expectations to accommodate their bad habits. If you adjust to their lax scheduling it can mean that you, too, will arrive late, but it might be better than the alternative, which is to drive yourself crazy over their bad habits. You can also try fibbing about the time. Tell a chronic latecomer that the dinner date is for 7:30 P.M. when it's actually for 8:00 P.M., and they might be ready on time. Eventually, of course, they'll catch on to this little game, and it won't work any more. Still other people have the habit of upsetting others' schedules with last-minute, unreasonable changes, cancellations or demands. These people are easier to deal with. Simply refuse to make further appointments with that person. For those who make last-minute demands that will affect your schedule, a simple, "I'm sorry, I'm busy," will do nicely.

Finding Quality Family Time

If you have trouble finding quality time to spend with your family, try re-instituting some old traditions and starting some new ones.

Bring back the daily dinner hour. Establish a consistent dinner time—say 6:30 P.M. each night—and insist that everyone be there. Don't commit yourself or your children to times that conflict with that hour. During dinner, don't answer the telephone, and turn off the TV. It may seem awkward and difficult at first, but once the dinner habit takes hold, you will find that it can be the most important part of your day. It guarantees you up to seven hours of quality time every week with your family.

Reinstitute the Sunday afternoon dinner. This is a variation on the daily dinner hour, only grander. Make Sunday dinner an event. You can have it at 2:00 in the afternoon, or at 5:00 every Sunday, but make the meal a big one, and invite a friend or relative over at least once each month to join you at the Sunday meal. And yes, the football game gets turned off during dinner.

Worship together. If attending services was once in your life, and you've left it behind because of your busy schedule, bring it back and take the family with you. Don't accept excuses (too tired, have something else to do, etc.), and if you want, stop off for a big family meal at a restaurant after services. That way you'll spend quality time together and establish a family tradition, too.

Work together. Make Saturday mornings the time for family chores. Everyone can pitch in to do housework, yard work, and shopping and errands. Cook and bake together, have everyone clean their rooms, or rake leaves together. Dad can teach kids how to do certain chores, and Mom can do the same. By working together, the chores will get done sooner, the children will learn important tasks and responsibility, and you will have spent time together.

Allocate special time for each child. Give one or two hours of your undivided attention each week to one child. If you have four children, one week Dad can spend time with one child and Mom with another. The next week the other two children get the special time. The third week, Mom and Dad switch and start over. This way, once a month, each child gets special attention individually from Mom and from Dad (they will soon come to look forward to their "special" time). Parents can use this time to get to know the special qualities of each child and to reinforce the individual bonds within the family.

Go out once a month with the family. On Saturday or Sunday, make plans for the entire family to take a special outing together. Do this once a month, and put it on the calendar in advance. Go to a movie, go hiking, or play miniature golf. It needn't take all day, but this family event can be planned for and looked forward to by the entire family.

The most important thing to do if you want to plan for and spend quality time with your family is to *honor your plans*. Don't change your mind or beg off at the last minute. If you do, eventually your family will know that you don't consider them important enough to spend time with, and eventually they won't consider you important either.

Finding Time for Romance

Are you so overwhelmed with the demands of your job, the kids, and the assorted other daily obligations that you never have time for romance? Believe it or not, you can reverse that pattern and make time for romance on a regular basis. Here's how.

Prioritize romance. As unromantic as it may sound, you must make romance a priority in your life. If you don't think of it as a priority, you'll never get around to it.

Stop working nights and weekends. If you can't do that, at least set aside Sundays or two weeknights when you absolutely do not touch work.

Share the household chores. If only one person is responsible for all of the chores and child care, he or she will always be too pooped for romance. Pitch in, and you'll both have more time for regular romantic rewards.

Learn to say no to the kids. You don't have to give in to every demand on your time.

If necessary, put a lock on your bedroom door. Children do not need to watch TV, play games or get dressed in their parents' bedroom, and they should be taught to knock before entering. Parents need that room for rest, recuperation and romance.

Teach your child to respect your quiet time. Buy a bag full of dollar items, and give a small child a timer. Set the timer for an allotted "quiet time" and promise the child a gift from the bag if they don't bother you until the timer goes off.

Go to bed thirty minutes earlier.

Turn off the TV for an entire evening or an entire Sunday.

Schedule at least twenty minutes of conversation time each day. It can be in the morning over breakfast, or at night at bedtime. Or, if the children aren't too small, take a walk after dinner with your spouse. Discuss the day's events, and keep the communication lines open. Say at least one positive thing. This can set the stage for a closer relationship and more romance.

Schedule a date for lunch with your spouse at least once a month.

Schedule a night out on a regular basis. Get out at least once a month. Twice a month is better, and once a week is ideal. Trade babysitting services with a friend, if sitting fees are a problem. You can spend money or not; go out to dinner, to the movies, or just look at the stars from the beach. The point is to go out and spend undisturbed time together.

Schedule a long weekend away alone at least once every three months. If you can pay taxes on a regular basis, you can figure out a way to make this happen as well. Alternate who does the planning for the dates or long weekends. You plan one, and your spouse plans the next one. This takes the burden of all the planning off of one person, and guarantees that each person will enjoy the date thoroughly — especially when they plan it.

Make it a point every day to say something loving to your spouse, and include a sincere hug. Like time, bits and pieces of romance can add up over the long haul, and make a significant difference in your life every day.

PUTTING OUT FIRES

The best excuse for not getting important things done during the day is often the fire fighting excuse. "I just couldn't get anything done, today. I spent all day putting out fires." "Putting out fires" describes time spent in crisis management. And, while engaging in crisis management may seem exciting (after all, look at all those crises you handled), most of the time, it represents poor management. Eventually, people who consistently manage crises ignore everything else and only handle those daily fires. You can put out a lot of fires every day, and it can save the barn from burning down. But it won't help you get the cows to pasture and to market at a productive price. There's no time to take care of long-term, ongoing business when you are constantly dealing with short-term, urgent stuff.

Determining the difference between urgent and important, and understanding what constitutes a true crisis, is critical to breaking the pattern of wasting time with urgent but unimportant tasks and spinning your wheels with a circle of crises every day. Urgent matters need to be tended to immediately. Important tasks can be done now or postponed. And a true crisis needs to be identified as something that if left untended could be disastrous. The trick is to be able to respond appropriately to the circumstances, be they urgent, important, or a full-blown crisis. To determine how you handle these matters every day, try asking yourself these questions.

Do I really need to take care of this now? Don't allow mundane or daily interruptions to assume the urgent mantle. A constantly ringing telephone, for example, might be ignored from time to time. Let voice mail take some messages while you take care of some of your more important priorities.

Will this contribute to the big picture, the future, my goals or the bottom line? If the answer is yes, then it's important—which means you can set it aside to handle something urgent or to deal with a crisis, but you should never set it aside for very long or eventually it, too, will become a crisis.

Do I have to take care of this personally? Don't automatically assume that just because something urgent rears its head that you have to deal with it personally. Perhaps you can delegate it to someone else. If a major client calls you angrily complaining about his bill, perhaps the accounting manager can smooth the client's feathers and solve the accounting problem. If you are a working mother and the school calls to say that your child needs to go home early, maybe your husband can pick up the child, rather than automatically assuming that since you were called, you should go.

What's the worst thing that will happen if I don't take care of this right now? If not responding immediately to something doesn't produce long-term negative consequences, postpone your response until you've finished with more important matters. If you will suffer consequences without instant action, either take action as quickly and as calmly as possible, or delegate it to someone else who can take care of it without turning it into a major crisis. If you have received a customer complaint that looks like it could result in legal action against you, then obviously you would want to take care of the matter immediately; perhaps litigation isn't necessary if you head the issue off at the pass. But if you have received a customer complaint that is frivolous or completely off-the-wall, you might want to address it later in the week, or delegate the complaint to someone else.

Avoiding Crisis Management

There are other ways to try to avoid falling into the crisis management trap, and to more effectively handle the crises that crop up from time to time. Consider the following.

Don't overcommit yourself. If you do, you won't have the needed resources and energies to handle the everyday problems that can turn into crises.

Stop telling yourself that you work best under pressure. This is just an excuse to let priorities slide until the last possible moment. Priorities deserve a better effort than that. Leave the no-brainers until the last minute instead of shuffling what you know are priority items to the bottom of the pile. You'll find your life littered with far fewer crises this way.

Keep on top of matters with regular progress reports. You'll be able to head off potential problems at the pass if you know how things are going at each stage of the project.

Get in the habit of thinking ahead. If something could become a crisis, give yourself lots of extra time to deal with the matter. Allow more time than you think is necessary to complete projects so that when a seemingly insurmountable problem comes up, everyone has plenty of time to regroup and get back on track. Don't wait until November to redo the roof if you live in Wisconsin, because the day after the shingles are ripped off, it will snow. Instead, line up the roofer in April to do the job in July. If he doesn't show up until the first of September, you've still got time to get the roof done — even with unforeseen problems — before the first snow.

Always ask yourself what could go wrong. Then have alternative plans in mind in case something really does go wrong. When plan A falls apart on you, simply shift to plan B. You'll be able to keep the crisis under control regardless of the circumstances.

Accept mistakes. If you don't, people will keep them from you, and things are likely to compound into a crisis. Hearing bad news early on makes it easy to correct the course of action and avoid a major crisis later.

Ask for help when a true crisis hits, but don't get in the habit of always living on the edge and always asking for help. People will get tired of helping you and start to duck your requests for assistance. Have a support system of friends, relatives and colleagues to help you out, and make sure you return the favor from time to time as well.

Look for the opportunity in every crisis, even if it's just a learning or growth experience. And once a crisis has been successfully handled, learn from it so that you don't make the same mistakes again.

Making and Keeping Appointments

Making and keeping appointments can throw even the best schedule off. Whether you're cooling your heels in the reception area or racing off to your own next appointment (because the last one made you late), how you handle appointments can make or break your day. These tips should help you make the most of those appointments.

Ask for the first appointment of the day. Your chances of being backed up in a holding pattern in the waiting room should be reduced significantly. When you make an appointment, always ask, "How long will it take?" This alerts the other person that you care about how you spend your time, and he or she may try harder to start and finish with as little wasted time as possible.

Set a time limit. Don't be afraid to set a limit on the appointment in advance. Say, "I can meet with you for 45 minutes; will that be sufficient?"

Or, if you agree to meet for lunch, be specific about the ending time as well as the starting time. Instead of agreeing to meet for lunch at noon, agree to meet for lunch from noon to 1:30 P.M. Time limits can help you in other ways. For instance, if you've had a hard time tying someone down for an appointment, suggest that the meeting be for only a brief period of time. "Could we get together for twenty minutes to go over the key points?" might be better received by a busy person than an open-ended plea like, "I really need to meet with you to discuss everything." If you secure a brief meeting, keep your word, and stick to the time limit. Your chances of obtaining future critical appointments will increase.

Call the day before to confirm appointments. Check again how long it will take. The confirmation call reinforces the time of the appointment, helps insure that it begins on time, and also protects you from no-shows.

Always include the phone number. When you note upcoming appointments in your schedule book, always include the phone number of the person you are meeting with, in case you are running late, or need to cancel or reschedule. Likewise, always carry the phone number of your pharmacy so that if your doctor issues a prescription, you can ask the nurse if he can call the pharmacy before you leave. The prescription should then be waiting for you when you get to the drugstore.

Take directions. Always take written directions with you when you go to an appointment (particularly if you've never been there before). Include the phone number of your destination in case you get lost. When you get back to the office (or home) put those directions in a file folder marked "Directions." The next time you go there, you won't have to waste time phoning in advance to get the instructions all over again.

Be prepared. Once at the appointment, don't make the other person wait while you dig in your briefcase or purse for papers or call the office for information. Have all necessary information with you, and have it in good order. Then, get to the point as quickly as possible. Time wasted with small talk only leads to everyone being late for their next appointment. (You'll find more valuable tips on how to save time in meetings in chapter eleven.)

For doctor's appointments, if you have insurance claim forms that you need to fill out, fill out one with all the common information, such as your name, address, phone number, policy number, etc., and copy it. As soon as you leave the doctor's office, simply fill in the date and reason for the visit along with the charges. Make a copy for your records and mail the form and receipt to the insurance company in an envelope that you have preaddressed and stamped in advance. This do-it-now method saves time by avoiding a confusing paper pile-up of insurance forms and medical receipts.

Plan for bureaucratic delays. Bureaucratic waste has elevated into a virtual art form. Delays waste money (usually the taxpayer's) and time (usually yours). When he formed the tongue-in-cheek International Association of Professional Bureaucrats (INATAPROBU), according to the *Daily Oklahoman*, Jim Boren issued three guidelines:

> When in charge, ponder;
> When in trouble, delegate;
> When in doubt, mumble.

So if you have an appointment with any government agency, expect and prepare for the worst. You are at the bureaucrat's mercy, and will probably be treated indifferently or rudely. Allow lots of time, wear comfortable shoes, take plenty of reading or a crossword puzzle with you, and muster up your reserve of patience.

Give tit for tat. If you spend an inordinate amount of time waiting for an appointment, consider sending a bill for your time. After all, time is money. Or, if people tend to cancel appointments with you at the last minute, you might want to charge them a cancellation fee. They'll be more considerate the next time they book an appointment with you.

On the other hand, just as medical professionals should be considerate of your time, so should you be considerate of theirs. Call in advance if you're going to be late or if you need to cancel your appointment. Don't take along another patient for the doctor to look at "while she's at it." And jot down a list of questions so that you can get right to the point and gather all the information you need without wasting anyone's time.

Don't cancel; reschedule. If you see that you can't make an appointment, call to reschedule. Most people don't mind changing the date, as long as it isn't done at the last minute. Also, if you're going to be late, call to see if your late arrival is acceptable. You may find that everybody would be happier to reschedule.

Be on time. If you really want to get to an appointment on time, turn your answering machine or voice mail on ten to fifteen minutes *before* you are planning to leave. This way, you won't get hung up on the phone just as you are preparing to leave.

Coping With the Day That Gets Away

Regardless of the best laid plans, sometimes the day gets away from you. Things start to go wrong and seem to get worse from there, and before you know it, you're dealing with one of *those* days at work that can only end in total exasperation.

The first sign that you are about to experience one of those days is when it starts late. You misplaced your keys, got out the door late, and ran into

REDUCING WAITING TIME

Sooner or later everybody is faced with waiting in line or waiting for an appointment. Try these tactics to cut down the amount of time spent waiting and to extend your patience to cover the times when waiting can't be avoided.

Call ahead. Call ahead and ask if there will be a wait, and if so, for how long. At least you'll know what you're facing; you may decide not to go.

Wait and go later. When something opens (such as a popular movie or a new play) wait a few weeks before you go. By then the demand will have been met to some degree, and the lines should be shorter and reservations easier to get.

Let people know you don't like to wait. When you make an appointment or reservation, ask if there is a wait, and don't hesitate to let the other party know that you don't like to wait. Say it nicely but firmly. Often, another time will be suggested—when there will be no wait.

Calm down. If waiting makes your blood pressure rise, learn to put a lid on it. Count to ten, pray, hypnotize yourself—whatever it takes to calm down. Remember, it's not worth giving yourself a heart attack. Either learn to wait patiently, or take your business elsewhere.

Always be prepared with something to do. Always carry something to read or do with you; when you are faced with unavoidable waits you can catch up on some reading, write notes or letters, crochet or work a crossword puzzle. It helps pass the time and can get something done at the same time.

the world's biggest traffic jam. Late to work, it seems like everything else is backing up on you with alarming speed as well. All it takes is one little unexpected problem that needs your immediate attention and the day begins to ominously turn into the day that begins to get away. Soon, you're about to miss a deadline, but the boss takes this time to have an informal chitchat with you that runs an excruciating forty-five minutes long. The school called to say one of your kids is sick, and since your spouse handled the last child-care crisis, it's your turn to do something. Or you don't have the supplies you need for the 5:00 presentation before the Board, so you have to drop everything and run all over town trying to find the proper materials. You can't find your biggest client's file, and she's expecting your call to discuss some details. Whatever. It's definitely shaping up to be one of those days.

The unhappy truth is that almost no one is immune from at least some out-of-control firestorm days. But you don't need to let it completely do you in. While it's inevitable that these days can be dreadful, how you cope with them can help you get through the day better and help you avoid having more of *those* days in the future than necessary. These techniques can help you cope.

Collect your thoughts. Take a few minutes to clear your head and organize your thoughts. While you're organizing your thoughts, give a few minutes' attention to organizing your desk; clear a space if you are drowning in clutter, and put some things away. You'll feel a bit fresher for it, and you'll be able to tackle your problems with more clarity and confidence.

Review and renegotiate deadlines. Review your to-do list as well as your deadlines, and immediately reprioritize what is in front of you. Eliminate or postpone things that can wait, and give only minimal attention to things that can be postponed with little effort. If you are about to hit the panic button because of a deadline that you are about to miss, don't. First, check with the people who set the deadlines to see if they can be changed; even an extra day's reprieve may be all you need. Even if you suspect your deadline won't be extended, make sure you let people know that you are running late on the project so that they can be prepared for any inconvenience. While people can be annoyed by missed deadlines, their annoyance is always much greater if they have no warning.

Explore alternative solutions. If you are going to miss a deadline because of other important things you need to do, see if you can find help from other quarters. Perhaps you need to take on some temporary help, or maybe you can delegate some of the more mundane things on your plate that you do more because you like to do them than because you have to do them. If your day is going to be further interrupted with a routine meeting, see if you can postpone or cancel it. If it's a weekly meeting that you always attend, see if you can send an assistant, or if someone will take notes for you.

Ask for help. Don't be afraid to ask for help, particularly if you have been helpful in the past. In a crunch, the unspoken rule is that if you've done favors for others, they owe you when you need a favor. So call in your chips and let people that you have helped help you. And if you are asking a favor, don't forget that in the future, the unspoken rule is that you will owe that person a favor in return. Make sure you pay up when asked, and don't allow yourself to get to the point where you have asked for so many favors so many times that people don't want to help you at all.

Learn from your experience. Every time you survive one of those days, take some time when it's finally over to analyze what went wrong so that you can prevent it happening again in the future.

Ultimately, when it comes to scheduling, sometimes it pays to take a day off for no particular reason. Call it a mental health day, and use it to recharge your mental energies and regroup your plans so that you can tackle your upcoming schedule in an energized and organized manner. Effective scheduling can mean an end to most tail chasing and the beginning of more time for yourself—not only for today, but for all the tomorrows to follow.

PART TWO

Overcoming Everyday Obstacles

Those who make the worst use of their time
most complain of its shortness.
— La Bruyère

Even though you recognize the Plan for Finding More Time for Yourself as a good one, now that you've come this far, you may find yourself falling back on your own personal repertoire of "yes, buts." "Yes, but I can't get anything done; I'm interrupted a million times a day." "Yes, but this plan won't work for me, since I am the only one who can do everything, and do it right (perfectly)." "Yes, but all the timesaving techniques in the world won't help me; I'm constantly swamped at work." Or, "Yes, but I don't have time to do it now—I'll get around to it as soon as I can." (You usually get around to it at the last minute.) And, "Yes, but I've got a killer job and I work seven days a week. There's nothing I can do about that."

These are but a few of the refrains that are trotted out to avoid dealing with everyday obstacles that stand in the way of finding more time for yourself. The truth is, a significant proportion of daily obstacles are the result of our own poor habits. If you know what you want, and understand the value of your time, you should be willing to replace the bad habits with more effective timesaving ones. If you are ready to prioritize, plan and balance the activities in your life, you won't let poor habits keep you from finding time for yourself. You can do this with Step 5: "Work on Overcoming Everyday Obstacles."

Chapters six through twelve will help you discover ways to overcome all of those bad habits you thought you would always have to accept. You may want to skip directly to the chapter that covers your particular problem area, or you can read the entire section so you can overcome and change time-wasting habits and pick up some new tips in areas that are already under control in your life.

WORK ON OVERCOMING EVERYDAY OBSTACLES

EVERYDAY, TIME-CONSUMING OBSTACLES ARE OFTEN THE RESULT OF POOR HABITS. THOSE HABITS CAN EASILY BE ELIMINATED OR REPLACED WITH BETTER METHODS THAT CAN EQUAL MORE TIME FOR YOU EVERY DAY. RESOLVE NOW TO CHANGE THE HABITS THAT ARE HOLDING YOU BACK AND REPLACE THEM WITH HABITS THAT WILL MOVE YOU FORWARD.

CHAPTER SIX

Pushing Past Procrastination

One of these days is none of these days.
—English proverb

Procrastination affects nearly everyone at some time in life. After all, why do something today that you can very well put off until tomorrow? Tomorrow you'll start on that sales report or do that pile of ironing. Next week is a better time to catch up on the filing, and at home, you'll clean out the basement next Saturday, for sure. And of course you'll write to your grandmother soon. Before you know it, procrastination is not just a habit, it's a way of life. Why not just put things off indefinitely, since chances are, you won't do them today or tomorrow?

HOW WE PROCRASTINATE

People rarely admit that they are procrastinating. They're always busy with "something else" that "must" be done. Procrastination takes many forms and involves many techniques. Here are a few of the common ways to avoid doing what really should be done:

- Stop to make a telephone call. Make that three telephone calls.
- Stop to take a telephone call. Make it last for an hour.
- Stop for a snack. Cripes, you're hungry.
- Stop to go through the mail. While you're going through the mail, take thirty minutes to go through the latest magazine, catalog or business journal.
- Run over to the neighbor's house to return that cup of sugar. Stay an hour at least.
- Go to a meeting that you don't need to attend.
- Put piles of important papers over here "just for now."
- Stop to look through that stack of photos you just found in the closet.
- Watch TV. Just need to see this one program, promise.
- Get up to leave your office and drop something off at someone else's

71

desk. While you're at it, stop by Bill's office to discuss the results of last night's game.

- Go to the bathroom and spend fifteen minutes reapplying your makeup and combing your hair.
- Interrupt your home-based business to do laundry. Four loads at least. Do it on the day your proposal is due. After all, you're almost out of underwear.
- Set a completely unrealistic deadline for yourself. That way, you can throw up your hands and give up before you even start.
- Always bite off more than you can chew. That way, you'll never have enough time to get everything done, and you can incorporate excuses and alibis about why you can't get things done into your daily speech and habits. Procrastination is truly a way of life for you.
- Always leave unpleasant but important tasks until the last minute. Tell yourself you thrive on the pressure of the last minute. Before the last minute arrives, pretend that all the unpleasant tasks in your life will somehow magically disappear.
- Do things you like to do instead of things you should do.
- Always put off routine tasks, such as opening the mail, doing the filing, and taking care of the house and yard.
- Wait for the "right moment" to do something.
- Make it a point to allow — even encourage — distractions.
- Put off paying bills every month for no particular reason.
- Keep putting things off until you have time to do them perfectly.
- Plan constantly, but rarely act on those plans.
- Surround yourself with mountains of clutter that make it difficult to start and complete a project in an organized and coherent manner.
- Always fall back on the king of excuses for not getting something done: "I just didn't have enough time!"

It's easy to procrastinate on dull, unpleasant or difficult tasks. But procrastination goes even further in many cases. Procrastinators are forced to be creative as they invent new reasons for not getting things done. Still once you figure out how to do it, it tends to stick, and becomes an automatic bad habit. Every time you put energy into procrastinating, you are wasting time. It doesn't matter that the job eventually gets done; if the time and energy devoted to creative procrastinating were applied to actually getting something done, you'd end up with a net bonus of more time for yourself.

Before you can begin to curb the time-consuming procrastination habit, you need to recognize and acknowledge why you may be procrastinating in the first place.

EXCUSES, EXCUSES

According to a report in the *Milwaukee Journal*, a Northwestern University professor filed an employment discrimination complaint against the university claiming he was wrongfully fired. The university did indeed fire the professor—after he had entered a plea of guilty to theft of $33,000. It seems the professor, in the apparent throes of paralyzing procrastination, continued to collect his mother's Social Security checks in their joint account for five years after her death. In his complaint petition against the university, the professor claimed the university discriminated against him, since he "suffered from the disability of 'extreme procrastination behavior.' "

Why We Procrastinate

- We manage to constantly overcommit ourselves.
- If we postpone something long enough, someone else will do it.
- By not having enough time we can excuse the poor job we do.
- We would rather be doing something else.
- The task at hand is too difficult or complex.
- We fear either failure or success.
- We don't know where to begin.
- There is safety in routine, so why do something new?
- The task is too time-consuming or overwhelming.
- We insist on results that meet our perfectionist standards, and there's never enough time to achieve those unrealistic results.
- Procrastination has become a bad but regular habit.
- We won't be able to see immediate results.
- The task is tedious and boring.
- We fear change or new situations.
- We fear being judged on our efforts and work.
- We don't know how to do the task.
- There is no deadline, so there's no rush to get started.
- Everything has snowballed to an unmanageable and overwhelming degree.
- We can't buckle down and make necessary decisions.
- We are hooked on the adrenalin flow of doing things at the last minute.

Great Escapes

Unfortunately, understanding the reasons for procrastination doesn't mean most people won't still try to escape doing their duty in a timely fashion. In fact, procrastination can be just another word for escape. When you automatically shift into a procrastination mode, you temporarily escape your responsibilities. Most often people procrastinate by doing something they don't need to do, or by doing something they like to do. Doing something you like to do is fine, as long as you're not doing it when you should be doing something else. And doing something you don't have to do just to avoid doing something you should be doing is also an illegitimate use of time.

According to Alan Lakein, author of *How To Get Control of Your Time and Your Life* (Random House), there are *seven common escapes* that people use to put off what they should be getting done:

Indulge yourself. Doing something you really enjoy. Buying a new hat or tie or book. Taking the rest of the day off to play golf. . . .

Socializing. Visiting with others. Lingering on the telephone. Renewing an acquaintance with an old friend. Making small talk every chance you get.

Reading. Catching up on the backlog of unread periodicals stacked on the side table. Skimming through material previously relegated to a bottom drawer as not really worth reading . . . or trying to make a dent in your pile of unread copies of the Sunday *New York Times* or Book-of-the-Month Club selections.

Doing it yourself. Spending an hour taking notes on a reference book rather than photocopying the three essential pages. . . . Doing something that could be delegated. Spending your time solving other people's problems. Delving into aspects of the job that don't really concern you.

Overdoing it. Supervising employees so closely that they can't get their work done. Keeping every visitor an extra fifteen minutes while you talk about your mimosa, butterfly collection, arthritis, or lack of time.

Running away. Expediting something that doesn't need it; hand carrying a memo to another branch office; paying your telephone bill in person. Taking a long coffee break; extending your lunch hour. . . .

Daydreaming. Planning how you're going to spend your weekend. . . . Wondering how you're going to spend the extra money from your hoped-for promotion. Recalling what a witty remark you made at a party yesterday.

Once you recognize why you procrastinate, the second step is to acknowledge how you procrastinate. Spotlighting your own personal tricks and habits means that you can then try to change them. All of your self-created diversions, from fiddling to fetching and noshing can gradually be eliminated from your daily schedule so you can get more done and have more time for yourself. Try incorporating the following tactics into your daily life to battle whatever tendencies you may have to waste time procrastinating.

OVERCOMING PROCRASTINATION

Admit it. The first step is to acknowledge that you are procrastinating, and try to determine why. If you know *why* you procrastinate, it can be easier to figure out *how* to stop.

Accept the challenge. Every time you catch yourself procrastinating, consider it a challenge to be conquered. Then fight the urge to put things off as if it were a game, with you the potential victor.

List your excuses. Make a list of the excuses you have for avoiding completing a task. Make another list of the consequences you'll incur if you don't do the job and don't do it on time. Finally, list the benefits you will reap once the project is completed. Keep the consequences, as well as the benefits, in mind at all times. If the consequences aren't particularly dire, perhaps you can delegate the job, or don't really have to do it in the first place. But if the consequences are meaningful, use those as a reminder to get going, and use the benefits as a motivator to get done. The excuses, once on paper should pound home the point that they are just that — excuses. Why not stop making excuses altogether? Dreaming up excuses for why you haven't done something is tiresome, and people are quick to see through the procrastinator's veil. Your bills don't get paid on time because you don't tend to them on time, not because you didn't get the bills in the first place. And don't use creativity as an excuse to avoid responsibilities. Just because you are an artist doesn't mean that you shouldn't tend to other, more mundane tasks and daily responsibilities.

Catch and correct yourself. In the course of the day make it a point to stop saying, "as soon as . . ." and "just for now." "As soon as my son leaves for college, I'm going to clean the attic." "As soon as I have the money to buy special labels, I'll do the filing." "As soon as I get a computer, I'll write my resume." Or, "I'll put these bills over here, just for now." "I'll set this project aside, just for now." "Just for now" ends up being indefinitely, and "soon" sometimes turns into never. Decide to do it. Now.

Make deadlines a way of life. Establish deadlines to complete tasks and projects, and write those deadlines down. Don't set deadlines too far in the future, since this is an open invitation to put things out of your mind totally until the last minute rears its ugly head. At the same time, don't sabotage yourself by underestimating the amount of time any given task or project will take. Be realistic about the amount of time required; then add more time to that estimate. Sometimes, however, you can force yourself to get things done, by setting dangerous deadlines. If your office is a mess, make an appointment to have an important client stop by next week. You'll be forced to organize your office before that important visit. And where appropriate, set deadlines for others so you are not at the mercy of their procrastination. Say, "If I don't hear from you by next Friday, I'll assume that I can send the report on as is." Don't make dangerous deadlines a daily practice. That kind of living is just an excuse to continue being a chronic procrastinator.

Inch by inch, it's a cinch. Schedule the time required for tasks and projects on your calendar. If a project takes five hours to complete, you might schedule one hour per day; at the end of the week, you'll be finished. For smaller tasks, take advantage of odd moments of time that may come up. Is there some small portion of the job you can do during that fifteen-minute lull after work? And for other jobs that are routine but not big enough to schedule, ask yourself how long it really will take. If you constantly put off emptying the dishwasher, ask yourself how long it will take? The answer is less than five minutes. Viewed in that context, it is easier to quit procrastinating and unload the thing.

Delegate or dump it. Be sure that the task at hand really needs to be done, and that you have to do it personally. If you find yourself constantly procrastinating in spite of yourself, maybe you really don't have to do it; perhaps you can delegate it to someone else. Or, maybe the task simply doesn't relate to your priorities, and, after careful consideration, you might even realize that it doesn't have to be done at all. Give yourself permission to let it go in that case.

Get organized. If, for example, you hate to pay the bills because you have papers and files all over the place, take the time to set up a simple system for keeping track of the bills as they come in, as they are paid, and as they are filed. You won't feel so overwhelmed if you stick to the system, and it will be easier to combat the tendency to procrastinate when the time comes to start writing checks. Make sure your working environment is pleasant, and that it suits you; also make sure you have any necessary supplies close at hand. Procrastination often begins in disorganized, depressed surroundings with inadequate supplies. (Part Three is devoted to getting organized; you'll find lots of systems and strategies for organizing your home, office and life in general.)

Don't overprepare. Prepare ahead for the job by assembling the materials and information you need. But don't spend unnecessary hours overpreparing — organizing or reorganizing your materials before you even get started on the project.

Be decisive. Avoid "paralysis by analysis" by making decisions in a timely fashion. Deciding something is always better than deciding nothing at all.

(See chapter eight for more advice on effective decision-making.)

Work your plan by setting priorities. Prioritize all the tasks, projects and new endeavors in your life. Follow up by controlling your tendency to constantly reprioritize so things fall in line with whatever you've selected to procrastinate about.

Match your energy level to tasks. Plan to work on tedious tasks when your energy level is at its highest. If you are a morning person, tackle those tasks then. With the worst over, the rest of the day lies more or less blissfully ahead. If you are more of a night person, hit those hard or unpleasant projects in the afternoon, when you start to feel alive. Don't try to do things you hate when you know you'll be bushed. It's just an excuse to throw up your hands and put things off to another time. Always do the worst first.

Tell others what you plan to do. Once you've made a public commitment to get something done, you're more likely to follow through rather than face the embarrassment of admitting that you procrastinated your way out of completing the job.

Just start. Getting started is often the biggest hurdle, and once it has been jumped, it can be easier than you think to keep going and finish the task. Even if all you do is assign fifteen minutes to getting started, at least you've begun. The following day, add thirty minutes to the project. By the third day, you may find yourself ready to work on the project without interruption until it is done.

Deal with only one problem at a time. Don't try to do several things at once. Instead, block out time—for instance, thirty minutes—and devote yourself to accomplishing at least some part of the task that needs to be completed. Then concentrate solely on the job at hand.

Don't allow distractions. Don't take phone calls, and don't stop to chat with someone else. Don't stop for a snack or get up and go into another room, and don't put one thing down and start to work on or read something else. Focus only on the job at hand, and nothing else for that thirty minutes.

Reward yourself. For every task or project that you complete—where you would have procrastinated—give yourself a small reward. Take a walk, watch TV, call a friend for a chat, or have a piece of cake. When you complete a particularly overwhelming project, up the reward accordingly. Buy a new dress, or get away for the weekend. Go out to an expensive restaurant, or spend all day Sunday in bed. Whatever. Live it up. You deserve it.

Don't start what you can't finish, and finish what you start. Finish one project before you start another. If you always find yourself surrounded with half-finished projects, such as craft projects, maybe it's time for you to let go of the idea that you can do so much. Begin only those projects that are

THE PRICE OF PROCRASTINATION

In his book, *Working Smart* (Warner Books), Michael LeBoeuf details the price we pay for procrastination.

Waste of the present . . . All the talking, hoping and wishing about the future isn't making the most of the present, and it certainly isn't building for the future. The past is history and tomorrow is only a vision, but the procrastinator wastes today.

An unfulfilled life. A fulfilled life means accomplishment and enjoyment each day. But procrastination is an immobilizer that blocks fulfillment. To the procrastinator there is always tomorrow, so today never has to count for anything.

Boredom . . . Boredom is a way of life and a great escape for not using present moments constructively. . . . Choosing boredom as a way of life is merely another way the procrastinator structures his time.

The anxiety of working under pressure. By waiting until the last minute, the procrastinator provides himself with numerous opportunities to fill his life with anxieties.

Impotent goals. Many procrastinators, like doers, have goals. Of course, the procrastinator never gets around to pursuing his goals, much less achieving them. Consequently, his goals aren't really goals but rather just a lot of hot air.

The constant plague of unsolved problems . . . Ignoring or failing to recognize and deal with most problems doesn't make them go away. Worse yet, unsolved problems live to create more problems. . . . Unsolved problems are much like vermin. If you don't make the effort to extinguish them, they can breed at an extremely high rate and compound your misery.

Continuous frustration . . . Frustration is not getting what you want out of life. Who needs that? Evidently the procrastinator must, because that's what he sets himself up for. Instead of taking action, he says to himself, "I hope," "I wish," "Maybe things will get better" and other such nonsense.

Poor health . . . Sweeping symptoms of medical problems under the rug and putting off getting them checked can be fatal.

A mediocre career . . . Many a procrastinator is content to stay in a lackluster position or career that he really isn't suited for. Missed business opportunities often result from procrastination.

A life of indecision . . . By being indecisive you allow yourself to become a slave to your future rather than the master of it.

Poor interpersonal relationships . . . Whenever a conflict arises the procrastinator shies away from further contact rather than trying to amicably resolve it with the other person. If a conflict can't be resolved, the procrastinator still does nothing. . . . In addition to the frustration of clinging to bad relationships, the procrastinator simultaneously forgoes the opportunity to form happy and meaningful relationships.

Fatigue . . . Although it may look easy, procrastination is not what it seems. It's an excruciating way to spend your time and energy. . . . [The procrastinator] works hard all day struggling with doubt, indecision, delay, frustration and boredom. After all that, it's no wonder he's tired.

Note: In the interest of accuracy, LeBoeuf's words have been quoted exactly. It is recommended that you apply the price of procrastination to women as well as men; the words *he* and *himself* can easily be interchanged with *she* and *herself*.

important and necessary, and commit fully to finish each one within a reasonable amount of time — every time.

Constantly giving in to procrastination only adds to the daily burden of feeling like there is never enough time to get everything done. Telling yourself that you operate better under pressure may or may not be based in truth. Even if you do function better under last-minute pressure, how does that affect those around you? Your family, your subordinates or your boss may not appreciate all that last-minute hysteria, and eventually it's bound to affect those relationships.

And whether you are postponing things at work, at home or those aspects of your life that contribute to your relationships or your own needs, the bad habits that go along with procrastinating invariably affect every part of your life. Conquering procrastination can mean more time to develop relationships, increase effectiveness and productivity, and find more time for yourself. Remember this anonymous quote: "Even if you're on the right track, you'll get run over if you just sit there."

CHAPTER SEVEN

Eliminating Perfectionism

People throw away what they could have by insisting on perfection,
which they cannot have, and looking for it where they will never find it.
— Edith Schaeffer

I f you find yourself constantly putting things off because only you can do them right, you have a time-consuming problem known as perfectionism. Insisting on perfect results is sometimes appropriate. If you are performing brain surgery, a perfect performance is definitely called for. If you are representing an innocent person who faces the death penalty on murder charges, it goes without saying that you want to present a perfect defense. But if you are mailing out five hundred brochures to potential new clients, it isn't necessary to make sure that every single stamp is placed precisely and perfectly on the envelope.

Why People Are Perfectionists

Perfectionists find all kinds of ways to waste time while striving for stellar results every day. Perfectionists are often motivated by some or all of these thoughts and ideas along with ways of doing things that only fuel the perceived need to be perfect:

- Perfectionists secretly compare their work to others', and always strive to do a far superior job.
- Perfectionists fear making mistakes.
- Perfectionists worry what others think of them.
- Perfectionists tend to do things over and over until they finally (if ever) get it done exactly right.
- Perfectionists are afraid to let anyone else do anything for them, lest they do it wrong.
- Perfectionists are rarely fully satisfied with how something is done — even if they did it themselves.

In addition to doing things over and over, the perfectionist often develops some unnecessary and time-consuming habits. Here are just a few examples.

Time-Consuming Habits of Perfectionists

- Rewrite a report five times before reluctantly handing it in.
- Insist that handwritten items be done only in their handwriting—which is painstakingly perfect.
- Spend extra time to trim the edges off of stamps and make sure that the stamp is placed precisely on the envelope.
- Refuse to do the filing until they can get the perfect supplies and do it themselves—perfectly.
- Demand that only certain colors be used in all areas—from ink to clothes to paint.
- Insist on using only the best, but hard to find, products when other more readily available products would be fine.
- Expect their spouses to do everything perfectly.
- Forbid anyone else to clean their house for fear they won't do it right, or will do something "terrible" like bump the wall with the vacuum cleaner.
- Paint the living room five times in six months, because the color is never just right.
- Insist that the children are immaculate at all times.
- Allow mountains of clutter to pile up, waiting for the time when they can go through it and put everything away exactly right.

The type and scope of these habits is endless.

A perfectionist doesn't just wake up wanting to be perfect. The ongoing struggle to achieve perfection is a learned behavior. People learn perfectionism from a parent who is never satisfied with what the child does or tries to do, or a teacher who spends all of his time with only the best students, rewarding them and ignoring the others. Advertising, which glorifies only the perfect in people, such as the thinnest body or the whitest teeth, is an ongoing spur to perfectionism, as well.

Perfectionism can also be used as an excuse to avoid doing something or, in the case of pack rat, to hoard possessions. If you can't do it perfectly, that's why it can't be done. And you couldn't possibly not hoard items that are, after all, so perfectly made, needed or useful.

Perfectionists also confuse excellent with perfect. In truth, they are not the same at all. Edwin Bliss, author of *Getting Things Done* (Bantam), points out that, "There is a difference between striving for excellence and striving for perfection. The first is attainable, gratifying, and healthy. The second is unattainable, frustrating and neurotic. . . . It is also a terrible waste of time."

So, if you find yourself falling prey to perfectionist tendencies, begin the process of retraining yourself to expect excellent rather than perfect results. While you're at it, you might want to drop your expectations even a notch further. For, while perfection is not the same as excellence, it is also handy to remember that excellent is great, but sometimes good is good enough.

LETTING GO OF PERFECTIONISM

To move from *perfect* to *excellent*, and from there to *good enough*, try to incorporate the following ideas into your daily routine.

Make a list. Write down all the areas that bring out the perfectionist in you. Try to reduce your standards in those areas first, even if you do it a bit at a time. If you insist that your kids dress immaculately at all times, start by letting them dress however they wish one day each week.

Lower your expectations. Most of the time you are placing unnecessarily high expectations on yourself. Try to whittle away at your concept of what perfect is. Understand that being average is not the end of the world; you can be both average and acceptable. Don't let your concept of average become a distortion. What many perfectionists think of as "average" is actually perceived as better than average by those around them.

Focus on the results. Whatever project faces you, keep in mind that results are usually much more important than the method used to achieve those results. Every letter you write doesn't have to be a literary masterpiece.

Just say no. Force yourself to stop giving in to perfectionist tendencies. Every day let at least one imperfect thing happen.

Recognize when enough is enough. Use the "going down for the third time" rule; if you've done something over the third time, it's probably time to let it go. Otherwise you'll find yourself drowning in perfectionism.

Consider a worst case scenario. Continually ask yourself "what's the worst that can happen" if you don't do something perfectly. If you don't get the icing on the cake in perfectly symmetrical swirls, what's the worst that can happen? Absolutely nothing. And, if you don't spend all that time fussing, you'll have a bonus — more time for yourself.

Accentuate the positive. Learn to value and appreciate what's right about what you do, and try to overlook some of what is not perfect. If you write a terrific letter but don't like the way the margins are set on the paper, appreciate the great letter, overlook the margins and get it in the mail.

Results count. Remember that effective and efficient are not the same as perfect. An effective person delegates tasks and projects, and is satisfied even if they aren't done perfectly, as long as they are done efficiently.

Divide and conquer. Break a job into small parts before you become immobilized by a large project that you think you need to do perfectly. Then tackle each small part and work efficiently for good — not perfect — results.

Learn to delegate. By giving away parts or all of a job, you are freeing yourself — cold turkey — from perfectionism. As long as someone else does it well, you don't have to worry about doing it perfectly.

Don't let mistakes devastate you. Mistakes are to be expected and are not considered character flaws. Mistakes are really just opportunities to learn something new. Learn from your mistakes just as an inventor or researcher does. Each error can put you that much closer to what you need to know to possibly change the world (or at least make a dramatic contribution).

A person who lives behind a veil of perfectionism is likely to find true satisfaction fleeting. Usually, the efforts that go into doing everything perfectly result in all pain and very little gain. It just isn't worth it.

CHAPTER EIGHT

Making Decisions

A decision is judgment. It is a choice between alternatives. It is rarely a choice between right and wrong. It is at best a choice between "almost right" and "probably wrong"—but much more often a choice between two courses of action, neither of which is probably more nearly right than the other.

    —Peter Drucker

The ability to make decisions competently is essential to buying more time for yourself, yet decision-making stops some people dead in their tracks. Just as we develop tricks and habits to enable us to procrastinate in dozens of small ways, so too, do we develop countless techniques to automatically avoid making decisions—large and small—on a daily basis. The energy required to continuously manipulate situations and avoid decision-making is put to far better use in making the decisions, living with them and learning from those decisions. You'll save time, worry and energy in the long run. Not only that, you may find more opportunities coming your way. Indecision is responsible for missed opportunities, just as it's responsible for mistakes. On balance, a mistake is something you can learn from, whereas a missed opportunity is gone and cannot be recovered.

Are You Indecisive?
People who give in to the time-consuming habit of indecision are always ready with a battery of excuses for why they can't decide. These excuses are often cloaked in these characteristics.

The Thinker. The thinker has to mull the potential decision over. And over. And over. This is the classic "paralysis by analysis" mindset that takes an idea and examines it to death. The thinker thinks about it and has meetings about it. Bob, the owner of a small business, knows one of his employees is incompetent. But he has to give the idea of replacing the employee a great deal of thought. Three months later, the employee has managed to single-handedly lose the company's biggest account through ineptitude. Bob is still thinking about whether he should consider looking for another employee to replace the incompetent one. Similarly, Mrs. Wilson can't decide which dress to buy for her daughter's wedding. She's seen three she likes, but she has to think about it. Which is the better value? Which looks best on her? Which will look nicer than the dress that the mother of the groom may wear? Mrs. Wilson waits so long to decide that all three dresses are sold and she has no choice but to dig something out of her closet, which definitely did not look better than the dress that the mother of the groom wore.

The Researcher. The researcher spends inordinate amounts of time gathering the facts, and any other information that can be dredged up regarding whatever needs to be decided. A magazine contacts a freelance writer to see if she would submit a proposal for a brief article on the panda that has just been acquired by the zoo. The writer researches the history of the panda back to prehistoric times. Not content with that information, she then calls the national zoo to ask for any and all information—including the balance sheet—on the zoo. And, while doing the research for the proposal, she also discovers that the panda is a big deal in China. So, of course, China needs to be researched a bit further. While all of this researching is being done, the magazine hires someone else. Mrs. Benson wants to enroll her children in private school, but she spends so much time researching the possible schools that the school year starts before she can decide which of the five schools is best, and her kids end up in public school. And Mr. Ross has been asked by the CEO of his company to suggest a more streamlined way of handling the administrative department. Mr. Ross then spends months requesting reports and studies from his subordinates and then asking them for even more paperwork to add to his information on the topic. By the time Mr. Ross gets back to his CEO, he's created more paperwork when the goal was to streamline and reduce paperwork. Not only that, he really doesn't have a clear idea as to exactly how to proceed with the CEO's request, and the CEO is impatient and more than a little miffed at Mr. Ross.

The Worrywart. The worrywart agonizes over any potential decision to near-death. They live by the "what ifs." "What if I toss this piece of paper? I might need it someday. What if I don't sign my children up for four extra-curricular activities apiece . . . will they be deprived or unhappy? What if I have a new brochure printed, I spend all that money, and nobody responds to it? What if I order roof repairs and the roofer doesn't do it right? What if. . . ." The what ifs can successfully stop the worrywart from making any decision in some cases. No papers are ever tossed, so now there are rooms full of boxes, bags and filing cabinets packed to the brim with papers that no one ever looks at. . . . No one even knows what most of the paperwork is about. The worrywart frets so much about how many and which extracurricular activities to register his children for that he doesn't sign them up for anything, and now they really are unhappy, not to mention underfoot all the time. Or, she can't select which activities, so she signs them up for all of them, and runs herself ragged driving the kids to the various activities. And he doesn't print that new brochure, and business is off even more than before. The old brochure is so hopelessly outdated that almost no one responds to it anymore.

The Escapist. The escapist is either afraid to make a decision or so hooked into the habit of procrastination that avoiding the deadly dawn of decision-making becomes normal. People who are afraid to make decisions are often timid and insecure or lack the self-confidence required to move forward on their own. So they map out as many escape routes as possible. "I can't get involved in that. . . . I don't have enough time. Fred knows more about that than I do; why don't you take that up with him? No one ever told me to go ahead on that; I've been waiting for an OK. I didn't think it was that important. My husband deals with that, and he's too busy right now." Before she knows it she is a master of chasing herself in a circle as she constantly works to avoid making decisions by putting it off, or pushing it off on someone else.

Why We Avoid Making Decisions

There are lots of reasons people delay in decision-making:

- The decision will mean a break in routine or habit, and change is always difficult to embrace.
- The decision means you'll have to do something you don't like, and who wants to do that?
- You believe that you will be judged adversely and/or disliked for your decision, and you'd much rather be popular.
- You're afraid your decision will be the wrong one or will have poor results.
- You're paralyzed by fear; you simply don't have a clue as to what to do, and you really wish someone else would do it for you.
- You are certain you don't have enough time to make the decision and to deal with the ramifications of it once it is made.

OVERCOMING INDECISION

Recognizing why we delay on decision-making can help reverse the tendency. And it is vital to build good decision-making skills — for small and large decisions — and use those skills on a daily basis. Poor decision-making skills not only waste time, they increase stress. All the busywork and worry that go along with delay tactics don't make the problem go away. Delay only intensifies unpleasant consequences. If your car is running a little hot, and you don't take it in to the repair shop this Friday, a small radiator repair job could turn into a very expensive engine replacement two weeks from Friday. That repair bill is really going to cost you. You'll lose money for the repair; time without the car, which will lead to enormous inconvenience; and you'll probably be so stressed over it that you'll lose a little sleep. Delaying decisions does not make them To avoid the unpleasantness that often results from deliberately delayed decisions, start changing your habits with the following tips and techniques.

Be proactive. Stop wasting time thinking about what you *should* do and what you *could* do. Consider instead that you should *and* could do something, then do it. The next time you find yourself caught up in wishing ("I wish I could . . . I wish I had . . . I wish I knew . . ."), try to put those wishes into action. Stop wishing so much, and start doing more.

Take the long view. When faced with a decision that will have short-term results, don't lose sight of your long-term goals, and whenever possible try to advance your short-term decisions along the path that will positively affect your long-term goals. If you want to lose fifty pounds, you should decide on your menu for next week now, and then make that decision without fail each week. If you plan good meals each of those weeks, in a year you could be fifty pounds lighter.

Don't let other people wear you down. Don't make a decision that goes against your grain just because the people around you wouldn't get off your back. You are right to impose an early curfew on your teenager, regardless of the wails of protest. Announce your decision, then stick to your guns. Eventually people will know you mean business when you make decisions and will stop campaigning to influence you or change your mind. And they will learn to live with those decisions, for better or worse.

Stop postponing decisions about small problems. Left to fester, they will only turn into large problems. If you can't decide what to do about how to handle your child's behavior in school, and do nothing for now, it could very well turn into a much bigger problem later where you are forced to do something that you don't want to do.

Know when to stop. Gather the facts before you make a decision, but don't overdo it. If you keep postponing the decision until you have more information, chances are, you'll never have enough. These days, the amount of information available is staggering, and you could be getting more of it indefinitely. Don't ask for three reports or studies when one will do. Likewise, if you need input from others before you can make a decision, limit that input to only those whose views are really germane to the situation. Gathering information from too many people only slows things down and causes unnecessary angst.

Set deadlines for assembling facts and making a decision. Then stick to the deadline. If you want to relocate, give yourself a deadline for deciding where you want to go. You'll base that decision on information you obtain prior to the deadline. Once that decision has been made, give yourself a deadline to actually relocate. Then do it.

Don't agonize over minor decisions. You don't need to spend fifteen minutes trying to decide what color of label to buy for your file folders or which rake to buy for the yard. Make the decision quickly and get on with it.

Understand the rewards of risk-taking. Taking risks is not necessarily a bad thing; indeed often it is a very good thing and can yield surprising results. If taking risks scares you, start small. Decide to buy some plants you're not sure of, or drive home from work on a new route. What's the worst that can happen? On the other hand, what's the best that can happen? Once you've survived the plant or driving experiment, move on to bigger and riskier decisions.

Don't fight change. Like it or not, change comes along with some regularity in nearly everyone's life. Fighting it by refusing to decide how to deal with it only makes accepting the change that much more difficult. If new management takes over your department, anticipate change, and decide how to accommodate it. If you don't, the new management is likely to decide to let you go.

Never lose sight of your overall objective. If your goal in life is to be a good mother and loving wife, remind yourself of that when you have to make unpopular but wise decisions at home. If you are single and aching to get married, think about that the next time you decide to turn down an invitation to meet new people so you can sit at home in front of the TV.

Use a tally sheet. If you're having trouble making a decision, make a list of the good and the bad things that might happen as a result of the decision. Review the list, and if the good outweighs the bad, go for it.

Do it now. Stop waiting until the last minute to make decisions. You make yourself and others crazy when you do that. If someone invites you to a movie on Friday, why wait until Friday morning to make the decision?

Then once you decide, be prepared to do. Do whatever it takes to bring the decision to life. If you decide to present a revolutionary new proposal to your boss, be prepared to follow up by seeing the proposal through to the action and completion phase.

Don't worry; be happy. Catch yourself every time you find yourself beset with worry. If you're plagued with recurring thoughts of "what if," try to get off those thoughts. Make the decision and move forward, otherwise the "what ifs" will have you on hold forever.

Stop overanalyzing everything. Most decisions can be made in the space of a few minutes or hours. Only a few decisions are worth more time than that. Pulling up your city roots and moving to the country is probably not a decision to be made hastily, but deciding which doormat to buy should be a five-minute affair.

Maintain your resolve. Don't waste time with second thoughts after you've made a decision. You'll just waffle on everything, and get little accomplished. Before you know it, you'll be losing sleep over every little decision, and it's far easier to make a decision and let it go or live with it.

Monitor the results of your decisions, and change direction when necessary. If the decision turns out to be a mistake, don't wallow over spilled milk. Learn from it, and move on. Your next decision will be a wiser one.

Decide to Decide

Remember that making a decision is making a choice. It means choosing from alternatives, and almost any alternative you select is better than always opting for the easy way out—doing nothing. Michael LeBoeuf, author of *Working Smart* (Warner Books), points out that making decisions means making choices and having control: "Every decision is an opportunity to gain some control over your future. However, when you put off decisions you are forfeiting that opportunity. Sooner or later circumstances will prevail and your right of choice will be taken away."

So the next time you are faced with making a decision, vow to reduce your stress level and increase the time you have for yourself. Don't say that you will deal with it next time, and don't keep telling yourself and everybody else that you'll do something "as soon as" you figure out what to do. Instead make the decision and do what needs to be done. By getting quickly past the decision stage and into the doing stage, you can move yourself closer to finding more time for yourself to spend however you decide.

CHAPTER NINE

Learning to Delegate

It takes no genius to observe that a one-man band never gets very big. To conduct a symphony you have to let others play. . . . A peak performer delegates to other people in order to multiply his or her own strengths.
— Charles Garfield

By the time I show someone else how to do it, I could have done it twice myself." This is an all-too-common refrain of people who are reluctant to delegate. Or how about, "They won't do it right. I just know I'll have to do it myself." And the truth is, whether you are talking about teaching your child how to make the bed or asking your assistant to take over some clerical work you've been doing, you're probably right. You could do it faster and better, but if you never delegate, you will always have too much to do, with too little time for yourself. And it is entirely possible that you will never realize your full potential—whether it is to be the world's best mother or to be an executive at work. Great mothers don't rate perfectly made beds as a priority, and chief executives do not busy themselves with clerical work that can be done by others.

Nevertheless, nearly everyone has, at one time or another, fallen back on one of many tried-and-true laments to justify their refusal to delegate:

- "Nobody else can do it right—I'm the only person who can do it correctly."
- "It would take someone else forever. I can do it in half the time."
- "I can't afford to pay someone to do it."
- "Even though it's an inconsequential task, I like doing it."
- "I like to be on top of everything myself."
- "That's ridiculous! I don't need anyone else to do my work."

Whether you employ one or all of these excuses, they tend to become an automatic litany that issues forth without question or discussion to explain why you have no time, and to reinforce your own importance, since you are the only one who can do the task. Yet people who delegate almost always have more time for themselves, and are generally considered to be far more important than people who do not delegate.

Moving past the excuses for not delegating, you can probably locate the real reasons you avoid using this timesaving device. The following list may help you identify your own points of resistance.

Why We Refuse to Delegate

- We are afraid of losing control.
- We want to do everything according to unrealistic perfectionist standards.
- We are afraid that if we ask others to do something they'll think we are a slave driver or they won't like us.
- We want to do it ourselves because it's easy and we like doing it — plus it means we can put off more important or difficult things until later.
- We believe that we really should be able to do everything ourselves, and that if we can't, it's a character flaw.
- We're certain everyone else is incompetent.
- We're afraid that if we delegate a project it will be done wrong and will reflect on us, or that we'll be blamed.
- We'd rather do everything ourselves because it makes us irreplaceable.
- We fill the role of martyr perfectly, and secretly enjoy the admiration or pity that goes with the role.
- We don't want to take the time to train people to do the job at hand.
- Often it doesn't even occur to us that something can be delegated because we just don't think in those terms.

Many of these negative and obstinate ideas about delegating create a self-fulfilling prophecy. If you like to waste your time doing all the minutiae, you'll find a way to do just that. And you will probably never advance beyond that. If you absolutely insist on doing everything yourself, you will. And, in the end, you'll be exhausted and have no time for yourself.

Delegating is a good thing, and everyone should try it at least once in their lives. More than that, wherever possible you should fit delegating into your life on a regular basis. By so doing, you will buy more time for yourself. If you're still not convinced, consider the following list.

Ten Good Reasons to Delegate

1. Delegating to get the job done — and done soon — is preferable to waiting indefinitely until you can do the job yourself. And it's definitely better than not getting the job done at all.

2. Functioning effectively is more important than functioning perfectly. Unless the task at hand is something like brain surgery, having someone else do a good—rather than perfect—job is often good enough.

3. Micromanaging everything instead of delegating the details can mean that someone else takes responsibility for the big picture. In the end, the big-picture person is nearly always more successful than the detail-obsessed person.

4. Controlling and doing everything yourself does not necessarily make you important. Mostly it just makes you anxious and tired all the time.

5. It makes more sense to worry about getting things done than it does to worry about being liked. Finding time for yourself through delegation should take priority over any popularity contests you think are attached to delegating. If you respectfully ask someone to do something, most of those fears about being disliked will prove to be unfounded.

6. Heroes and martyrs are admired and sympathized with. However, the label hero or martyr is generally applied to people who do things like save lives or live in leper colonies. Refusing to delegate so that you will be seen as a hero for doing everything just isn't in the same league as the real martyrs. You might get a pat on the back, but don't delude yourself. You're no hero.

7. Nearly everyone and anyone can be asked or trained to do something. This includes children, teenagers, spouses, support staff, senior citizens, and all manner of independent services—from household help to errand runners to yard care services.

8. It does take an initial investment of time to train someone, but once that person is trained, you'll be rewarded with more time for yourself.

9. It is not a sign of weakness to delegate. It's a sign of responsibility, vision and good common sense.

10. No one person can do everything. This means you.

It can take some convincing when someone is dead set against delegation—whatever the reason. You may have been on the receiving end of delegation and hated it, or perhaps you've given it a stab yourself once or twice, and the results have been rocky at best or miserable and unhappy at worst. The problem usually is simply stated: People just don't know *how* to delegate effectively. But delegation is a skill that can be developed, and as it's developed you'll experience more success—whether you're trying to use more people to handle your business or to get the house cleaned once a week. To help you develop good delegating skills, and turn it into a positive experience, use these guidelines.

DELEGATING DOS
Do:

- Get over your fear of losing control.
- Set objectives, and keep your eye firmly fixed on those goals.
- Give up time-consuming tasks that you do just because you like them — but that others can do easily.
- Give up any guilt feelings that you might have that make you think you "should be able to do it all yourself."
- Spend your time solving problems rather than placing the blame on others for those problems.
- Encourage others to take risks and stretch beyond their current capabilities.
- Say what you mean, and mean what you say when giving directions. Make your instructions specific and comprehensive. Remember that people are not mind readers.
- Provide training and any supplies or tools that may be needed to complete the job successfully.
- Make your expectations realistic and achievable. This may mean reducing your expectations somewhat from time to time.
- Set consistent standards for everyone.
- Invest in trust. Once people are trained, they need to feel valued and trusted in order to do their best every time.
- Indicate resources that might be available to help complete the project.
- Establish consequences for a job that is either poorly done or not done in time. And, just as important, praise someone for a job well done.
- Make yourself available for advice as needed.
- Establish key points at which you will review the work that's been done. Without being judgmental, correct any problems or change direction as needed at that time. Then have the person proceed to the next stage.
- Set a good example at all times; make sure you are organized and productive and that you handle yourself and your work in a realistic and professional manner. Others will tend to follow that example.
- Keep a page in your planner or a notebook for each of the people or services that you routinely delegate to. Note the date you make the request, and describe the task or project to be completed. The people you routinely assign work to should also keep a similar log so that they can also effectively prioritize assignments as you delegate them. Regularly review progress and make notes on that page regarding the project. Establish a date for completion, and when the job is done, cross

that task or project off that person's page.
- Communicate openly and make it clear that you have written the details (including the deadline) down. Encourage the person completing the task to do the same. This eliminates that ever popular refrain, "But you didn't tell me to do that!"
- Praise achievement publicly.

DELEGATING DON'TS

Don't:
- Get sidetracked or obsessed by details someone else can handle.
- Insist on perfection. Look instead for results that are excellent or good.
- Focus on how something is done; concentrate on the results.
- Worry about being disliked or perceived as a slave driver. Focus instead on distributing work fairly and equitably.
- Be demanding or unreasonable in tone or action. Be firm but respectful.
- Delegate to someone who is incompetent or chronically disorganized. On the other hand,
- Be afraid to give people a chance to prove themselves to you and to improve their own abilities, competence and organization. Empowering the people around you only adds to your strength.
- Allow those who do work to avoid responsibility for the results of their work. Insist on personal accountability.
- Be immediately or overly critical. Expectations can be adjusted, and mistakes can almost always be corrected if caught in time. Praise what was done right, and review errors later or when you begin the next project by saying, "This time I'd like to see it done this way."
- Always delegate trivial or mundane tasks that involve no responsibility and require hours of tedium. People will only come to resent both you and the tasks you give them.
- Delegate to someone who is already clearly overburdened. Be flummoxed, however, by someone who claims to be swamped, but who is really camouflaging a moderate workload with lots of clutter and complaining.
- Allow yourself to be put off by the amount of time it will take to train someone. Remember that training is only an initial time investment, which will eventually pay off in more time for yourself.
- Allow upward delegation. Upward delegation results when you permit someone to become overly dependent on you. This sets the scene for them to return to you, mid-project, saying, "Can you give me more help on this?" Or, "Since you're doing such and so anyway, can you

take care of this as well?" Besides the interruption of your time, this ploy all too often results in some job or part of a job being insidiously transferred back to you. Disallow these tactics by saying no or by providing only enough guidance to help that person solve the problem or complete the project alone.

- Set unrealistic or unreasonable deadlines. On the other hand,
- Accept any bogus excuses for missed deadlines.
- Be influenced by personality when you delegate. Delegate according to capability, not personality.
- Lose sight of that all-important big picture. That's the one with the big rewards at the end of the rainbow.

DELEGATING AT WORK

At home and at work, those delegating dos and don'ts will help you develop the skills you need to get things done without doing them yourself.

But the art of delegation at work—whether you are the person doing the delegating or the person being delegated to—is an art that should be practiced to perfection. Many a ladder to success has been toppled due to the inability to handle delegation properly. Alec Mackenzie, author of *The Time Trap* (Amacom), paints an all-too-common view of delegating in the workplace by quoting the anonymous author of *Functions of an Executive*:

As nearly everyone knows, an executive has practically nothing to do except,

to decide what is to be done;

to tell somebody to do it;

to listen to reasons why it should not be done, why it should be done by someone else, or why it should be done in a different way;

to follow up to see if the thing has been done;

to discover it has not been done;

to inquire why it has not been done;

to listen to excuses from the person who should have done it;

to follow up again to see if the thing has been done, only to discover it has been done incorrectly;

to point out how it should have been done;

to conclude that as long as it has been done, it might as well be left where it is;

to wonder if it is time to get rid of a person who cannot do a thing right;

to reflect that he probably has a wife and large family, and certainly
   any successor would be just as bad, and maybe worse;*
to consider how much simpler and better the thing would have been
   done if one had done it oneself in the first place;
to reflect sadly that one could have done it right in twenty minutes,
   and now one has to spend two days to find out why it has taken
   three weeks for somebody else to do it wrong.

This amusing scenario needn't be representative of your delegating experience. Knowing you should delegate is not the same as knowing how to delegate for best results. Whether you are asking a member of your support staff to do some research and write a comprehensive report or telling your youngsters to make their beds and clean their rooms, how you handle the request, and your follow-through, can make all the difference. Done right, delegating means that tasks are completed with good results, and you benefit personally by freeing more time for yourself. Along with the Delegating Dos and Don'ts, use these tips to help you master delegation at work.

If You Are Delegating

Match the job to the person. Make it a point to know who does what especially well. Don't expect everything from one person. Don't give administrative work to a salesperson who hates being inside, and don't ask your secretary to make sales.

Start early. Don't delegate late in the day unless it's absolutely necessary. Instead, have an uninterrupted meeting for ten minutes or so first thing each morning. Go over the status of what has been delegated, and hand out new projects and tasks at this meeting. Then allocate extra time and attention for review and problem solving if necessary.

Don't confuse delegating with dumping. People know when they are being dumped on, and they will resent it.

Don't pass the buck. Passing the buck to avoid responsibility will eventually catch up with, and backfire, on you. In the meantime you will not be making friends and influencing people—you will be alienating them. Why work at annoying others?

No ego trips allowed. Don't delegate just so you can make yourself feel important. True importance comes from much more than arbitrarily telling others what to do.

Don't delegate responsibility without also granting some authority. With-

---

*This is a direct quote; today, of course, it is just as likely that *she* has a husband and a large family.

out at least minimal authority, a person can only work in frustrating fits and starts, and productivity and quality can suffer as a result.

Focus on what needs to be done rather than how it should be done. Let go of overseeing and dictating every little procedure that goes into accomplishing a task. Tell yourself that as long as you get the results you require, the procedures for achieving those goals (unless they are somehow detrimental to others or take too much time) are not your concern.

Be honest. Don't fib about the nature of the task being delegated. If it's drudgery, don't pretend it's glamorous.

Promote a spirit of teamwork. Consider increasing your effectiveness dramatically by delegating everything that can be done by someone else. Make people feel they're part of a team. Help them see the big picture so they know what they're working toward and feel like an integral part of the team that achieves key goals successfully.

If You Are Being Delegated To

Don't be afraid to ask questions. Especially important are the following:

What is my authority and how far does it go?

What exactly is my responsibility?

How am I doing?

Be a troubleshooter. When you run into a problem, try to think of at least two solutions before you take it to your superior. You'll get more attention, be taken seriously, and ultimately increase your chance of promotion by showing that you are a thinker and problem-solver as well as a doer.

Get a second opinion. If you become overloaded with tasks, make a concise list and present it to your manager. Ask the manager to prioritize the tasks, and follow those priorities. Likewise, if you are always busy and your boss constantly dumps last-minute projects on your desk, ask him to prioritize the new projects or tasks for you. Go over what you are already doing with your boss and ask where the new work should be on your to-do list. If more than one boss drops work on you, follow this same procedure, letting them tough it out among themselves as to whose work is most important.

Always write things down. Don't think or say, "I'll remember that." If you write everything down (even in the presence of your boss), you are guaranteed to remember everything (just consult your notes), and it may impact the boss who always says, "I told you that the other day," when she actually did no such thing.

Repeat instructions aloud. This tells your boss that you understand exactly what's expected and how to proceed.

Ask for deadlines. In addition to the final deadline for the entire project, each segment of the project should have a deadline. Schedule your work so that you can meet those deadlines.

Be courageous. Don't allow the fear of seeming incompetent stop you from trying to take on new projects or come up with new solutions to old problems. Remember the adage, "nothing ventured, nothing gained."

Suggest improvements. If you have ideas about how something can be streamlined, present them to your boss in a tactful manner. Don't let yourself be sidetracked by a fear of rejection. It's a job, not a date.

When in doubt, ask. If you don't know how to do something, either ask your boss or someone else who may have the correct answer. It's not a strike against you to ask questions, but doing something wrong (because you wouldn't ask) is always remembered in a negative light.

Get and stay organized. It's impossible to effectively and efficiently handle multiple responsibilities and tasks if your desk and your files are a mess all the time. (See Part Three for specific ideas and advice on this subject.)

Share information. Don't try to ensure your job security by setting yourself up as the only person who knows how to do something, or as the only person who understands the filing system. Doing this will only mean that you'll definitely stay at that position (rather than being promoted to a better position), and besides, one day, when you least expect it, somebody will reach the end of the rope regarding your domain. They'll be sick of not understanding how something is done — and waiting for you to do it — and they'll find somebody to establish a new system. With this new system you might just find yourself out of a job.

Delegating, once you get the hang of it, can be addictive. After all, why do something you hate and don't want to do, particularly if your time is better spent on more important matters. And if you're being delegated to, handle the work smoothly and you may work your way into a better position because you've done such a good job. The big payoff can be more time for yourself!

DELEGATING AT HOME

Regardless of their best efforts to delegate, many people find delegating at home to be the most difficult. Trying to get the children to help out and do their part can mean putting up with everything from tears to tantrums to outright manipulation and blatant avoidance. By the time the average parent wades through the angst of, say, getting the twelve-year-old to take out the trash every day, it really does seem that doing it yourself is the saner solution. But when you give in to the trash, you have taken the first step down the path that leads to doing it all yourself. Your twelve-year-old, having savored the victory of upward delegation (delegating the trash back to you through his manipulation), will only go on to use the same tactics to get out of other chores. When, where and how do you draw the line?

You can deter task avoidance at home if you get into the habit of delegating effectively and consistently. Whether you are delegating to a four-year-old or a teenager, use these tactics to stick to your guns, and get things done at home.

Stop feeling sorry for your kids. Unless you have adopted cruel and inhuman delegating techniques, the children's plaintive wails over their chore list are without any merit whatsoever. Ignore their complaints completely.

Be prepared to reduce your expectations initially. A poorly made bed is not as good as a well-made one, but it's better than an unmade bed. Remember, practice makes perfect.

Expect to explain not only how but why things are done a particular way. Training time with children can be lengthy but ultimately rewarding, so don't give up early.

Put aside your worries about infringing on others' time. Your spouse's time may be valuable, but so is yours, so don't be afraid to ask for, and expect, help.

Let family members know what is expected of them in advance. If you want your teenager to do three loads of laundry every Saturday, don't wait until Saturday morning to issue the order.

Break jobs down into manageable pieces. If children are too small to thoroughly clean their entire room, ask them to put their clothes away or pick up their toys and put them away. Slightly older children can clear the floor of objects and make their beds. Teenagers can pick up their rooms weekly and dust and vacuum as well, and if company drops by, you won't be embarrassed.

Get everyone involved. Remember that many hands make light work. Don't make one family member help out with the housework more than other members. Since everyone enjoys the benefits of a well-run, clean household, each person should contribute to maintaining these benefits. After all, each member of the family eats the food, uses the bathroom and likes clean laundry. Therefore, as soon a child is old enough, he should help with at least those vital areas of housework and meal preparation. Once everyone gets used to that concept, there's no reason family members can't all help with the rest of the house and yard work, too.

Use positive reinforcement. Compliment completed tasks, and from time to time, issue positive reminders. Agreeing to a request provides a good opportunity to issue a positive reminder. If your child wants to go to a friend's house for a sleep-over, you can respond, "Well, you've done such a good job with your chores for the last week — and without being reminded — that, yes, you can go." This spontaneous reward and compliment issued whenever possible can work far better than paying family members with money for doing what they should be doing in the first place.

Don't let anyone claim sainthood for helping out. Since the people who routinely do the housework, meal preparation, yard work and errands have never been able to lay legitimate claim to sainthood, other family members who pitch in shouldn't be elevated to the status of saint either. Family members who expect to be glorified for their effort only add to the workload. Who needs to feel guilty about having a saint cook a meal or vacuum a floor? You'll feel obliged to do it yourself. Don't tolerate the symptoms of sainthood, should they appear — it sets a very bad precedent. You'll end up spending time and effort building the saint's ego with expressions of your undying gratitude for at least a week or so, adding to your mental exhaustion. A simple thank-you should suffice, and you should expect more of the same help on a regular basis. Period.

Use a chore list and calendar. Write down who is supposed to do what for at least a week at a time. Post it for everyone to see. This way, you can bypass that ever popular, "Nope, it's not my turn to load the dishwasher (or feed the pets or whatever)." Rotate the chores so everyone gets the benefit of learning how to do everything (according to age and capability) that goes into taking care of themselves at home.

Keep an eye out for sabotage maneuvers. The husband who cleans the bathroom once and does a pathetic job of it is likely doing it poorly on purpose (especially if he was in the service, where almost everyone gets some latrine cleaning training). Give him a break by giving him the opportunity to do it over again and again. The same approach works with kids who deliberately do a chore poorly. Learn to live with the poor results for a few days or a week, then make sure the same person gets the same chore again. Eventually, they'll get the message that sabotage tactics don't work since they only have to live with it, and do it again next week.

Live by this rule: Except for babies and very small toddlers, no one is too young or too male to help out around the house.

Hire help. If you're drowning in chores with not enough family hands to help out, hire someone else or a service to do the work. Even if only occasionally, this investment has a major payoff. You'll be buying more time for yourself to enjoy as you see fit. Unless you have no money whatsoever, stop wasting energy fussing about the price for such services. Instead, find creative and affordable ways to delegate as many chores and errands as possible. Then relax and revel in your free time.

The Household Chore List

Owner of Creative Time Plus in Torrance, California, Ann Gambrell addresses the problem of the household chore list in her seminars for working women. According to Gambrell, everyone can and should do something. "I believe that every member of the family should be prepared to share the love and the dirt, equally," says Gambrell. Generally speaking, she says you can create a household chore list centered around the following capabilities and potential contributions from each family member.

Three- to four-year-olds make great fetchers. They can get the mail and the newspapers from the porch and they can fetch diapers for the baby. They can also help set the table, fold napkins, and fold small towels and washcloths when you do the laundry.

Five- to seven-year-olds can gather laundry, fold much of it, and hang some of it up as well. They can set the table, and clear it after a meal. They can take the newspapers to the recycling bin, feed pets, and clean up after them. They can also make their own beds and keep their rooms tidy. They like to sweep outside walks and can also help rake and bag leaves in the fall.

Eight- to twelve-year-olds can do all of the above, plus more yard work, such as planting, pulling weeds and mowing, depending on maturity. They can dust and vacuum, load and empty the dishwasher, and take out trash. They can make and bag their own lunches, and help dress and care for younger ones. In safe areas, they can run to the store on the corner, and they can clean mirrors and windows (they love squeegees and spray pumps).

Teens can do all of the above, plus their own laundry (including ironing). They can feed the babies and babysit, and help prepare food and snacks. Teens that drive can gas up the family car, run errands and shop for groceries (be sure to give them a list).

Husbands can get the coffee on in the morning and start or prepare dinner at night. They can grocery shop (with a list), and can take the kids shopping for clothes (they will never understand what you go through until they undertake one shopping mission on their own). They can handle or supervise recycling and trash take-out as well as yard work. They can clean the windows and screens as well as other heavy cleaning, such as cleaning the basement or garage. They can maintain the family cars, and help with the errands, such as picking up the cleaning. They can clear the table and empty the dishwasher. They can help the kids with their homework and get them their breakfast. They can change diapers and bathe the smaller children. They can volunteer for car pool duties and attend parent-teacher conferences. They can also vacuum and clean the bathroom.

Gambrell points out that a fair chore list makes it easy for everyone to know what is expected of them, and while it sometimes takes a little time for everybody to get with the program, Gambrell firmly believes that starting children out early with a chore list makes training them to accept and do the chores a simpler matter. Guilt shouldn't even enter the picture for the work-

WHERE TO FIND HELP

At home or in the office, for short-term or long-term projects, help may be closer than you think. And it needn't cost a fortune. Here's where to look.

Senior citizens. Check local community centers, and ask friends and relatives if they know anyone who wants to stay active with some extra work.

Teenagers. Post a notice at the local high school or any place teens congregate. Check with neighbors who may have teenagers as well.

Friends. See if you have friends that you can trade some chores with. If she likes to cook but hates to clean, and you like to clean but hate to cook, she can put together some meals to be stored in your freezer, and you can give her house a good cleaning once a week.

Temporary employment agencies. Look here for part-time help when you need extra help for a short time at the office.

Professional services. Today there are services to do just about everything, from free shopping services at major department stores, to dog walking and errand services. Check the ads in your local publications to find these services that can be hired for small one-time or regular projects (such as a day of errands, or walking Fido every morning) or for major projects that are just too time-consuming or overwhelming (such as moving or reorganizing your entire home or office, which can be streamlined with the help of moving services or a professional organizer).

Remember that *delegating* is just another word for *doing*. The beauty of it is that the doing gets done by others so that you can have what you really want—more time for yourself.

ing woman, claims Gambrell. "Instead of feeling guilty, women should be glad to delegate chores, knowing that by doing so, she is helping her family learn and retain the life skills necessary to take care of themselves both now and in the future." She believes that allowances can be fraught with peril. Once you start paying, they tend to expect it for everything, and are happy to not do something, saying "just deduct it from my allowance." If you ask them to do something extra, they're likely to ask, "What do I get for that?" Don't pay, advises Ann. What they get for doing their chores is a roof over their heads, a bed to sleep in, and food to eat. And a family that appreciates and loves them.

CHAPTER TEN

Eliminating Interruptions

In heaven when the blessed use the telephone they will say what they have to say and not a word besides.

—Somerset Maugham

There's probably no one who hasn't, at some time or another, been busy all day, but accomplished nothing significant. The day starts with the best intentions and plans, but before you know it, it has been interrupted. Many times. With each interruption, your distraction increases, and the potential for getting things done decreases. Interruptions all seem legitimate, giving credence to the refrain, "I just couldn't get to it today; I was interrupted a million times. . . ."

At home or at work, interruptions become so common that we tend to accept them as a normal part of daily living. It never occurs to us that perhaps we could put a stop to many of these interruptions, and in so doing, buy ourselves much more time. Curbing interruptions starts with determining exactly what those interruptions are. Common complaints about interruptions often include:

- The phone rings at home, and it's supper time. Nevertheless, you get up from the table to answer the phone.
- At work, mail is put into your in-box twice a day. Both times, when you see the mail arrive, you stop what you are doing to go through the mail.
- Your toddler has a million ways to interrupt you during every waking moment. His needs must be addressed immediately.
- You are spending Saturday cleaning out the garage, and a buddy comes by and talks you into going to the sale at the hardware store.
- During the course of a business day, at least a dozen times someone pops into your office, saying, "Got a minute?" You always say yes, and the visitor's question always requires more than a minute.
- The phone rings on your desk. You have to answer it—it could be a

client, or perhaps even a welcome social call. By the time you hang up, at least ten minutes have passed. And this happens all day long.

- Someone calls you for advice. Although you doubt they'll take your advice, you're flattered and spend forty-five minutes dispensing your special brand of wisdom.

Although it's easy to tag interruptions as being out of our control, the reverse is true. Interruptions can be controlled, and in many cases, eliminated. But first, it's important to recognize the role we play in allowing, and in some cases, encouraging interruptions.

Why We Allow Interruptions

- We hate to say no.
- We like to feel important or needed.
- We welcome a distraction or diversion.
- We like to socialize.
- We want to be liked.
- We want to be polite.
- We're bored.
- We're curious.
- We're lonely.
- Being interrupted constantly adds to pressure, and we think we work best under pressure.

Of course you can't eliminate all interruptions. Before you can reduce the number of interruptions in your daily schedule, you need to analyze the types of interruptions you receive. There are two types of interruptions: *necessary* and *unnecessary*. Necessary interruptions include work-related interruptions that pertain directly to your job description, and emergencies. Customer calls are a necessary interruption, but can they be handled by someone else? If so, they don't have to interrupt your day. A meeting called by your boss must be attended, and if the school calls to say that your child has been in an accident, obviously you need to tend immediately to that interruption. Your father has a heart attack, the firm's biggest client calls out of the blue to tell you he's thinking of switching firms, your dog gets hit by a car, or the building catches on fire. All necessary interruptions. Drop everything and give them your full attention.

Completely unnecessary interruptions, on the other hand, are far more common. Peppering the day are invitations to stop what you're doing—to automatically deal with each and every interruption as it comes along. The phone rings far too often, and you always answer it regardless of what you are doing. Drop-in visitors are common in your office or at your desk; they stop by to chat about anything and everything—from the results of the football game to a date they had, to the sales report due this Friday that has everybody hot under the collar. You make unnecessary phone calls, and drop by others' desks because you are bored or need a diversion. You run out to the grocery store, and see a sale sign in a dress shop on the way, so you make a quick detour that takes thirty minutes, and you know it's a useless interruption since you can't possibly afford to buy anything. Interruptions such as these are all too common, and easily dispensed with.

To reduce and even eliminate many of the interruptions that litter your days, try using these tactics to bring your schedule under control.

OVERCOMING INTERRUPTIONS

If you didn't commit to keeping a time log when it was first suggested in chapter one, now is the time to set one up. (If you have already started a time log, refer to that one now to pinpoint the interruptions that trip you up the most.) Although it will be time-consuming, keep a log for one week, noting each interruption you incur during the day. At the end of the week, tote up all the interruptions. Before you categorize them into necessary and unnecessary, list the types of interruptions you run up against on a regular basis. Then start whittling away at all the unnecessary interruptions, and reducing the necessary interruptions by managing them better.

There are four main types of interruptions that tend to be a bugaboo for nearly everyone: the drop-in visitor at work, the telephone, self-interruptions, and children. You may not be surprised to see these kinds of interruptions popping up often on your list of crazy-makers. If so, you will want to take advantage of some of the techniques and information that follow.

Interruption #1
The Drop-In Visitor at Work

When someone stops by your desk or office and chirps, "Hi, got a minute?" say no. If they tell you "it'll only take a second," don't believe it. It always takes longer than a second, and if you're in the middle of something, you'll lose your momentum if you stop to talk to the drop-in. If possible say no, you don't have the time. Then ask what the topic is, and if it's important, arrange to discuss it at another time. Don't be afraid to be specific about time limits. You could ask, "Will fifteen minutes be enough time?" If the visitor says no, or waffles, suggest that an appointment be scheduled at a later time.

If the visitor's question can be handled by someone else, refer him to that person. Do this even if you can handle it—there's no need for you to kill ten minutes on something that is someone else's responsibility.

The minute someone drops into your office unexpectedly (or stops by your desk) to chat, stand up. It's a hint that's hard to miss. If necessary, start walking away from your desk. Tell the person you were just leaving, and ask if "we can talk as we walk."

Get to the office at least thirty minutes before everyone else so you can have some uninterrupted time to deal with your paperwork and get your priorities straight for the day.

Try to avoid storing information in your office that others need to see regularly. Your office will start to take on the tone of a library, with people popping in and out at will, saying, "I just need to see that XYZ manual."

Take some time to figure out *why* you're being interrupted, instead of dwelling on *who* is interrupting. You may find a common reason for the interruptions that can be eliminated. If your secretary is always interrupting you to get needed information, perhaps that information can be typed up and put into a brief manual for the secretary to keep on his desk.

If you have an assistant or secretary, try to post them — like a guard — outside your office and have them screen visitors, stopping them before they get inside your door. This is an old-fashioned way of doing business, but it is loaded with benefits in time saved by avoiding needless interruptions.

Remove some chairs from your office. If people can't sit down when they come in to chat, they won't stay for very long. If some other important person or client comes into your office, you can always rustle up a chair from someplace else. If you're afraid you won't be able to locate an extra chair when you need one, you can always keep one in your office in the corner. Load it up with files or reference manuals. People will be reluctant to take it upon themselves to unload the chair in order to sit; on the other hand, if someone important drops by, you can empty the chair quickly.

You could also rearrange the furniture in your office. Since people are less likely to stop into your office if they can't make eye contact, place your desk so you sit with your back to the door. If that's not possible, at least put the telephone behind you (such as on a credenza). This way your back will be to the door when you're on the phone, and people will be less likely to interrupt you.

At least some of the time, close your office door. If your office has an open-door policy, ask if they'll consider implementing a "quiet hour" that allows closed doors and no interruptions for that hour. But don't get in the habit of closing the door too often for too long. If you do people will start to think that the only way they can get to talk to you is to interrupt you and the closed door will lose its significance.

Don't let the drop-in visitor get off the subject that they initially stopped in to discuss. Stick to the topic at hand, and don't be tempted into digressing on to other irrelevant subjects such as how incompetent George is, or the results of last night's ball game.

If it's your boss who is doing the interrupting, of course you have to pay attention. But if she goes on too long, you can bring it diplomatically to a close by noting that you are in the middle of that regional report she asked you to do, and you're doing your best to get it ready in time for the board meeting this Friday. Most bosses will put the report ahead of chatting, and leave.

Cut the query short. If you start to answer a question and your answer leads to another question, and another—cut the conversation short. Say, "You know this is a bit more complicated than I thought, and it needs more than a few minutes to be discussed properly. I'm in the middle of something right now, and can't give the problem my full attention. Let's make another time to get together and discuss it."

Set parameters at the beginning. When the visitor says that he needs to talk with you, say, "Fine, but I've only got about five minutes to give you right now. I'm preparing for a meeting, and I have to leave soon."

If you have important work to do, try to find an alternative site—even if only for a few hours. See if the conference room is available (and don't tell anyone that's where you are going). You can even claim a dental appointment on occasion and do some work from home or from the library.

Consider scheduling visiting hours, and have people schedule time with you for anything that will take more than five minutes.

If you know you are going to be interrupted by a chronic windbag, pre-arrange with a co-worker to come into your office and "remind" you of another appointment in five minutes.

If someone is stopping by your desk for socializing purposes only, and you want to socialize, but need to get your work done, arrange to meet them on your coffee break or at lunchtime. That way you can socialize guilt-free and uninterrupted by work.

When someone stops by to discuss something, tell them you are busy right now, but you can stop by their desk in about twenty minutes. Then go to their desk. It is much easier to get out of someone else's office without wasting time than it is it get them out of your office.

If someone from outside the office stops by unannounced, and if he's not an important client, don't invite him into your office. Meet him in the reception area or the hall. Shake hands and ask how you can help. Met this way, most people will either get right to the point, or mumble something about just being in the neighborhood, and then depart. You can go back to your office without having wasted too much time.

When a visitor comes into your office, announce to your assistant when you'll be done. Saying, "We'll only be about fifteen minutes" to someone else within earshot of the visitor usually makes an impression that helps the visitor get to the point and then leave.

If your assistant tends to interrupt you dozens of times during the day, set up a meeting first thing every morning to go over the results of yesterday's work as well as the projects on tap for today. Make sure that you give her your undivided attention during this time. Doing this should reduce the interruptions from the person substantially.

Hang a sign on your door that says "Quiet time—come back at 10:30." Then make sure you're available at 10:30 to handle all questions.

Interruption #2
The Telephone

Using the telephone to call out (rather than take the time to write, for example) can be a great time-saver. Unfortunately, using the telephone to receive calls can be a constant source of interruption and irritation and a bona fide time waster. Therefore, remember the Golden Rule of the Telephone: Just because it rings doesn't mean you have to answer it. Most of the time answering the phone is a reflex action, born of habit and fueled by curiosity. The automatic need to know (who is calling and why) needs to be curbed before the phone will stop ringing.

Get an answering machine or voice mail; when you are busy train yourself to let the equipment take a message. You can return the calls later.

Screen your calls. You can avoid unimportant calls in several ways; along with the automatic answering equipment, you can have your secretary or assistant screen your calls. You can also ask your spouse to do it, and teach your kids how to screen calls that are unimportant or can wait.

Get to the point immediately. When someone calls you, say hello, followed immediately by "How can I help you?" This should help the caller get right to the point, keeping time-consuming socializing to a minimum.

Announce your time constraints at the beginning of the conversation. Say, "I only have five minutes . . . I'm on a deadline," followed by, "How can I help you?" This politely lets the caller know you will allow the interruption but only up to a certain point.

When someone asks if this is a good time to call—and it isn't—say so. When someone asks "Are you busy?" or "Am I interrupting something?," if you are busy or they are interrupting, say so. "Yes, I am busy right now." Then offer to call back later, or ask the person to call you at another time.

Recognize when you are welcoming the interruption of a phone call because you are all too happy to spend a little time procrastinating. Then don't blame your dashed schedule on the many phone calls. Blame it on your

SUCCESSFUL TELEPHONE SCREENING

If you've got someone who can screen your calls for you—whether it's your assistant, your spouse or your children—how they do it is important. Graceful screening techniques can give you some uninterrupted time without offending the caller. Try these methods:

Never, ever, ask the caller their name before announcing that the person they want to speak to is unavailable. Say, "Dad can't come to the phone right now; who is this please?" Follow that up by asking, "Can I take a message?"

If there are people you never want to speak to under any circumstances—such as a particular salesperson—make sure your assistant knows this and can screen the call by always announcing without hesitation that "Mr. Jackson isn't available right now; may I take a message?"

If the person answering your phone is your assistant at work, or is mature enough at home, have them gather as much information as possible when they take a message. "Can I tell her what this is about?" is always helpful and gives you a chance to be completely prepared when you return the call. If you have an assistant or secretary who answers the phone for you, have them offer to help the caller. Your assistant can say, "She's not available now, can I help you with something?" Much of the time, it's a simple matter that doesn't really need your full attention or action.

If there is some uncertainty as to whether the caller should be put through, have your screener say, "He's tied up right now, do you want me to interrupt him?" This puts the responsibility of interrupting you squarely on the shoulders of the caller; most times the person will realize that the call isn't that important and simply leave a message.

If someone else answers and screens your calls, see if they can handle at least part of the call or refer it to someone else. If someone calls wanting the latest sales figures, your secretary may be able to refer them to someone in sales who may be able to provide the figures or at least try to assemble the information and give it to you so you have it in front of you when the person calls again.

If the caller does have a question that would require only the briefest of answers from you (such as a yes or no), have the person who answers the phone say, "Let me see if I can interrupt her to get your questions answered." Then let that person pass your response on to the caller.

Always have the person who takes the message ask the caller when the best time is to call back. Otherwise you'll be playing telephone tag for a week.

propensity to procrastinate and welcome the interruptions. Stop procrastinating first, then work on reducing the telephone interruptions.

Quit assuming that every time the phone rings it's an important call. Half the time it isn't. Stop worrying about missing out if you miss a phone call. They can always call back.

End a conversation by saying that your spouse is waiting. For some reason this excuse packs a powerful punch. Saying, "Jeez, I gotta go, my husband [or wife] is waiting for me, and he's gonna kill me if I don't get off this phone," works wonders. Rarely will you find a caller that will keep talking with the vision of a foot-tapping spouse lurking nearby.

Don't ever tell people to call you at their convenience or "any time." Always tell them the best time to call you, or establish a specific day or time to call regarding the matter.

At work, if at all possible, group your incoming phone calls. Let people know when the best time to reach you by phone is, and when you're generally not available. If you like a bit of quiet time to work on paperwork first thing in the morning, tell people, "The best time to reach me by phone is from 10:00 A.M. to noon." Then make sure you are available to receive calls at that time. Have your secretary or answering equipment take messages until 10:00. You may want to get a telephone that has a clock and times your phone calls. If you don't want to do that, you can use a three-minute egg timer or stopwatch to time how long your calls take. You'll be surprised at how quickly the time wasted on the telephone mounts up, and seeing it in front of you each time you are on the phone can be a real eye-opener that can motivate you to develop better ways of handling phone interruptions.

Ask someone if you can put them on hold before you do it. Say, "Can I put you on hold for a minute, or shall I call you back?" Conversely, when someone automatically tries to put you on hold, and you don't want them to waste your time, don't be afraid to speak up. When they ask if they can put you on hold, say no, and give them your number and ask them to call you back within the next fifteen minutes. Also remember that the call-waiting feature on a phone can be considered as obnoxious as the hold button. If you find yourself interrupting a conversation more than once or twice to take a call coming in on call-waiting, you may want to offer to call your party back when things aren't so busy. The clicks and interruptions annoy many people, and can be considered disrespectful. If you are the caller who keeps getting interrupted with the clicks and your party keeps excusing herself to pick up call-waiting, you might want to suggest that you continue the conversation at a later time when she isn't so busy. Why should you wait on the line through several clicks and calls?

If you need to get some important work done and need some quiet time, see if you can arrange an exchange of phone-answering duties. Someone else will answer your phones in the morning, and you'll answer theirs in the afternoon.

Let people know you are ready to hang up by saying something like, "Before we hang up, I just want to remind you about the car pool next Thursday." This alerts the caller that you are ready to ring off.

When you want to end a conversation, tell the caller you have a call coming in on the other line and must go. If you're tied up with a chronic caller who is long-winded, and asking, "How can I help you?" or announcing that you "only have five minutes" is fruitless, try the coward's way out. "Accidentally" hang up on yourself in the middle of one of your own sentences. Oops, phone problems again.

If you must make calls to request information, make those calls early in the day so people you contact have time during the day to assemble the information and get back to you before day's end. The same rule works well when you need to have an important conversation with someone. The early bird catches the worm. Calls placed early in the morning are much more likely to be returned before the end of the day than calls that are placed later in the day when everyone is beginning to bog down with the day's tasks and obligations.

When you call someone, make sure you announce yourself completely. "Hello, this is Janet Wilson calling for Rick Burnett." You can also say, "Is he available to answer a quick question?" If you are returning his call, say so. Providing this information immediately can help insure that you will get through to a busy person, and will save time between you and the person who answers the phone.

If you call someone to discuss items for an upcoming meeting, keep the discussion brief. Otherwise you may find yourself going into the subject in too much detail and wasting time at the meeting by rehashing what has already been said. Simply point out that you can discuss it further when you meet—and end the phone conversation.

If you need to contact several people by phone with the same information, you can save time by using a telephone chain technique. For example, if you need to notify the ten people on your committee regarding the date, time and place of the next meeting, call three of them and ask each of them to call three or four specific people to pass the information along.

When you take someone's phone number, make sure you get their extension number. If they have voice mail, you'll save yourself time listening to a long menu of options by immediately punching in their extension number.

Whenever you leave a message for someone, make it a point to ask the name of the person taking the message. This request makes just enough of an impact on the message-taker to help guarantee that your message will get through.

If you must leave a message on someone's answering machine or voice mail, repeat your phone number twice so that they won't have to stop and back up the tape if they missed your phone number the first time. Conversely, use your voice mail or answering machine message to help direct the caller to leave a complete message. For example, you might ask callers to leave their phone numbers. This way, if you are out of the office, you can return the call, even if you don't have their number with you.

When you leave a message for someone to call you back, along with letting them know the best time for reaching you, also leave instructions as to what they can do if you aren't in. For example, you can tell someone, "If I'm not in, just leave your mailing address on my voice mail. Let me know which products you're interested in, and I'll get the information out to you right away."

Especially if you work in sales, you might want to use your voice mail or answering machine as a reminder and follow-up device. If you're out, simply call your own machine and leave a message for yourself. When you get back to the office or back home and check your messages, you'll hear your verbal reminder to yourself. You won't be jotting information down on a scrap of paper to be either lost or forgotten. For example, you can tell yourself to send the new catalog to a prospect and recite the prospect's name and address into the phone. When you're back at your desk you'll hear the message, address the envelope, and get the material right out. If you regularly send out information keep some envelopes next to the phone. As soon as a voice mail or phone request is received, address the envelope so that information can go out immediately. To keep a record of the addresses, simply photocopy the envelopes before you drop them in the mailbox.

If you have your business in your home, don't hesitate to set parameters on the hours during which you will answer your phone for business matters. (A home-based business should have its own phone line.) If you answer the phone whenever it rings, your clients will soon discover they can call you at all hours, any day of the week. And that's just what they will do. They'll be calling at 9:30 P.M. on Sunday without hesitation. On the other hand, if your voice mail notes that business hours are from 9:00 A.M. until 7:00 P.M., Monday through Friday, your clients will learn to call within those hours, and not think less of you for it. Indeed, taking calls until 7:00 P.M., rather than 5:00 P.M., is often looked on as an extra service not afforded the client by most vendors and service people.

Don't feel obligated to hear a telephone solicitor out. Some of their spiels are quite lengthy, so if you're not interested in the product, cut the call short by saying that you're not interested, and promptly hanging up. This goes against the grain of some well-mannered ways of thinking, but is it really good manners for someone to interrupt your privacy at will (and usually either during or after dinner) to try to solicit money or foist a product on you?

If you really want to eliminate telephone interruptions in a meaningful way, change your phone number and get an unlisted one.

Interruption # 3
Self-Interruptions

One of the biggest time wasters is self-interruptions. It is important to sit up and take notice not only of how others interrupt you, but also how you interrupt others and yourself. Reining in the following self-created interruptions can save lots of time every day:

You stop to make a phone call. You don't need to make that phone call, but you do it anyway. You need a break, you tell yourself. Not only have you interrupted your workflow, you've also interrupted somebody else with your unnecessary phone call.

You stop to eat when you're not really hungry. This unnecessary interruption can lead to unnecessary pounds.

You surround yourself with clutter so that you have to periodically stop to search for something. This interruption can occur repeatedly in the course of the day, and can eat up anywhere from three to twenty minutes or so each time.

You never miss a coffee break, and think nothing of extending it by ten or fifteen minutes when you have something important you should be working on.

You stop to look at the mail the minute it arrives, even though that mail will still be there one hour from now or later this afternoon.

You get sidetracked by picking up something to read, and decide to read just one article. Trouble is, the article takes fifteen minutes to read and has nothing to do with what you should be doing.

You procrastinate any way you can. Go to the bathroom, and stop off at Louise's desk for a quick chat (ten minutes) on the way back to your desk. Watch the noon news. Stop to call a talk-show radio program you've had on in the background. Daydream.

You stop to do routine things that could wait. If you're cleaning out the basement, you go upstairs to answer the phone, and on the way back downstairs you notice that the living room furniture could use dusting. So you stop and dust. At work you stop a major project to spend an hour or more on routine clerical work that can wait.

THE INTERRUPTION CIRCLE

If someone tends to call you several times a day regarding bits and pieces of information pertaining to a particular project, ask them to keep track of all their questions and information, and then plan to spend time once or twice each day to go over all the information on the phone. Otherwise you'll become part of an interruption circle that has a life of its own, with you as a co-conspirator. Here's how it works:

You're working on the fund-raiser with Sharon. You call her up to go over the estimates for printing the program. After a five-minute discussion, you hang up. Thirty minutes later, you think of something you forgot to tell her. Without thinking, you automatically pick up the phone and call her back. What have you just done? You have interrupted Sharon. Why did you do it? Because you didn't want to forget what you needed to tell Sharon, and because maybe she'll do something with the information right away. So, rather than make a note, you took the quickest route to relieving yourself of the information and burdening Sharon with it.

It doesn't stop there. Sharon, having been interrupted, assimilates the information, and an hour later that triggers an idea. She should tell you about this idea, she thinks, so she does what comes naturally — she picks up the phone and calls you. This is call number three so far today about the program; this time you have been interrupted.

Back and forth goes the circle of interruptions, calling and interrupting each other to avoid keeping track of your own reservoir of information, and in the hope that things will be magically done instantly as a result of the calls. The truth is it could have all been handled in one call at the end of the day. Not only that, both you and Sharon are very busy, and with all the interruptions all day long, nothing was done to move the program for the fund-raiser closer to completion.

Be aware of your own tendencies to interrupt your work, and you are well on your way to curbing them. Unfortunately, there are no quick tips for making these self-interruptions go away. The only surefire solution is to stop doing these things, pronto.

Interruption # 4
Children

Children will interrupt you endlessly unless taught to do otherwise. Once trained, however, even very small children can learn to respect small blocks of time during which they are not to interrupt you. Start by making sure they have plenty to do for a set time. If you want an hour to yourself, put your four-year-old in her room with lots of toys and projects, and tell her you expect her to stay in there for an hour while you do some reading. At the end of the hour, promise to read to her.

Set a timer for the amount of time you want undisturbed. When the timer goes off, the child gets your full attention.

Put a latch on your bedroom door. Except for very small children, kids do not need to roam in and out of your bedroom interrupting you when you are trying to rest, get ready for work, read or spend quiet time with your spouse.

As soon as age and size permit, start training children out of the "gimme" habit. "Gimme a drink of water." As soon as they can reach the sink (help out with a small stool), they can get their own water. Keep an unbreakable glass handy for those occasions.

Have kids save their multitude of questions and commentaries for "family time," which can coincide with dinner. If your ten-year-old wants to spend fifteen minutes telling you about the funny dream he had last night, tell him to wait so Mommy can hear it too, during family time at dinner.

For kids that are constantly tugging at you to "come look at this," get them in the habit of saving it for the end of the day, when you'll both take a personal "tour" to see everything they have done. Then look at the sand castle in the back and the way Barbie's dollhouse has been rearranged.

Use a reward system. For small children who are being trained to respect uninterrupted time with a timer, you might consider buying a bag of dollar items that you can keep in a closet. Every time they have spent a reasonable amount of time (at least an hour) respecting your quiet time, let them grab a gift from the bag.

Training children not to interrupt your time is only an extension of training them not to interrupt you when you are speaking. If you can get them to do one, you can teach them to do the other. Remember that, and use whatever rules, gimmicks or gadgets you need to get them to stop interrupting for every little thing.

As you take a closer look at how you are interrupted, and how you interrupt others, start thinking about how you can take control over those interruptions so that you're no longer powerless over your day and its many interruptions. Learn to handle necessary interruptions effectively and reduce or eliminate unnecessary interruptions, and you'll find yourself with more time for yourself every day. Guaranteed.

CHAPTER ELEVEN

Making Meetings Count

The Masters of Neo-Leisure (goofing off) are Hollywood film execs.
All days are divided into three parts; the breakfast meeting, the lunch
meeting, and the dinner meeting—all connected by drive-time.

   —Karen Karbo

At work, one of the biggest time eaters is meetings. There's the Monday morning sales meeting, and the client lunch meeting. There's the training session you are required to attend, even though you can't see how it is going to help you make more money for the company. There's the meeting you call twice a month to go over problems and make decisions with your staff, and there's the meeting that some other department head calls that, simply because of your job title, it seems you are required to attend.

Once a meeting starts, almost everyone agrees, at least half of the time spent in it is actually wasted time. Peter Drucker, author of *The Effective Executive* (Harper & Row), judges meetings more harshly. "Meetings," according to Drucker, "are by definition a concession to deficient organization. For one either meets or one works. One cannot do both at the same time." He acknowledges that meetings become necessary when the knowledge needed is not readily available and must be "pieced together out of the experience and knowledge of several people." And there are other reasons for having meetings.

The Purpose of Meetings:
- To solve problems.
- To reach a decision or to come to a consensus.
- To coordinate activities.
- To boost morale.
- To share information.
- To dispense educational and training information.

While those are good reasons for a meeting, more often than not, meetings are called for the vaguest of reasons. And, like sheep, all who are called, thinking of themselves as the chosen ones, stop everything and attend the meeting whether they need to or not. Michael LeBoeuf, author of *Working Smart* (Warner Books), thinks that we spend too much time attending meetings that are absolutely useless. Following are some of the hidden reasons that go into a useless meeting, according to LeBoeuf.

WHY WE HAVE SO MANY USELESS MEETINGS

To provide an audience for someone. Some people like to hear themselves talk so much that they just have to share it with a group. The late Senator Everett Dirksen was delivering a lengthy discourse at a Senate committee meeting. After being interrupted several times by a colleague, Dirksen turned to the interrupter and said, "My dear sir, you are interrupting the man I most want to hear."

How many meetings have you attended where all you did was listen to someone's view on everything from world economics to the mating of Great Danes with Chihuahuas? Far too many, I'm sure.

To socialize. There are very few of us who can tolerate working alone for extended periods of time. Meetings provide a great excuse for us to get together and quell any pangs of loneliness we feel. . . . Everyone would be better off if they just threw a party, but that's only for special occasions. We can't afford to admit to ourselves that we aren't getting anything done, so we meet and socialize under the guise of committee work.

To escape being effective. Meetings are an excuse for poor work or no work at all. . . . You can dodge unpleasant tasks or turn in assignments late and say you were too busy to get around to them last week because your time was taken up in meetings. Since meetings are an acceptable way to structure work time, you appear to be an ambitious, caring soul with many irons in the fire.

Habit. The only real reason for having many meetings is that it's always been that way. Regularly scheduled meetings are often prime candidates for wasting time. People are usually resistant to change, and traditions tend to live on long after their purpose has passed away.

To pass the buck. Very often a decision can, and should, be made by an individual but he [or she] is reluctant to do so. As a result he forms a committee and asks them for a decision or a recommendation which he automatically adopts. If the decision meets with an ill fate, the buck can be passed to the committee, and no one is held responsible.

To fool people into believing they are participating in important deci-sions. . . . Many committees do make use of the capabilities of people to make important decisions. However, all too often the boss forms a committee to make recommendations and then does whatever . . . he wants, or worse yet, tells the committee what kind of recommendation he wants. The meetings are usually held in the spirit of "All in favor say 'aye,' all opposed, say 'fired.' "

MAKING THE MOST OF MEETINGS

Attendees often have murky recollections of the purpose of meetings, largely because so many of them are indeed, useless. The one thing that everyone is certain to remember is whether the meeting ended early or late. When meetings begin and end, and what transpires in them can be either an effective use of time or a waste of it. Whether you are the person calling the meeting, or being asked to attend, there's a lot you can do to see to ensure you don't waste any more time than necessary with meetings.

If You Are Arranging the Meeting

Schedule fewer meetings. Ask yourself if there is a cheaper, more efficient way to handle matters, rather than automatically suggesting a meeting. And don't have meetings just because it's always been that way. Perhaps the Monday morning meeting really isn't necessary after all. Eliminating nonproductive weekly meetings will increase overall productivity, not to mention morale.

Before you call a meeting, consider the cost of that meeting. If you bring twelve managers together, and each of them earns $50,000 a year, each hour of the meeting has a cost factor of $300. And that doesn't include the cost of fringe benefits that each manager receives. If you've got a $50 decision to make, there's no need to spend $300 in meeting time to do it.

Don't call a meeting unless you need advice from everyone there. Only certain issues truly benefit from group discussion and dynamics, and if your reason for calling a meeting doesn't need that type of involvement, don't call the meeting; call key people instead. See if you can solve problems and make decisions with them over the phone or in brief conversations. You don't need to take up the accounting manager's time to go over the new brochure and decide how many to print. The bulk of the meeting will be about design, and the need to decide numbers is worth about five or ten minutes. A phone discussion with the accounting manager is all that's needed for that decision.

Keep the number of participants in the meeting to a minimum. The more people in attendance, the more time-consuming the meeting will become due to the number of people putting their two cents' worth in.

Let participants know in advance if you want particular questions answered or problems solved at the meeting. Send out a memo with an itemized list of questions. If you want to know how to increase sales on the new widget, say so by asking the attendees to come to the meeting with three specific ideas on how to increase those sales immediately. Surprises waste time in a meeting and merely prolong the time needed before action takes place. It's far more effective to give people the opportunity to come to the meeting fully prepared.

Distribute a detailed agenda in advance of the meeting. Along with the points to be discussed, you'll want to list the decisions to be made, and the problems to be solved during the meeting. Allocate a specific amount of time for each topic, and let everyone know what that time is. You can give twenty minutes to discussion about the budget, for example, and another twenty minutes to go over the new marketing plan. With the time limit, people tend to get to the point much faster. (If the meeting is off-site, include a map with the agenda so everyone is clear about how to get there.)

Schedule meetings right before lunch or near the end of the day. Everyone will be intent on finishing and getting out the door and the meeting will move along with miraculous speed. Scheduling at these times also means that the participants' day won't be broken up needlessly.

Always start on time, and don't go back over material for latecomers. It won't be long before everyone gets to the meetings on time. An extreme technique is to lock the door after the meeting has started. This means latecomers will have to go through the embarrassment of knocking to be let into the room. This educates chronic latecomers almost immediately, and eliminates outside interruptions that can waste time and drag the meeting off its track. Other techniques for handling latecomers can also be tried. Ask them to provide something essential to the meeting, such as donuts that are needed before the meeting starts. You can also schedule the most interesting topic first; or schedule the chronic latecomer's presentation first. Any one of these tactics should work. If you've got a real tough case on your hands, try implementing all three of these techniques at once. Finally, if several people are always late, consider listing "late arrivals" on the minutes next to the list of "attendees."

Open the meeting with some "housekeeping" announcements. These announcements can include reminding everyone to stick to the agenda, and to let them know when there will be breaks and when the meeting will end. Establishing these "rules" at the top of the meeting can often make the meeting easier to control so that it can be productive and end on time.

Don't serve food unless you have to. It's distracting and time-consuming.

If attendees aren't at the food table, they're thinking about when they can get back to it.

Be specific. When you announce the coffee break, don't be vague about the length of time. Instead of saying, "Let's take a break of about fifteen minutes or so," say, "Let's break now and reconvene at 10:30."

Keep it short. Short meetings are generally more effective than long affairs. Wherever possible, don't let the meeting run over two hours.

Stay on schedule. If people tend to spend the first ten or fifteen minutes of a meeting kibitzing, you can reclaim that time by getting started and getting the meeting over with. Get people going by checking your watch, and announce the time to the room. "Well, it's 9:30, let's get started." People can always socialize after the meeting if they want, and you can either join in or go back to work at that time.

No interruptions. Make it a rule not to accept interruptions from outside the meeting room during the meeting. Phone calls, questions from your assistant, and drop-in visitors should all wait until the meeting is concluded.

When people want to speak during the meeting, ask them to stand. It tends to prompt them to get to the point quicker, and make their comments brief.

No reading allowed. Don't allocate meeting time for participants to read documents and reports. Any written materials that pertain to the subject at hand should be circulated in advance with the agenda so that participants can read that information before the meeting.

Use visual aids. If you're going to need equipment (such as a flip chart, projector or marking pens), use a checklist to make sure everything is in place prior to the meeting. Rounding up equipment once a meeting's begun wastes everybody's time.

Cut the troublemakers off at the pass. If you have someone who tends to monopolize the conversation at a meeting, consider asking them in advance to help you elicit more from the quieter members of the group. Thus, focused, the person could be a helpful facilitator rather than a big mouth who drives everyone crazy and wastes time to boot.

Don't ramble during the meeting. It wastes time, and drives everyone crazy. If others can't get to the point, help them along by suggesting a vote on the issue, or by tabling it for the next meeting's agenda. You can say diplomatically, but resolutely, "that's not on the agenda for this meeting, but if you'd like to have it placed on the agenda for a future meeting, I can look into scheduling it for discussion then." If two people in the meeting persist in long discussion and disagreement, move the meeting along by suggesting that they take it up further with each other after the meeting.

Use a designated writer. If part of the objective is to make decisions that will result in written material (such as policies, reports, letters, etc.), don't start drafting the material at the meeting. Group authorship is one of the biggest time wasters around. Instead, agree on key concepts and appoint someone to draw up a draft and circulate it for comments, redrafting the document as necessary after circulation.

Take minutes and vow to reach a decision on each agenda item. Once the decision is made, immediately assign responsibility for follow-up action. After the meeting, distribute the minutes so that those who couldn't attend are kept abreast of what happened. Make sure you circulate a copy of the meeting's minutes as soon as possible after the meeting. Along with the minutes, you can include a brief list of "Decisions Made" and "Actions to Be Taken" along with the date, time and place of the next meeting. This keeps everybody on track and moving forward, and helps eliminate rehashing old business at future meetings. If you have a problem getting someone to take minutes, either alternate the chore, or give it to the person who arrives last.

Allow people to leave after their point of business has been discussed. If their input isn't critical to the rest of the meeting, they are usually very appreciative of not having to stay.

Schedule the next meeting. At the conclusion of the meeting, take a few minutes to either announce or decide the date, time and place for the next meeting (if one is required). Everyone can then mark their calendars, and plan and prioritize accordingly. It may also be a good idea to circulate an evaluation sheet for the participants to fill out before they leave. Comments and input regarding the success of the meeting can be a valuable tool to help you tighten the next meeting and save time.

Set a time in advance for the meeting to end and stick to that time. This way, everyone can plan the rest of their day with confidence.

The meeting should have now moved your people from the discussion to the *do* stage. Follow up by insisting on action and results; otherwise you'll just have another meeting to rehash the same old stuff.

If You Are Attending the Meeting

Even if you did not arrange the meeting, but are required to attend, you have some control over the amount of time you spend in that and other proposed meetings.

Just say no. Before you automatically make plans to attend a meeting, ask yourself if it's really necessary for you to be there. If it isn't, try to get out of it by saying no tactfully. You might want to propose that your input can be provided in other ways—by phone, by report, or in short conversations with key people, for example. Or see if you can send a representative to the meeting in your place.

Try to find out in advance what exactly is expected of you at the meeting. This way you can be prepared, and save your time as well as everyone else's by getting right to the point and providing the necessary input. As soon as you are invited to a meeting, ask if you can have handout materials in advance, so that you can come better prepared to discuss and act on the issues at hand. Then gather the necessary material well in advance so you aren't desperately trying to find paperwork at the last minute. Get to the meeting early so you can find a seat and organize any materials you brought with you. The best way to keep materials relating to a meeting — particularly if the meeting occurs on a regular basis — is in a three-ring binder. You can use index dividers to separate reports, minutes, to-do and action lists. The binder eliminates fumbling with loose papers and files during the meeting itself. With a binder, pen and notepad you'll be prepared and professional at the meeting, instead of rummaging through your briefcase, digging through files and papers, and borrowing pens and papers from others in the room.

If there are several topics of discussion at a meeting, and only one concerns you, see if you can leave once that issue has been addressed. (You can point out that you'd like to get right to work on your end of the project, for example.) It's always a waste of time to cool your heels in meetings while others are droning on about topics that aren't related to you or your area of expertise.

Avoid impromptu meetings. When someone asks to meet with you, don't be shy about asking why. Ask, "What will we be discussing?" Often, you'll find the requestor doesn't have a clear answer to the question, and will admit that perhaps a meeting isn't necessary right now after all. It may even be possible to make a quick decision on the spot, putting the notion of a future meeting over the issue to rest once and for all.

Don't schedule your appointments too close to meeting times. If a meeting runs over, it will make you late for your next appointment, and your entire day will become discombobulated.

Avoid down-time. In a large meeting, where your full attention isn't necessary, and your behavior won't be noticed, catch up on some reading or write letters. Make it a point to look involved when necessary, of course.

Be prompt. If you are running late, call to let the people you are meeting know that. They may want to reschedule, or they may revise the agenda to handle other issues before yours.

Similarly, if you are due at a scheduled meeting at, say 10:00 A.M., and the other party isn't there by 10:15 A.M., leave. Unless the other party has called to explain their tardiness or to reschedule, it makes no sense for you to waste your time waiting. Leave word that you left after waiting fifteen minutes. Eventually your reputation for punctuality will spread, and people

GOING OUT FOR A MEETING

Meeting people in places other than the office can be a frequent and time-consuming occurrence. Perhaps you have to travel to the coast to meet with people in the branch office. Or you ask a client to lunch. Although a certain amount of business may be transacted, much time will probably be wasted. Here are some suggestions for saving time.

Have a breakfast meeting instead of a lunch meeting. Everyone is more alert, the service is quicker, and there's no consumption of alcohol. Most people are anxious to get on with their day, so they get to the point so they can get out of the restaurant and into their office.

If you must have a lunch meeting, select a restaurant where you know the service is fast and the room is relatively quiet. Then either plan an early lunch (between 11:30 and noon) or a later lunch (after 1:15). You'll avoid the congestion that slows service during the normal lunch hour. If you want the meeting to be brief, don't drink. Having drinks before the meal tends to slow down service, and dull the senses. When you get back to the office, you won't be as alert, energetic or productive as you should be, and you'll end up frittering away the rest of the afternoon.

If your lunch meetings tend to be too sociable or meander more than you'd like, consider meeting at your office for thirty minutes first to go over the most important business, and then go out to lunch together. This way, if social chitchat takes over at lunch, you've got the most important business of the meeting behind you.

Ask for the check when the waiter brings the food so you won't waste time chasing after it later.

Rather than one long meeting, consider meeting over coffee two or three times each week. The coffee shop will probably be nearly empty, and you can go over information quickly and without interruption.

Always reserve dinner meetings for only the most important of clients or colleagues. There is almost no way to hurry the time spent over dinner, so unless you really want to impress someone, or take someone out who is in town from somewhere else, don't do it.

Save travel time by having a conference call instead of an in-person meeting. Since each person is paying for the call, it can motivate everyone to get to the point in a hurry.

Alternate places of meeting. If you do business with someone regularly and need to meet from time to time, make it your office one time, and her office the next. This shifts the convenience factor equally, and gives each party a bit of extra time (that would have been spent commuting to the other office) on a rotating basis.

will make a concerted effort to be on time for meetings with you.

Give tit for tat. If a professional (such as a doctor or lawyer) consistently makes you wait more than fifteen minutes past the appointed time of your meeting, let them know that your time is equally important and waiting is inconvenient for you. If they make you wait more than thirty minutes, leave and take your business with you. Or, send them a bill for your time. By the same token, once you meet with the professional, be brief and concise. Stick to the pertinent facts so that you don't waste their time and make them late for their next appointment.

Plan for bureaucratic delays. If you have to meet with any government agency, expect and prepare for the worst. You're at their mercy, and chances are you'll have to wait and may be treated rudely. Allow lots of time, wear comfortable shoes, take plenty of reading, work to catch up on, or a cross-word puzzle, and summon as much patience as possible. There is just no way to spend your time efficiently when you're dealing with a government agency.

When it comes to meetings, always remember to do unto others as you would have them do unto you. Don't ask for, or go to, a meeting unless you have to. And once you're in one, get to the point, so that everybody can get out of the room as soon as possible and get back to using their time to get some real work done.

CHAPTER TWELVE

Working Wisely

Those who work smart are not loafers looking for the easy way out. Rather, they are people who make the most of their lives and thus create greater personal satisfaction for themselves and those they come in contact with.
— Michael LeBoeuf

Work takes up the majority of most people's time, but the old axiom that "work expands to fit the time available" is only half true. Most people are convinced that they have much more work to do than could ever be done in the time available. Getting everything done is often tied to being organized in the workplace. A disorganized desk, for example, is not only inefficient, it's demoralizing, and like most clutter, tends to overwhelm. This feeling is often difficult to overcome, and the result is that more and more time is spent trying to sort out the disorganization on a daily basis. Since time is money, how you spend your time at work can translate into more or less money as well. For example, promotions will likely go to the people who are the most effective managers of their time and work. Those people who don't manage time and work output well will be passed over.

Why People Work Too Much

If you seem to be working all the time, including evenings, weekends and holidays, you are working too much. There are myriad reasons for having to spend so much time working, some of which have already been addressed in this book. Inordinate time consumed for work can usually be directly linked to at least some of the following reasons.

- You're a perfectionist who takes twice as long to do everything in order to do it perfectly.
- You refuse to delegate and therefore spend all of your time doing everything yourself.
- You procrastinate regularly, which means you're constantly doing

things at the last minute and find yourself swimming frantically in a sea of crises nearly every day. Crisis management takes up more time than effective daily management.

- You are indecisive, and because of it, problems pile up to a dangerous level. Solving them when they become an emergency always takes longer than it would have if you had made the decision to take action early on.

- You don't prioritize and plan, so you have no control over your daily schedule. Because of this, unexpected problems or delays can mean that your day, or for that matter, your week, is thrown completely out of whack. You are always spending any spare time trying to catch up with routine matters.

- You are chronically disorganized, which means that you spend time nearly every day looking for, or losing something. This time-consuming habit feeds on itself; the more disorganized you are, the more time you waste.

The first step in learning how to work wisely and find more time for yourself every day is to take a good look at your work habits. If you regularly practice any of the methods listed above, changing those habits will mean that you can work smarter not harder, and still have time left over for yourself. You may need to review some of the information in this section to overcome those obstacles in the workplace. If disorganization is your only problem, the next section of the book, Getting Organized, will help you tackle that problem so that you can save time by being organized every day.

But perhaps the habits listed above are only part of the problem. You may not be working wisely for one reason: You are a confirmed workaholic.

Time-Wasting Habits of the Workaholic

If you are a workaholic, it is a near certainty that you are wasting time and that you do not have any spare time for yourself or anyone else. If you recognize any of these tendencies in yourself, you may be a workaholic.

- You work nearly all the time, from early in the morning to late at night. Holidays and weekends often find you at work as well.
- You don't like vacations. All that empty time makes you a little nervous.
- You have a multitude of ways to deny that being a workaholic is a problem. For example, you say, "What's wrong with working hard? There are worse things in life."
- You are an overdoer and an overachiever. You constantly overcommit yourself, and feel secretly proud that you can do everything yourself.
- You like to be in control of everything, so you do everything yourself.

- You are a perfectionist who refuses to delegate, preferring instead to do everything perfectly yourself.
- You are compulsively organized, and spend an inordinate amount of time every day organizing and reorganizing everything.
- Since you "have so much work to do" you find yourself chronically disorganized, with a good portion of your day spent wading through the chaos that is in your home or office.
- You never really relax. If nothing else, your mind is usually spinning with thoughts about the problems facing you at work.

Although many people are often faced with working long hours (for various reasons), there is a distinct difference between working long hours and being a workaholic. You may have to work long hours because you have a special one-time project that needs to be completed, or because the office has just downsized and dumped someone else's work on your desk. Short of getting another job, usually working long hours in these cases cannot be helped. But, if you approach work compulsively, and can't stop without feeling restless, bored or nervous, you are probably obsessed with or addicted to work. You are a workaholic.

What's Wrong With Working a Lot?

Is it really bad to be a workaholic? In most cases, yes. Workaholics often work long hours for all the wrong reasons. Those "reasons" lead to bad habits that become, for the workaholic, impossible to change. The benefits of workaholism are virtually nil. Working constantly insures that the workaholic has no time for anything or anyone else. While workaholics are working, life is passing them by (which secretly relieves many workaholics).

The obsessed workaholic is often passed over for promotion as well, because the workaholic is addicted to the *process of doing* the work, not the *results*. Generally, the workaholic prefers to work alone, eschewing teamwork. What the workaholic tends to overlook is that promotions are often based on many things, including process, politics and teamwork. And one of the most important factors that goes into promotions is the record of results produced. The workaholic is so immersed in the details of the doing of the work, that he loses sight of the importance of results. Consequently, the results often suffer; they are delivered late, done poorly, or buried altogether in the sheer volume of work that the workaholic surrounds himself with. Canadian time-management consultant Harold Taylor may have put it best when he noted that "working long hours does not make you effective any more than hanging out at McDonald's makes you a hamburger."

It's not easy to change the addictive and time-consuming habits of workaholism, since the reasons a person escapes in workaholism can be complex and personal. The psychological reasons for the behavior are best explored by professionals in the field. But if you're a workaholic who really wants to change your daily habits so that you can find more time for yourself every day, you might try to put these practical techniques to work for you.

OVERCOMING WORKAHOLIC TENDENCIES

Make a concentrated effort to replace bad work habits with good habits that will save time. Learn to delegate daily. Make decisions in a timely fashion. Reduce and eliminate perfectionist tendencies. Get organized. Prioritize and plan regularly. Curb interruptions and streamline meetings. You don't have to eliminate all your bad habits overnight, but work on changing them bit by bit on a daily basis.

Reduce your work hours in small increments. If you work seven days a week, next week force yourself to work six and a half days. Do that for two weeks, then move to working only six days a week for two weeks, and so on, until you are working a reasonable amount of time.

Give yourself a daily deadline for stopping, no matter what. If you routinely work late, give yourself an enforced quitting time, even if it is as late as 9:00 P.M. This is better than working until midnight on some nights, and working until 9:30 or 10:00 P.M. on others. Gradually move your quitting time by half-hour increments until you are quitting by 6:00 P.M. or so every night.

Give yourself a targeted goal for reducing the number of hours you spend working. If you work ninety hours a week now, give yourself a goal of a fifty-hour work week within twelve months. Then work toward that goal by reducing your work week in small increments every month.

Learn to relax. Force yourself to do nothing for an hour. Then increase that time. Take a weekend mini-vacation away from the telephone. Don't take work with you. Keep practicing until you reach the point where you can relax for some time each week and can take at least three or four such vacations each year.

Improve Procedures

If you're not a workaholic, and you're still working too much, chances are the culprit is poor procedures, or worse, no procedures at all. Paperwork and the tasks that go with it can all too easily fall prey to the time-wasting effects that are generated by lack of proper procedures. At work, take a good look at how you and your staff process the paperwork and daily tasks. This examination usually results in exposing some truths that can be real eye-openers. Duplication of effort, inefficient and outdated methods, and individual incompetence can often be pinpointed by analyzing each and every procedure. Once the problems are illuminated, you can replace the inefficiencies with methods that can increase productivity. Write the new procedures down, and make sure that you have a manual for them that anyone can access. Put one person in charge of the manual. A streamlined operation makes changes and revisions in procedures often. Those changes should automatically be noted in the procedure manual, and outdated methods removed.

The initial procedural examination may seem overwhelming. If you and your staff can't find the time to do it, hire a consultant to do it for you. It's one of the easiest things to justify financially. (Every time I've completed a task analysis and procedure manual for a company, the amount of money saved through the elimination of duplication and inefficient procedures and personnel has far exceeded my fee.) Not only that, having a manual makes training new personnel that much easier, providing a handy reference for them when others aren't available to answer specific questions.

Once you have written procedures in place, make it a habit to question what you and your staff do. Is it really necessary, or can it be eliminated? Is it a duplication of effort? Can you simplify the task or combine it with another one? By doing this rather than automatically adding tasks without question, you can be more productive and have more time for yourself.

Remember that although by necessity work will take up a good portion of your time, it doesn't have to be all-consuming. The rewards you will reap by working smarter not harder, and by eliminating any workaholic tendencies you might have, can include not only more time for yourself, but also a more successful and rewarding work life and career.

PART THREE

Getting Organized

All my possessions for a moment of time.
— Last words of Queen Elizabeth I

Organized people seem to float through their days, knowing where everything is, and always getting out the door and to appointments on time. Disorganized people are left to watch in wonder and annoyance, telling themselves that they are "too creative for all that get-organized stuff." While proclaiming the "disorganized is better" mantra, they are avoiding the truth, which is that daily disorganization is one of the biggest time wasters in anyone's life. If you're drowning in piles of paper or are overwhelmed by clutter, like it or not, you spend nearly every day facing up to the obstacle that disorganization creates. It takes longer to find things; you spend more time trying to maintain some semblance of order; and for some, much time is devoted to an elaborate cover-up so that others don't realize just how out-of-control everything is. Once disorganization takes hold, chaos rules. And the obstacle that a mountain of backed-up paper and clutter creates seems impossible to overcome.

The truth is, disorganization can be overcome, though it may take a fair amount of time to get things under control initially. If clutter and piles of paper have been allowed to accumulate over weeks, months or years, even more time is required to tackle the tedious task of digging out from under that backlog, getting organized, and setting up simple systems to keep things in order from now on. I've written several books on getting organized. If you have a serious clutter or paper backlog that seems completely insurmountable, you might want to read *How to Conquer Clutter* or *Conquering the Paper Pile-Up* (both Writer's Digest Books). Regardless of the apparent enormity of the task, however, simplifying and streamlining your surroundings is a must. This brings us to Step 6: "Simplify and Streamline Your Life by Getting Organized." Chapters thirteen through fifteen will give you the basics you need to overcome this final obstacle so that you can get organized, set up simple systems to help you stay organized, and reap the benefits of more time for yourself each and every organized day after that.

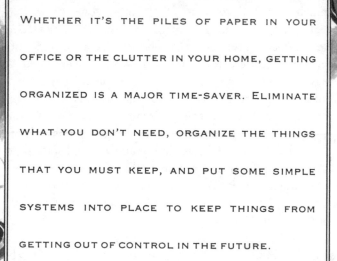

6

SIMPLIFY AND STREAMLINE

YOUR LIFE BY GETTING

ORGANIZED

WHETHER IT'S THE PILES OF PAPER IN YOUR

OFFICE OR THE CLUTTER IN YOUR HOME, GETTING

ORGANIZED IS A MAJOR TIME-SAVER. ELIMINATE

WHAT YOU DON'T NEED, ORGANIZE THE THINGS

THAT YOU MUST KEEP, AND PUT SOME SIMPLE

SYSTEMS INTO PLACE TO KEEP THINGS FROM

GETTING OUT OF CONTROL IN THE FUTURE.

CHAPTER THIRTEEN

Conquering Clutter

Those of us who are Messies frequently fail to realize that the reason we find it so hard to part with the clutter around us is that we derive so much comfort from it.
—Sandra Felton

One of the biggest time wasters of all is clutter. A little clutter never hurt anyone, but clutter tends to multiply and before long, you're dealing with mountains of it at every turn. There are reasons for the accumulation, of course. You've been too busy, and things backed up on you. Or, maybe you never learned good organizational habits. It's easy to learn simple, effective organizational techniques that will help you keep on top of everything with relative ease. But clutter becomes a much bigger problem if you are deliberately covering up the mounting hoard of things with excuses. Luckily, the excuses are easy to spot, since almost everyone who is knee-deep in clutter uses the same refrains.

Most excuses, alas, are just that — excuses. If these excuses are part of your repertoire, you need to consider the following realities so you can find more time for yourself rather than for the care and feeding of clutter.

Excuses for Clutter

Excuse: "I might need it someday." **Reality:** Then again, you might *not*. And even if you do need it, won't it be easy to replace it? Keeping everything on the off chance you might need it someday leads to a veritable warehouse of things. If you do need something, replace it. Chances are good you won't need it someday.

Excuse: "It will be worth money someday." **Reality:** Really? When? And how much money will it actually be worth? Exactly how fast is it appreciating? Is its value appreciating as fast as the cost of the storage space you are paying for to keep it? There is a slim chance it will be worth money someday, but unless it is an extraordinary item — such as an antique and rare piece of furniture — it will never pay off in enough money to compensate you for the cost of the storage space required to keep it for who-knows-how-many years.

Excuse: "It will come back in style if I wait long enough." **Reality:** Clothing designers, many of whom seem to try to make up for a lack of originality with an abundance of raw nerve, may indeed bring something back into style in the next ten years or so. But it will doubtlessly be in a slightly different fabric and a slightly different cut, and you will look a little nerdy around the edges.

Excuse: "It was a gift." **Reality:** It's the thought that counts. There is no law that says you have to hang on to a gift that doesn't suit you forever. Give it to someone else (such as charity).

Excuse: "I paid good money for that." **Reality:** We all make mistakes from time to time. Learn from this mistake, and vow not to repeat it. In the meantime get rid of the evidence.

Excuse: "As soon as I lose twenty pounds, I'll be able to wear it again." **Reality:** This is true, and if you are dieting and exercising religiously, you will be able to wear it again. But if you are just fantasizing about losing twenty pounds, get rid of the clothes.

Excuse: "It's still perfectly good." **Reality:** If it's so good, how come you never use it? "Perfectly good" means nothing if you're talking about something you never use.

Excuse: "I inherited it." **Reality:** Just because you inherited it, you don't have to keep it. After all, the giver is gone. If you're not using it, the person you inherited it from won't care if you give it to someone else.

Excuse: "When it's fixed it will be good as new." **Reality:** When, and more important, *if* it gets fixed, it may or may not be as good as new. You will never know unless you actually fix it.

Excuse: "They don't make things like that anymore." **Reality:** There's a very good reason for that: Nobody in their right mind would have one. Besides it doesn't matter how well made it is if you never use it.

Excuse: "It would cost a fortune to replace." **Reality:** Probably. But just think of all the money you'll save by dumping it and *not* replacing it with anything.

Excuse: "It brings back memories." **Reality:** There's certainly some room in everyone's life for some mementos to bring back those supposedly elusive memories. But selectivity is required. After all, old tax returns bring back memories too. How many memories do you really need?

The Dollar Cost of Clutter

While you're making excuses, the clutter is wasting not only your time, but your money as well. That's because clutter that never gets used gets stored. And storage space costs money—whether it's in your closets, garage, basement or a storage unit. That space is, after all, what your monthly rent or mortgage payment is for. Think about it. How much space is required to hold those magazines and newspapers going back years? Three square feet? Four square feet? How about the clothes you never wear? Are they using up two feet or five feet of hanging closet space? What about all those paper mementos going back twenty years? They may be in boxes in the garage, but those boxes are still costing you money for the square footage they occupy. Is your never-used clutter taking up 10 percent of your space? 20 percent? 30 percent? Some simple arithmetic will show you how much of your monthly mortgage or rent payment goes to store useless clutter. Just figure the percentage. For example, if your monthly payment is $650 and your clutter occupies 10 percent of your space, you are paying $65 per month for clutter, or $780 per year.

If you've reached the point where you think you have to move because you "need more space," think again. How much money per month is that extra space going to cost you. $100? $200? $500? Unless you have extra children with no place to sleep, it's a good bet that all you need the extra space for is to store your expanding cache of clutter.

It doesn't take an accountant to figure out that you can save money by eliminating clutter. First, you won't have to move, which will save you moving costs, deposit expenses or escrow costs. Then you'll save the money you would have added to your monthly rental or housing payment. (Don't forget to multiply that times twelve to come up with your yearly savings.) Add these sums for a total savings. You are looking at roughly the dollar cost of clutter.

The Time Cost of Clutter

Clutter eats up time in bits and pieces, and if you're overwhelmed with clutter, chances are, you have adapted without question to working around it in an automatic but time-consuming manner nearly every day. Here are only some of the ways clutter actually costs you time.

Searching. If you are surrounded by clutter, you are always misplacing things. At least twice a day, you have to stop and look for something like your keys, your purse, your glasses, the cleaning ticket, a phone number or address, a piece of paper and a pen that works, the tickets to tonight's game or this month's past due utility bill.

Time wasted: approximately 20 minutes each day

Sifting. If you've got a closet full of clothes because you never get rid of anything, three-fourths of what's in there probably doesn't fit or is inappropriate. Before you can pull yourself together in the morning, you need to sift through the clothes you can't wear in order to put together an outfit you can wear. And, if the closet is particularly crammed, you may have to iron whatever you pull out of the closet before you can put it on.

Time wasted: about 10 minutes each day

Supervising. If your children's rooms are choked with clutter and they are not instructed to keep their things organized, it will take far more time than would otherwise be necessary for them to get ready for their day. If they are small children, you will have to supervise and become actively involved in the frustrating daily hunt for the missing shoe, glove or school project lost among the clutter.

Time wasted: at least 10 minutes each day

Shining. Clutter needs to be cleaned. If you have a collection or tend to display knickknacks or other clutter in abundance, you have to dust it and clean around it. This takes time that could be devoted to something else.

Time wasted: at least 20 minutes each week

There are other ways that clutter impedes progress and wastes time, of course, but even with these examples you can see an enormous amount of wasted time.

Total time wasted:	300 minutes per week
This equals:	5 hours per week
Which adds up to:	20 hours per month
Which adds up to:	240 hours per year, or
	10 full days of wasted time each year!

GETTING ORGANIZED—WHERE TO START

To find more time for yourself, you may first need to conquer the clutter in your life. If you're ready to get organized, and can't quite figure out where to begin, you'll need to start by setting up the proper attitude and atmosphere. Tackle one room at a time at home, or one area at a time in your office. (Chapter fourteen will give you the techniques you need to tackle paper and office clutter.) Put the following rules into effect.

Don't allow distractions. No visitors, phone calls, TV, or stopping to read an article in a magazine that you pick up. And stay out of the kitchen or commissary. Stop and eat only at meal time.

Do one area at a time. If you are cleaning out a closet, just work on that closet; don't walk into another room and start doing something else until you are finished with that closet.

Allow enough time to make a dent in the clutter accumulation. If your accumulation of clutter is substantial, don't try to conquer the clutter by devoting an hour here and an hour there to the problem. You'll find it difficult, if not impossible, to make much of a difference. Set aside at least a half-day to get started; a full uninterrupted day is better.

Don't try to keep everything! Hoarding is physically and mentally exhausting, and you'll never conquer your clutter unless you can learn to let go.

One of the biggest obstacles to conquering clutter is deciding what to eliminate. Go through all of your clutter. As you pick up each object, ask yourself the following questions to help you decide whether you should *dump it*.

Deciding to Dump

Is it a duplicate? If it is a duplicate of something you already have, and you really don't need more than one, *dump it*. Keeping duplicates of things "just in case" invites an overabundance of clutter in your life.

Is it broken beyond simple repair? If it is broken and has been for some time, either get it fixed *immediately* or *dump it*. Hanging on to broken things — such as broken clocks and appliances — is tantamount to hanging on to junk. If you don't get it fixed, give it to a charity that will fix it and sell it. You can also dump bits and pieces of things that you have been meaning to glue back together for years.

How much will it cost to store it? Remind yourself constantly that hanging on to things you don't need or use costs money to store (the cost of square footage). It also costs money in some cases to insure it, and it often takes time to clean it or clean around it. If it takes more time and costs more money than it's worth to keep, then cut your losses and *dump it*!

Do I use this? If you don't use it, lose it. Give it to someone who will use it. Get rid of that Exercycle you haven't touched in years, and pass on that third set of dishes that has been choking up the cabinets since the day you got married thirty years ago. Give it away, but *dump it*!

Is quantity more important than quality? If every available surface is covered with knickknacks, do you really need that quantity? Have you kept every Christmas card you have ever received? And do you automatically hoard all empty mayonnaise jars because you might need one someday, and now you have twenty-three in the kitchen cupboards? If you must keep these things, keep only a selection. Save a few Christmas cards from each year (limit yourself to a half dozen or so of the most special), weed your mayo jar habit down to a realistic four jars, and tell everyone you're not collecting knickknacks anymore so that they stop buying them for you on the holidays.

A PLACE FOR EVERYTHING

Once you've set aside the time to conquer the clutter in your home, along with your determination to dump what you don't need, you'll need to find

---

LETTING GO OF CLUTTER

If you have a hard time figuring out what to toss when you are going through your clutter, start by pitching, recycling or giving these items away:

- Keys that don't go to anything
- All gift boxes over a supply of two dozen maximum
- All shopping, paper and plastic bags over a supply of two dozen maximum
- Old, dried up cosmetics (these harbor bacteria)
- Exercise equipment that you haven't used in years
- Silly souvenirs
- Spices you never use
- Gadgets and gizmos that are more mysterious than useful to you
- Broken appliances you haven't used in ages
- Exhausted lingerie or droopy drawers
- Shoes that hurt your feet or back
- Clothes that are too small, out of date, or so boring you won't wear them
- Worn out and mismatched socks and stockings with runs
- Boxes of baby clothes (your children are grown and long gone)
- Toys that the children have completely outgrown
- Craft materials and half-finished projects that you gave up on many years ago
- Duplicates such as corkscrews and can openers
- Anything that is dried up, moldy or otherwise ickified

---

a place for everything and then put everything in its place. This can be difficult when clutter has usurped nearly every available inch, creating an unending mass of chaos and confusion. Caught hopelessly in the middle of the muddle, you may find yourself barely able to start, much less find a place for everything. These guidelines should help you figure out what belongs where.

Make a commitment to organizing the clutter in one complete area without stopping. Either set aside a half-day (minimum) or tell yourself that you won't stop until two closets or the garage or the bathrooms are done.

Set up large cardboard cartons labeled Charity, Toss, and Elsewhere. When you come across something that goes in another room, put it in the Elsewhere box. Put those things in the proper room at the end of the day.

Otherwise you'll end up running all over the house, interrupting yourself over and over as you transfer items to other rooms.

Empty the target area of all clutter. Pull it out into another area (such as the hall or the bed), sorting as you go.

If you're not sure where something belongs, think about keeping items as close to their point of first use as possible. Dishes should be in cabinets near the sink or dishwasher, pens and paper belong near the telephones and in the desk, and videotapes should be kept near the VCR. Although you don't want to keep duplicates you don't need (such as two lemon peelers), sometimes it makes sense to keep certain duplicate items in different areas of the house. For example, keeping scissors in the bathroom as well as in the desk can eliminate time spent searching for and moving the scissors every time you need to clip something.

Group like items together and store them in containers. For example, all of the underwear gets put back in the same area with drawer dividers to keep it separated. All of the bobby pins and hair clips and accessories go together in containers in another area.

When you are finished, take the Toss box out to the trash. Bag it tightly so that no one in the family can dig through it to retrieve items. Put the Charity box in the car, or call for a pickup so that you get rid of it as soon as possible. Put the box marked Elsewhere into the hall to be sorted and carried into other rooms.

Reward yourself when you are done. Keep repeating the process until you have licked all of the clutter in your home. The reward system is limited only by your desires and imagination. Some rewards you can give yourself are:

- Lunch at an expensive restaurant
- An ice cream sundae
- An afternoon movie
- A manicure or a pedicure
- A day at the beach or park with a good book
- A massage
- A facial
- A round of golf
- An evening out

With every conquest, give yourself a well-deserved pat on the back. Because while you've eliminated clutter, you have simultaneously given yourself the best reward of all—more time for yourself.

GETTING ORGANIZED IN EIGHT WEEKENDS

If you feel like you are so backed up that you'll never catch up, and you can't figure out how you'll ever find the time to tackle getting organized around the house, you might want to break it into projects and do it over the next few weekends. Although you'll be forfeiting your weekend time for the next few weeks, once you have eliminated the clutter and caught up with everything, you will have more time than ever for yourself. Here's how to plan some weekend organizing and catch-up projects.

Weekend #1 — Closets. Clean and organize all of the closets in your house. Get rid of clothes that are too small or outdated. If you haven't worn it in more than a year, you probably never will, so those items can go as well. Get rid of shoes that hurt your feet or are outdated. Rehang everything in groups; shirts in one section, slacks in another, skirts together in another part of the closet. Fold and gather all sweaters, and keep things like workout clothes together on one shelf. Organize the linens and get rid of tattered or never used sheets and towels (they can make great rags or drop cloths). Go through the junk in the hall closet and either get rid of it or put it where it belongs so that your coats and other outdoor clothing fit into the closet and are easy to get to. Be sure to check the fit and style on the hats and coats; if the item is out of style or outgrown and never gets worn, give it away.

Weekend #2 — Cabinets and Drawers. Clean and organize all the cabinets and drawers in the house. Thoroughly go through the bathroom and kitchen cabinets and drawers, and sort through the linen cabinet. Get rid of old makeup, appliances you never use, and duplicates you don't need. Organize what's left and put it back into the cabinets. Make use of organizing containers such as dividers, turntables, and containers such as plastic boxes and bins when you return things to the cabinets.

Weekend #3 — Basement or Attic. These are areas that are often the last outpost for clutter and items that you truly never use. Start early in the morning and pull everything out of the attic or basement, then put back only what you need to save or use. Throw everything else away or give it to charity. If other people are using your basement or attic space for storage, call them and tell them to pick up their things before you start. Make sure you dispose of any toxic items responsibly, and if you must store mementos in these areas, repack them in clean boxes with clearly written labels on all sides and store the boxes on shelves, rather than stacking them on top of each other on the floor.

Weekend #4 — Garage. If you use your garage to store all the things you never use (mainly because you don't have an attic or basement to serve this purpose), use this weekend to clean out the garage (use the guidelines outlined here under Basement or Attic). Additionally, if your car needs attention, now is the time to clean out the trunk and glove compartment, and get the car washed and serviced.

Weekend #5 — Fix Everything. Get everything fixed. Gather everything in the house that needs to be repaired, and take it to the appropriate repair facility or call a repairperson to come in. Clothes should go to a tailor or seamstress, small appliances need to go to appliance repair shops, jewelry goes to the jeweler, and the clock to the clock repair shop. Don't waste your time or your money repairing things you won't wear or use, and don't try to fix everything yourself. You probably don't have enough time or talent to fix it all, and the time you save will be well worth the money spent for repairs.

Weekend #6 — Paper. Don't wait until tax time to organize all of your household paperwork. Get all of your receipts for the year in order now, and when filing time rolls around, you'll be well ahead of the game. While you're at it, throw out all of the accumulated junk mail and catalogs that have been piling up. Go through any boxes of papers or files that you have, and purge unnecessary papers too. Put what's left into neatly labeled file folders or boxes so that the next time you need to put your hands on a particular piece of paper you won't spend twenty minutes searching for it.

Weekend #7 — Read. Get rid of all those backed-up, outdated magazines, newspapers, catalogs and journals that you simply don't have time for — the accumulation is just too big and overwhelming. If there is an article you must read, clip it and throw the rest of the periodical away. Then spend the rest of the weekend catching up on some reading that is really important to you.

Weekend #8 — Correspondence. Catch up on all of your back correspondence. Write letters, notes or cards to all of your friends and relatives who are always complaining that you never write. Stock up on stationery, cards, postcards and postage, and put it all in a portable basket so that you can carry the basket to your bedside or easy chair and keep up with your correspondence by getting a note or card off with some regularity. This is also the weekend to go through all those stacks of correspondence that you've collected over the years. Get rid of most of those hundreds of greeting cards that you've held on to (no need to keep three hundred Christmas cards after all), and keep only the most important and meaningful correspondence as mementos or family history.

DON'T LET CLUTTER IN THE DOOR

Once you've caught up on the backlog of clutter, you'll want to keep on top of it so that it doesn't back up on you again. Use these tips to help you save time for yourself by spending less time with clutter in your life.

Learn to let go. As lives change, needs change, but somehow, objects accumulate with no regard for the changed circumstances. Think about this when you shop, and don't even consider buying things that merely take up valuable space and give you nothing in return.

Buy what you need, not what you want. Clutter starts when you begin buying things you want but don't need. You may *want* that fancy gourmet popcorn popper, but you really don't *need* it. There's no cupboard space left to store it in, so it will have to sit on top of the counter will all the other paraphernalia that is cluttering up that space. If you don't eat popcorn that often, you can do what you've always done—cook it in a pan on top of the stove.

Ask yourself where you are going to put the item before you buy it. If you don't have a place to put the item, don't buy it. There's no point in buying one more hat if you already have ten you don't wear, and you don't have a shelf or hook left to store the hat on when you aren't wearing it.

Forget the Joneses. Stop and think before you buy something just to keep up with the Joneses. Half the time it just ends up being clutter, and face it, the Joneses won't be there to pay the bill when it comes due.

Don't buy things just because they are on sale. Many a closet is cluttered with great buys that don't go with anything and are therefore unwearable. Ditto kitchen and bathroom gadgets that get purchased on sale and never used. Let *use* rather than *price* be the deciding factor in your purchases. If you won't get a lot of use out of it, don't buy it, regardless of the price.

Use the in-and-out inventory rule. When you buy something new, before you put it away, select something old to get rid of. New toys replace old toys; new clothes replace old and outdated things; new books take the place of those you have read and can now generously give away. Stick to this rule, and you'll never find yourself overloaded with clutter again.

Do It Now

Clutter is often a direct by-product of procrastination. Once the clutter starts to mount, the natural tendency is to make excuses about it. Everyone sees through those excuses (even if they don't tell you directly), and the overall result is that nothing is solved, and the clutter continues to mount until it is an out-of-control obstacle. To circumvent this unhappy cycle, vow to deal with the clutter *now* instead of *later*. Make these habits a part of your daily life.

Decide to decide what you are going to do with that next piece of clutter that you pick up. Stop procrastinating; tackle your clutter now and keep on top of it on a daily basis. Stop putting things all over the place "just for now."

Be a giver. Give things away, right away. Friends, relatives and charities

TAKING IT WITH YOU

There comes a time in everyone's life when consideration is given to what should be passed down to heirs. Generally older people are faced with several kinds of abundance; they have an abundance of experiences, an abundance of memories, and an abundance of things—all collected over a lifetime. Experiences add to wisdom; memories can be passed down to become history and remembered forever; and things (such as furniture, pictures, diaries, letters, trip souvenirs) become part of an estate to be sorted through and decided upon. If you are at this stage in your life and find yourself a bit overwhelmed by the prospect of deciding who will get what, these guidelines can help.

You are the best person to decide. We don't do our heirs any favors when we leave behind a lifetime of things. Papers, documents, knick-knacks, old clothes, mementos and heirlooms can add up to a daunting and very painful chore for our loved ones when they find they have to sift through it all and make decisions shortly after we have passed on. It is far kinder for you to make the decisions than to leave it to your heirs.

Family history is important. Old diaries, letters with biographical or geographical information, and photos that are clearly marked with names and dates all contribute to the family history. These should be neatly organized, labeled and passed on to the person in the family who is most likely to keep the history intact. If some of the documents are deteriorating, you might want to copy them or read them into a tape recorder and pass the tapes on instead of the papers.

Give some things away now. Often we automatically hang on to things that are fine items but are no longer used. You may have more than one set of dinnerware, for example, with some of the china pieces being heirlooms that have been passed down. Although these items are lovely and have family significance, you no longer entertain, so the china sits unused in the cupboard. Is there a young couple in the family who would love the beauty and history of this china? Perhaps they are just beginning to entertain and can't afford nice pieces themselves. Pass the china on. And take those things with no significant value that you never use directly to your church or local charity.

Organize critical documents. As you sift through your papers, pull out the important items, such as real estate documents, birth and marriage certificates, insurance policies, and investment papers. Put them in order and make a concise summary of what you have, and make sure that at least two relatives or your lawyer has a copy of the documents and know where they're kept. This will ease their burden as they deal with paperwork in your life once you are gone. And the rest of that paperwork? Get rid of as much of it as you can. Clippings, magazine articles of interest, coupons, and all the rest of the miscellaneous paper means nothing to anybody. Get rid of a small stack each day, but do get rid of it.

Getting organized now, and passing things on will clear the clutter from your life and will ease a painful burden that your loved ones might otherwise have to face later. It will renew in you the joy that giving brings. And it will streamline your life so that you have more time to do what you want to do with the rest of your life!

all appreciate a giving person far more than they do a pack rat. Make an ongoing effort to get rid of things you never use by keeping a Charity box on hand. Toss things in the box as soon as you realize you're not using them anymore, and make a periodic run to the charity to drop off your castoffs.

Use it or lose it. If you're not using it, get rid of it. Period.

Keep everything in its place. Find a place for everything and keep everything in its place. Make this a habit to live by. Another good rule is: Don't put things down; put them away.

Stop and pick up the room. When clutter starts to get out of control, stop whatever you're doing and take twenty minutes to pick up that room. Put everything in the right room—you can put it away within that room later. Toys go in the kids' room or the playroom, dirty clothes and towels go in the hamper or laundry room, dirty dishes go in the dishwasher, papers and magazines go in a reading stack, and jackets go in the coat closet. Later, when you have more time, you can put things away more specifically (toys in toy chest, newspapers in the recycling bin, etc). You can clean at that time, too. In the meantime you will have controlled the clutter and made an immediate change for the better in how the room looks without taking hours to do a thorough cleaning.

Clutter is a fine example of the "less is more" concept. The less clutter you have, the more time, money and energy you will have for yourself. So if you really want to have that time, money and energy for yourself, simply eliminate unnecessary clutter, and organize and keep only those things that contribute positively and actively to your life today. Life is too short to live it on behalf of your many *things*. Live it for yourself.

CHAPTER FOURTEEN

Conquering the Paper Pile-Up

Excessive record-keeping is a symptom of insecurity and defensive thinking. It indicates that you are less concerned with attaining objectives than you are with documentation, and that your thinking is oriented to the past, not the present.

— Edwin Bliss

P aper is a time-consuming fact of life that can eat away at even the best of time-management intentions. Although a lot of the paper that comes into our lives is something we would probably rather do without, the daily deluge still arrives, demanding your time and attention. The constant barrage of paper can make it difficult to find the time to figure out how to manage the problem, let alone actually *do* something with all that paper. If you haven't taken care of yesterday's or last week's mail, there is no way you're going to have time to take care of the paper that gets dumped on you today. Along with the demands on your time comes the clutter that paper so often turns into — and clutter, as you know, is a tremendous time waster. Before you can say "booby hatch," you find yourself staring down piles of paper collapsing on top of tables, desks, filing cabinets, bookcases and refrigerators. It may even be popping out of drawers, boxes and bags.

Once the paper starts to back up, it can be a fearsome sight indeed. Even worse, if you spend just ten minutes a day looking for a missing piece of paper or file, you will have wasted over sixty hours a year — that's two and a half days! Take a look at those piles, and you're likely to find some or all of the following:

Unopened Mail	Memos	Forms
Catalogs	Faxes	Stationery Supplies
Trade Journals	Reports	Magazines
Newspapers	Bulletins	Receipts
Bills	Lists	Cards

| Letters | Schedules | Recipes |
| Children's School Papers | Brochures | Coupons |

Paper Personalities

Clearly, we have not yet reached the promised land of the paperless society. Computer printers all over the world are kicking out enough paper to wallpaper the planet in printouts. Faced with an overwhelming amount of information and paper, people tend to develop their own particular "paper personality," complete with a set of habits that can be self-defeating because they are time-consuming and nonproductive. If you recognize yourself in any of the following "paper personalities" you may want to consider changing some of the habits that hinder rather than help you find more time for yourself on a daily basis.

Information Nut. Paper carries information, of course, and the abundance of information now available has given rise to the definitive phrase "information anxiety." This, roughly defined, describes what happens when a person feels obligated to soak up as much information as possible on a daily basis, and when this becomes impossible or overwhelming, feelings of obligation turn into anxiety. The information-anxious folks adjust their stress level upward several notches with every few inches of paper that are added to the piles of information yet to be absorbed. The papers multiply at a frenzied rate, and it isn't long before the panic button is activated. There simply aren't enough hours in the day to keep up, but a compulsive need to know drives this personality type to continue collecting "valuable" information.

Paper Pack Rat. The paper pack rat also has a problem with paper, but is blissfully immune to anxiety regarding the piles and stacks. The pack rat religiously continues collecting every conceivable type of paper until one day the health or fire department is called in. Then the anxiety kicks in big time. The "reasons" for collecting are varied, with some apparently more sanctified than others. Take, for example, Mom. Giving in to unbridled motherly pride, Mom keeps every single piece of precious paper that every one of the children brings home. She collects coupons and recipes that she forgets to use. She has catalogs and magazines she has no time to read stacked all over the house. A filing cabinet seems like a ridiculous thing to have in the house so the papers get piled, tacked and stacked all over the house. But when the refrigerator, walls, tables and countertops are loaded with the stuff, something must be done. Or there's Dad, who has years of hobby- and business-related papers that he can't turn loose. He's a history buff, so he's got papers, journals and magazines that accumulate in boxes, bags, cupboards and corners. Ask him what they are about, and the answer is a vague but emphatic "important things!" He keeps all the papers he ever accumulated on his sales contacts over the years—and he's been selling for fifteen years. Some of the information is out of date, but Dad is insistent. "Don't touch those, I might need them some day!" Eventually the basement, garage, attic and spare room are chock a block with papers. It's a fire hazard, and there's no room for guests or the car. D-day has arrived. Dad has to deal with those papers—not just push them from one area to another.

The Besieged. The businessperson or department head has been chugging along nicely for some time, but suddenly it's cutback time. The company is downsizing; lean and mean is to be the new operative word. People are let go, and their paperwork is shifted to others' desks. Now the power of paper raises its ugly head. The remaining employees have to pay attention and figure out not only how it was handled, but why it was processed in the first place. Paper pushing and its procedures suddenly assume top priority for those besieged by the additional paper burden. They were behind to begin with, and now the piles of paper are taking on a hopeless hue, leaving the besieged to sink into a "poor me" despair that solves nothing and just puts them farther behind. Ultimately the reasons for the layoffs are negated by lower productivity and (often) profits. Finally someone recognizes that perhaps the real answer to efficiency may be to streamline the paperwork, which should have been done before anyone was fired in the first place.

Bad Habits

Whatever your particular paper personality, there are three common bad paper handling habits that many people fall prey to.

The Stacker. Stacks papers, magazines and files in stacks and feels that since the stacks are upright (not toppling over), the papers are in good enough order and will silently wait until the miraculous day when the Stacker has time to get to all those stacks. This rarely happens, however, once the stacks start to multiply. When stacks are everywhere—including the floor—chances are good that the bugs will get to those papers before the Stacker does.

The Stasher. Stows papers inside drawers and cabinets, unperturbed by the old "out of sight, out of mind" rule of thumb. The Stasher plans to get back to those papers, but before she gets to them, other papers are piled on top and the whole mess is topped off with take-out menus, old newspapers, and the sales reports from six months ago. Not only does the Stasher forget about the nature of the papers stashed, no one else has a clue as to where these documents are. Depending on the importance of these papers, this may or may not be a problem. If the stashed papers consist mostly of junk that could be tossed, the biggest problem is that the Stasher has desk drawers and cabinet space that is sorely wasted. If the papers are important, it's only a matter of time before circumstances conspire to create a scenario where those papers rise up and bite the Stasher on the behind.

The Spreader. May start with stacks and stashes of paper in varying quantities. Whatever the origin and regardless of the amount of the paper, the Spreader makes it a point to spread the paper over every available surface within five minutes of his contact with that paper. Now the Spreader *looks* busy, and in a way, this is true. Because now, at least several times a day, the Spreader will have to stop and scrabble around the mess to try to locate some important document that's buried who-knows-where.

Stacking, stashing and spreading are quick and easy to do, but those habits leave their perpetrators feeling constantly overwhelmed and overworked. Left to deal with the daily chaos of lost documents and unmanageable piles of paper, most people with bad paper habits just throw up their hands and give up.

GETTING ORGANIZED—WHERE TO START

Whatever your situation, dealing with paper takes time every day. While paper is an unavoidable fact of life, chances are, you are spending far more time than necessary on it. There are lots of terrific techniques and simple systems that can streamline all of the paper in your life. If you spend some time nearly every day looking for a piece of paper or a file, you need to get organized. If you've got magazines, newspapers and catalogs that go back several months or if you're sitting on several weeks' worth of mail that you haven't acted on, or if you can't see the tops of your desk, counters, tables or any horizontal surface because of the piles of paper, you'll need to spend some extra time getting organized. But doing this will help clear your mind and clear your calendar. Once the paper in your life—both at home and at work—is under control, you can save time every day by using simple systems to help keep on top of that paperwork. You'll benefit by being more organized all the time, which means you can be more productive. You'll be under less stress (no more spending time every day looking for some elusive paper or file), and you'll have the time you need to spend on more important matters.

To get organized, first tackle any backlog that may be piled all over the place. Gather all of the loose papers and files. Get all of the papers from the top of your desk, as well as papers stacked or piled on top of the filing cabinet, bookcase and floor. If you are dealing with a paper problem in your home, make sure you check each room and gather all the papers that are stashed on bureaus, in closets, and on the refrigerator and kitchen counter. Put all of the papers into one huge stack. If your stack is so tall that it will topple, get some large cartons and put the papers in them.

Four-Step Paper Sorting System

Once you've assembled all of the loose papers and files in one area, sit down and methodically go through the papers, *one piece at a time*. Begin by remembering this simple paper processing principle:

There are basically only four basic things you can do with a piece of paper. Understand that, and sort your papers into these four categories:

To Do
To Pay
To Read
To File

Recycle or throw the rest away. (To get yourself in the proper frame of mind for this, put a large garbage bag at your side.) Put anything that is recyclable into a stack, and either put it in the recycle bin at the end of the day, or put it in your car so you can drop it off at the recycle center as soon as possible. Do not let it sit around the house because you think someone else wants it. (That's just an excuse to hang on to it.)

It's important not to get sidetracked with worry at this point. You are only *sorting* now, so don't start worrying about how you should respond to the latest correspondence from your attorney, or why the credit card company didn't give you that credit that was supposed to go through. To make the most efficient use of your time, don't let other things distract you. Don't take or make phone calls, don't start reminiscing over photos or letters, and don't start reading a magazine article. Don't give in to the impetuous idea that you just have to go out for a bite to eat after only an hour's effort. *Just sort.*

To Do. Once the entire pile (or piles) has been sorted, go through each category again. Begin with the papers in the to-do pile, and ask yourself these questions:

Do I really need to do this? If not, get rid of it by filing it or dumping it. (But don't use your files as a dumping ground. As a general rule, 80 percent of everything you file you never look at again.)

Is it too late to do this? If so, get rid of it by filing it or dumping it.

Do I really want to do this? If the answer is no, find somebody else to do it, even if it costs you money. Use that time to do something more important or something that you really want to do.

Does anybody care if I do this? If the answer is no, then you shouldn't care either. Dump it.

The papers that are left in your to-do pile after you've gone through it should now be only the papers that you *really must do* something about.

KEEPING UP WITH YOUR READING

Once you've dumped as many magazines, newspapers and journals as you can, these tips can help you keep up with your reading.

Learn to speed read and be selective about what you read. Don't feel obligated to read something just because you always have (such as a particular magazine) or because someone passed it along to you (such as a lengthy article that someone mailed you). If it isn't something you need to read or want to read, get rid of it.

Learn to scan things like reports and proposals before you set aside time to read them more completely. You may not have to read the material any more thoroughly since it doesn't apply to you or because it is something that won't be developed any further anyway.

If trade journals and other reports are routinely routed to you, see what you can eliminate. Get your name removed from the routing lists for those materials you really don't need to read. If you get regular reports (such as weekly sales reports, for example) perhaps you can change the routine so that you only receive the reports if there is a significant drop or increase in sales.

Don't buy more books and publications if you've already got a stack waiting for you back at the office or at home that you still haven't read.

If you are hanging on to a magazine just because there is an article in it you have to read, clip the article and staple it, and put it in your to-read basket. Toss or recycle the rest of the publication. Tomorrow over breakfast, or during a break, you can read it. Keep a pair of scissors and a stapler in your to-read basket so that you can weed out magazines regularly.

Set aside a specific amount of time to read on a regular basis. I like to spend two hours every morning reading (I get up earlier to fit it in). If I wait until the end of the day, I'm too tired. Other people find that an hour or so before retiring is the best time of the day to fit in reading time.

Break down your reading. If you can't read an entire book, and don't know when you'll ever have the time, schedule enough time to read two chapters each week, and in six weeks or so, you will have finished the book.

Always carry reading material with you. You never know when you'll have to spend time waiting, and you can keep up with your reading in bits and pieces by reading during these unexpected periods of time. If you commute via train or bus, or if you fly frequently, you'll be able to get in several hours of reading time each week.

Listen to books on tape while you drive to work. You can "read" and drive at the same time, and might be able to "finish" a book in just a few days.

Check the table of contents of magazines before you buy them. Don't become distracted by flipping through the publication. If you do you'll find yourself involved in articles that may be interesting, but are not articles really want you to spend your time reading.

If you spend time perusing several publications looking for articles on a particular topic of interest, consider hiring a clipping service instead. They'll send you just the articles you need.

Once each year, reevaluate the subscriptions you receive. Try to eliminate at least one subscription. And never order a new subscription unless you let an old one go.

To Pay. Next, go through your to-pay pile again. Ask yourself these questions:

Has this already been paid? If it has, mark it paid and file it.

Is there a problem with this bill that I need to look into? If the answer is yes, you might want to move it into your to-do pile so that you can make the call or do the research necessary to straighten the problem out before you actually pay the bill.

The bills in your to-pay stack after you've gone through it should be only the bills that you *really must pay*.

To Read. Next, go through your to-read pile. Whatever you do, *do not* allow yourself to stop and read the magazines, journals or catalogs in this pile. Instead quickly scan the table of contents or cover, and ask yourself these questions:

Is there a sound reason for me to read this? If the answer is no, dump it.

Do I have time to read this? If the answer is no, and you don't *have* to read it, dump it.

Is this out of date? If you've got reading material with outdated information in it (such as old catalogs, sales materials and journals that have been replaced with new editions), dump it.

Do I have more than three months' worth of issues here? If you have magazines backed up for three months, bite the bullet and get rid of at least one month's worth. It's hard enough to catch up and keep up with the reading in your life without stockpiling it.

To File. Finally go through your to-file pile. When you did your initial sort, you were probably convinced that you had to hang on to these papers and files. Now it's time to rethink your decision. While you are reviewing that pile, keep in mind the following.

Filing costs money

- A good filing cabinet can run from one hundred to several hundred dollars.
- With allowance for an opened drawer and standing room, a filing cabinet requires at least seven to eight square feet of floor space. If you're paying, say, $10 per square foot for that space, you're allocating $70 to $80 in space costs for one filing cabinet. Even if all you do is store papers in boxes, those boxes are taking up expensive space.
- If you pay someone to file, add even more money to the tab. A file clerk who is paid $10 per hour and spends three hours each week sorting and filing would cost you in the neighborhood of $1,560 per year.
- Supplies, including manila folders, labels and hanging folders also get added to the filing tab. Even discounted supplies add up. Figuring low, a price of five cents for the manila folder, forty-eight cents for the hanging file, and two cents for the label, still leaves you looking at a supply cost of fifty-five cents for every new file you make.

With these prices firmly fixed in your mind, make a commitment to decide what to do with each piece of paper once and for all. Papers and files that are kept can be put in one of several different types of filing systems.

Archival files are generally kept in a transfile box (available at office supply stores) and stored in a closet, warehouse, garage or off-site storage unit. Papers that should be kept and stored include financial and legal papers that you are required by law to keep for a specific period of time, but that you are not using on a regular basis. To evaluate which of your important records need to be kept and for how long, check with your certified public accountant, your attorney, or the IRS. Once you have decided to store records, make sure that the storage area is clean, dry and free of bugs and other vermin. Otherwise all of your records will eventually get ruined. Resist the temptation to store your records in odd-shaped cardboard boxes that you might be able to scrounge up. Stacking these boxes presents several problems . Because they are usually not uniform in size, you can't stack them all together and in order. When there is extra space inside the box, the stacks tend to collapse on the bottom boxes. The flaps make it a pain to get into a box and close it, and the boxes are harder to move since they don't feature the handles that transfile boxes have.

Permanent files include papers that you might use as a resource on a regular basis as well as current financial, legal, and business or client files. These should be kept in filing cabinets as close to your work area as possible.

Action files are files that you are actively involved with on a daily basis. These can be kept in a two-drawer filing cabinet next to your desk (for easy access) or, if you don't have more than about a dozen or so of these, they can be kept in the file drawer that you may have in your desk.

Project files are files that you are currently working with while you are developing and completing a particular project. You may be assembling a lot of information to put together a sales presentation. You can divide your information by category as you receive it, and put it into project files. These files can be kept in your desk file drawer or in a rolling file cart that can be pulled close to your work area as needed. When the project is done, keep whatever is necessary for back-up purposes and store the files in your current or archival files. Your project cart or drawer will then be ready to receive files for your next project.

Circular file. Finally, there are the papers that you put in the to-file pile that really belong in the circular file. This file is also known as the trash. The beauty of it is that you don't have to spend the time or money to set up a file before you put the papers into the trash can or garbage bag. No expensive filing cabinets or square footage either. No storage boxes. Just *dump it.*

Setting Up a File
Use the following guidelines to set up your files.

1. Use a manila file with a clearly marked label on that file.
2. Put the manila file into a hanging file; make sure the label on the hanging file matches the label on the manila file. This label goes on the *front* of the file, not the back. (This is so that when your hand touches the file you automatically open the folder to the right place. Tags on the back take your hand to the *file* behind the one you really mean to get into.)
3. Don't overstuff the files; when a file gets full, start another one. You can break them down by category or by date (perhaps the first six months' activity can be in one file, and the next six months' will be in the second file).
4. Never remove the hanging file from the drawer; it serves as a permanent marker for where the manila file goes in the drawer and eliminates misfiling. If you need the file, pull only the manila file out of the drawer.
5. Put all the files in the drawer filed simply by alphabetical order.

DECIDING TO DUMP

If you have trouble letting go of paper, or can't decide what to dump, ask yourself the following questions as you pick up each piece of paper to help decide whether you should *dump* it.

Is it a duplicate? If it is a copy of something you already have, *dump it*! Keeping copies "just in case" is unnecessary. And forget about sending some of the copies to your friends, relatives and colleagues. They've got enough paper in their lives; they don't need more from you.

What's the date? If it is hopelessly out of date, *dump it*! This includes catalogs from two seasons back, invitations for events long since passed, and address and price lists that have changed.

How much will it cost me to store it? Remind yourself constantly of the cost of paper storage, and if you'd rather spend your money elsewhere (like on a trip to Europe), *dump it*!

Is the information on this paper relevant to my current lifestyle? If it goes back to when you were a hippie, and now you are a yuppie, *dump it*!

How often will I need to refer to the information on this piece of paper? If you don't know the answer to that question, but want to keep the piece of paper "in case you need it someday," *dump it*! That's an excuse, not a reason.

Do I really have time to read this? Be honest. Do you really have time to read all of those magazines and all of that junk mail? If not, *dump it*. Your time can be put to far better use; why waste it on trivia?

Will I really use this information? Will you really try out that new recipe, or are you just clipping it out of habit so you can stuff it in the drawer with all of those other lip-smacking untried recipes? Will you ever take a trip to Tahiti, or are you just filing it in a fantasy file? If you know you won't use the information, *dump it*!

Can I live without this piece of paper? If you were wiped out by fire, flood or some other immediate natural disaster, would you need this piece of paper? If you know in your heart that you don't really need it, and could live without it, then do the right thing, and *dump it*!

ORGANIZING YOUR DESK

Once you have sorted all of your papers, tossed what you don't need, and filed what should be kept, you will want to set up your desk to give you the most efficient workspace possible. Start by setting up some baskets to hold papers on and around your desk.

Desktop Baskets

To Do. Put your remaining to-do items in this box. Keep this box on your desk within easy reach.

LETTING GO OF PAPER

If you have a hard time deciding what to toss when you are going through your papers, start by pitching or recycling these items:

- Old travel brochures
- Newspapers that are more than a week old
- Expired coupons
- Misprinted stationery
- Old road maps from other states
- Catalogs from two seasons ago
- Any magazine more than three months old
- Old college papers and textbooks
- Boxes of Christmas cards you've received over the years
- At least half of all the children's papers you've hung on to
- Business cards from people you don't know and don't care to know
- Recipes you know you'll never have the time to try
- Duplicate paperwork
- Outdated wall calendars
- Invitations with the date long passed
- Old checkbooks from closed bank accounts (cut them up first)
- At least half of those pink phone-call slips representing all of the people who have called you and whose call you never returned
- Old business cards from your previous jobs
- Outdated mailing and address lists
- Cartoons and copies of cartoons
- Articles that were clipped and copied just because you liked them
- Expired warranties and instruction books for things you no longer have

To Pay. If you pay bills, put your bills (to be paid) in this box. Keep this box on or near your desk so that you never forget about it.

To Read. Put any remaining publications, periodicals or journals that you need to read in this box. Do not put this on your desk; like the to-file box it is best placed on the floor under, or next to the desk, or behind you on the credenza.

To File. Put any filing that you still have to do in this box. Do not put this box on top of your desk; your desktop is a workspace, not a storage space. Put the basket under your desk (mark it clearly so that it is not mistaken for trash) or behind your desk (on top of the credenza, for example).

In/Out. If you have in- and out-boxes, try placing the out-box behind you on your credenza so that it doesn't take up valuable workspace on your desktop. If this isn't possible, try stacking the boxes one on top of the other (posts are provided for this purpose) so that you use up the least amount of desktop space for these boxes.

The best desktop boxes to purchase for your to-do and to-pay papers are either wire or wood. To maximize space, always consider adding posts (available to buy with the boxes) to stack the boxes. Lucite or plastic boxes provide the least amount of space and benefit because they don't have stacking posts; they stack directly on top of one another, making it difficult to put more than a few papers in each bin. These plastic boxes are good for holding forms, however. If you use lots of different forms every day, you can stack six to ten boxes that will hold several copies of each form very nicely.

Your to-file and to-read boxes should be the roomiest boxes or bins you can find. You may want to use large wire baskets, or you may want to get large bins (available at home supply stores) to hold one or both of these categories. You may even want to use a small cardboard carton for either of these groups of papers.

Personal Items

Once the papers are sorted into the boxes, take a look at the personal items you have on and in your desk. Personal items include everything from tea bags to shoes and boots to photos and awards. Put the awards on the wall or on a bookcase or shelf. Put a small selection of photos on a bookshelf or credenza, and if you must, one photo on your desk. Remember that this is a *work*space, where personal touches are nice but should definitely be kept to a minimum. Nobody needs to see your entire family tree in photographs, from Great-Aunt Minnie down to Puff the pooch. If you're short of space, check these family photos out first. They may be crowding you out. Any food should be kept in the kitchen or cafeteria. If this isn't possible, consider getting a very small picnic basket or cooler that you can tuck under, or next to, your desk to hold your lunch rather than letting it occupy precious drawer space. Shoes or boots, too, are more aptly stored discreetly under the desk rather than in a drawer. A plant is fine (but don't go for the jungle look) so long as it is in good shape and doesn't create clutter.

Equipment and Supplies

Make sure that your equipment is suitable and in good working condition. You need a sturdy but comfortable chair, adequate lighting, and equipment (such as an adding machine or answering machine for example) that works well. Also make sure that the drawers in your desk and credenza open and close without sticking. Keep only enough supplies on hand in and around your desk to cover your needs for a few weeks. All other supplies (such as extra stationery, boxes of paper clips and rubber bands, etc.) should be stored neatly elsewhere in a cabinet or on a shelf. Use drawer dividers to maximize and organize the space inside the smaller desk drawers. And take the time now and again to browse through a comprehensive office supply catalog to see what is available that can further help you keep your desk and work area organized. And whether you work at home or in an office, always have a *large* trash can next to your desk and use it often!

Keep instructions for all equipment either right next to it or under it (the instructions for the phone system can probably go under the phone, but the troubleshooting guide for the copier will need to be on a counter or shelf next to it). Tape the name and number of the vendor and the repairperson somewhere on the equipment so that you can call the minute there is a breakdown. When you buy new equipment, make it a point to immediately get rid of the old machinery. Either donate it to charity, sell it or toss it. It just takes up space if you're not using it and don't intend to use it in the future.

If you use reference books and manuals regularly, they can be stored on a shelf mounted above the desk. If they are used only occasionally they can be stored on a bookcase or in a credenza.

Furniture

Always keep convenience in mind when you select and arrange the furniture in your office. Put as much within reach as possible, including the phone, adding machine, reference materials that you need every day, and at least a drawer or two that will hold files (a two-drawer filing cabinet next to the desk is good). If you have to get up to get something, or put something else away, chances are you won't—you'll just toss it on another pile. So put as much within reach as possible.

Make sure the furniture you select is functional. Your desk should have several sturdy drawers, and preferably at least one file drawer. Filing cabinets should be of good quality with full suspension drawers (which means the drawers can open to a full extension). You'll want this; otherwise you can't reach the files in the back of the drawer. If you have a lot of household or charity paperwork that you handle from home, try to set up a functional work station rather than an overly fussy one. An expensive French antique desk with two itty-bitty drawers is not going to help you; you'd be better off to set up a workspace by setting aside a corner space in the kitchen. If you don't have an office (either at home or at work) you can "stake out your territory" and give yourself a bit of privacy by surrounding the area with bookcases, shelves, or even screens or portable walls. If you don't like the idea of filing cabinets at home, consider a two-drawer cabinet in a soft color that you can put into a closet or next to your work area. If you don't have room for the sorting baskets (maybe you're managing at the kitchen table) buy a rolling wire basket system from a closet or home supply store. The unit holds several baskets as well as hanging files, and can be easily stored in a closet when not in use.

CONTROLLING PAPER

Once you've conquered the paper pile-up, you'll want to keep it under control to forever eliminate the time wasted trying to manage unmanageable piles of papers and files. Use these tips and techniques to master paper and save time every day.

Open your mail. Open and sort the mail the day you get it. Throw away all junk mail, junk inserts and envelopes, and sort the mail into To Do, To Pay, To File, and To Read.

Go through your in-box. Go through your in-box at least once a day. Look at each item and make a decision immediately. If you can get rid of something with almost no effort, do it. If something just needs your signature, sign it and put it in your out-box. If dealing with the item will take more than a few seconds, put it in either your To Do, To Pay, To File, or To Read box.

Don't ask for information you don't need. Stop thinking that you have to be totally informed and aware. Limit the amount of information you try to absorb, and stop feeling guilty about what you're missing.

Streamline memos. If your company is memo-happy, don't automatically keep every memo you receive if several other people have it too, or if it doesn't really have any impact on your immediate job function. Don't allow yourself to write more memos than absolutely necessary (and control yourself when it comes to business letters as well). The next time you sit down to write or read a memo, you might want to think about a survey conducted by Robert Half that found that top executives spend 22 percent of their time (or as much as eleven work weeks a year) writing or reading memos. The one hundred executives polled said that 39 percent of the memos were a complete waste of time. That adds up to approximately one month a year spent on unnecessary memos!

Be realistic about your reading. Evaluate your subscription list on a regular basis. If you find yourself falling behind in your reading, let some of those subscriptions go. Have someone screen some of your business reading if you can, and do some screening yourself by clipping only the most important articles for reading, and throwing the rest of the periodical away.

Route things immediately. Don't sit on things that are supposed to work their way down a routing list. If you get a journal to read and you are only one of six people on the routing list, read it and move it along. If you don't have time to read it, move it along, and add your name again to the bottom of the routing slip. This way it doesn't get buried on your desk while others are waiting for the material.

Prioritize. To ensure that you don't let your to-do box turn into a dumping ground, start each day by going through the box and prioritizing what needs to be done. Move the most important papers to a priority position in the center of your desk. Then deal with those first before you look at new mail and paperwork that might come in that day.

Quit procrastinating. Procrastination is time-consuming and often represents the beginning of the end. If you find yourself procrastinating on your paperwork, try to do the worst first. Or tackle it in small segments. Work on a five-hour project one hour each day. Inch by inch, it's a cinch. Or better yet, let somebody else take care of it for you. Delegate it.

Stop being a copycat. Resist the urge to copy everything you have on paper. Every time you photocopy something, you're contributing to the blizzard of papers blanketing the human race. And don't put extra copies in the files "just in case." One copy in the file is plenty.

Quit dumping papers rather than making decisions about them. Quit using your files as a dumping ground for papers that you can't decide what to do with. Remember that 80 percent of everything you file you will probably never look at again.

Use the KISS Rule. Don't waste time setting up overcomplicated filing systems. For example, a complex, multicolor coded system or a system keyed to a thirty-page numerical index is usually not necessary, and it is time-consuming to maintain. Use the KISS rule—Keep It Simple, Stupid.

Learn to let go. Be selective about the papers you keep, particularly where mementos are concerned. Choose a special sampling of paper memories and let the rest of your paper past go.

Purge your papers regularly. Make it a rule to purge your files and papers at least once a year, and more often if possible. When you have a file out, clean it out.

Don't put papers in pending files. Don't keep a pending file or basket unless it has to do with shipments arriving or being sent. Things placed into pending often become lost or happily forgotten forever. These items go in the to-do or the to-pay box, where you'll see them every time you work on any of the papers in those categories.

Do your filing regularly. See to it that the filing is done at least once a week; otherwise it piles up and never gets done. It's not exactly the world's most pleasant task, and it's easy to avoid, but once it piles up, it becomes difficult to have an accurate picture of any one account. You may have the file for your credit card in your hands, but you can't straighten out the bill properly because the filing is so backed up that the last two months' worth of invoices are not yet in the file; they're in the to-file pile.

Get organized every day. Spend five or ten minutes each day tidying up your work area and prioritizing your paperwork for the next day. Put any loose papers into the appropriate box, and make sure your desktop or work area is clear of unnecessary paper clutter. The following day will get off to a much better start if your desk is organized and you are not faced with overwhelming piles of paper.

Finally, do what many successful executives do; ask yourself how you can rid yourself of each piece of paper that comes your way. Toss it, act on it, or pass it on, but work hard to figure out how to get rid of it as quickly as possible every day so that you can have more time for yourself rather than devoting it to the paper in your life.

STREAMLINE THE PAPER IN YOUR LIFE

There are hundreds of timesaving techniques that can be used to streamline the files and papers that you work with regularly. Time-management consultant Harold L. Taylor lists a good selection of them in his publication, *Time Worp, 750 of the World's Greatest Time Saving Ideas*. Here's a sampling.

Write brief memos and reports. Outlaw letters over 200 words in length.

Have sample letters on hand so you won't have to keep composing new ones for similar situations. . . . Use form letters for the routine, repetitive and relatively unimportant correspondence.

When composing long letters, itemize and number the ideas. This saves time in writing, reading, and replying. Always put the important information at the start of your letter. And end by telling the reader exactly what you want him or her to do. . . . "Get back to me as soon as possible" is too vague. Take the initiative. Use the "unless I hear from you" approach, rather than waiting weeks for a reply. . . .

If you are making several drafts of a manuscript or report, use different colored stock so you can quickly identify the final draft. When correcting errors on proofs, mark the words being changed using a yellow highlighter so you can quickly verify later that all the changes have been made.

Ask for exceptions or deviations from plans and summaries — not entire reports. To thin out distribution of reports, don't issue them for several weeks, and see who misses them.

When routing correspondence, the last line should indicate its final destination. If the end of the line is the wastebasket, say so.

If posted memos don't get read, consider placing bulletin boards in the company washrooms.

When filing paperwork, record a "throw-out" date on it. . . . Place the most recent correspondence at the front (of the file) for easy access.

Never label a file "miscellaneous." It becomes a tempting dumping ground and makes retrieval more difficult.

When flyers, envelopes, brochures, etc., are stored in closed cartons, identify the contents by taping a sample on the outside. When keeping inactive files, clearly mark the contents of each carton along with the date they are to be destroyed.

Keep a file copy of brochures, flyers and other mailing pieces. Make corrections or improvements as they come to your attention. This will insure that the changes are made when the time comes to reprint the item.

If you must have files or reports on your desk, store them in vertical racks rather than in piles. If you keep frequently used catalogs, store them in alphabetical order in magazine holders. Throw out the current one as soon as the new one arrives. Whenever you receive a telephone directory or catalog . . . or new roster for an association . . . that you must keep, immediately toss out its predecessor.

Don't let everyone keep copies of the same paperwork. Assign one person only to keep past issues of newsletters, minutes, catalogs, etc.

Have your mail date-stamped as it is opened. Review your mail at a set time each day. Don't grab for it the moment it comes in. If you can't resist grabbing for each piece of incoming mail as it arrives, move the IN basket off your desk—preferably out of sight. If you read your junk mail, do it during low energy time, such as just before quitting time.

Keep a photocopy of all valuable . . . papers—such as a driver's license, car insurance, birth certificate, credit cards, and the contents of your wallet. It will be easier to report and replace lost or stolen papers. Keep the number of credit cards to a minimum. You will have less chance of losing them . . . and fewer bills to pay at the end of the month.

CHAPTER FIFTEEN

Giving Yourself the Electronic Edge

In the clock culture, human beings believed that material accumulation would pave the way toward an earthly cornucopia. In the computer culture, our children's generation is likely to regard information accumulation as the surefire route to everlasting salvation.

—Jeremy Rifkin

Today's conventional wisdom is quick to declare that if you want to save time and get organized, use high technology. Get a computer or a fax. Put a cellular phone in your car. Drag a mobile phone along with you all day so you never miss a call. High tech today means unsurpassed speed and maximum availability, which supposedly equals massive amounts of time saved. If you aren't on the electronic bandwagon, chances are, you know someone who is, and that person is urging you to stop being such a dinosaur and get yourself upgraded electronically.

Availing yourself of all the electronic wonders on the market today — from special telephones to laptop computers — can indeed free your time. But there are pluses and minuses to consider when looking at electronic wonders as time-savers, because these machines can also be great *users* of time. If you make efficient use of technology, you will be able to save time; an overindulgence or overdependence on machines, however, can wind up wasting far more of your time than those machines will ever save.

Regardless of the changes that occur almost daily in the world of electronics, some considerations need to be taken into account before you use machines to get organized. In addition to your budget, you might want to keep these pros and cons in mind as you turn to electronics to give you a time-saving and organizational edge that really will suit your lifestyle.

COMPUTERS

When used as a tool, the computer is an amazing organizational and timesaving machine for certain tasks. It is particularly good at word-processing, data storage, and accounting. Desktop publishing, too, has made self-publishing everything from flyers to reports laden with charts and graphics accessible to nearly all personal computer owners. These are some of the things that are definite time-savers that you can realize with a computer:

- Storage and organization of business information
- Address lists that are constantly updated
- The ability to send out mailings with computer-generated labels
- Editing and rewriting important or lengthy documents or reports with relative ease
- The ability to keep up-to-the-minute accounting and inventory records
- The ability to send messages over computer lines instantly (E-mail)
- The capacity to create and store large amounts of data in an organized way
- The ability to generate multiple copies of documents with only slightly different information (such as the address and salutation) on each document
- The capacity to access a vast amount of reference information

The possibilities of even more timesaving features are limited only by the computer and software market at any given time. The speed at which the technology is upgraded and changed is remarkable. Today, you may be able to perform twelve timesaving functions; tomorrow there may be a new computer or program that will help you perform twenty.

The Downside of Computers

Today, however, an honest look at computers brings up some definite questions regarding how much time computers *save* and how much time they *waste*. While the temptation may be to emphatically endorse computers as a major time-saver, there are several pitfalls that can mean that you *waste* time on a computer.

For example, it's all too easy to think that a computer will solve all of your paper problems in the wink of an eye. Buy a computer, the thinking goes, and all of the mountains of paper in your life will be magically transformed into electronic data. Wrong. First, the data has to be *entered* by a human being onto the computer (and this might mean you). The papers will not beam themselves mystically onto the computer, the computer operator spends wads of time entering or scanning the information; this time expended is directly related to the size and number of piles of papers being computerized.

A computer makes it possible for you to access far more information than you need. Information anxiety can be quelled with a flip of the finger, which in turn starts the computer and the printer spitting out reports on everything, from, say, the balance in your checkbook to how many widgets the plant sold in Siberia last Tuesday, to the names of all the dinosaurs that roamed the earth once upon a time. Along with all the extra information you can buy (such as encyclopedias on CD-ROM) you may get completely carried away, and add gobs of your own personal garbage. You spend days, weeks even, wasting time entering information you don't need to have computerized — from a recipe collection that you never use to an inventory of all the types of nails and screws in your workshop in the garage. This endless doodle is also known as GIGO — Garbage In, Garbage Out — and is an enormous waste of time.

If you have a computer you may also belong to an on-line service that lets you "talk" to strangers over the computer. It's easy to get caught up in this, and before you know it you're addicted — staying up until three in the morning to talk to, and fantasize about Donna, with whom you have a computer relationship.

Once you buy a computer, if the software doesn't already include one, you'll eventually come to believe that you must have games on the computer. Then you play the games when you should be doing something else. This can lead to an addictive reaction that has you back into the game during every little bit of spare time you can find. Soon you have no spare time; the games waste it all.

A computer can lead you into the temptation to overdo. Where a two-page proposal may have been fine in the past, you now feel that a twelve-page proposal complete with charts and graphics is in order. The truth is, the two-pager will probably still get you the job, but it's too late; you're well into creating ten more pages, and spending far more time than necessary on the project.

A computer can be a perfectionist's handmaiden in compulsive editing and rewriting. A letter that you might have sent out with only one minor rewrite now gets rewritten four times before it passes your reluctant muster. Each rewrite after the first one is a waste of time that could be spent with more important matters.

Adjustments can be endless with a computer. If you don't like the margins or tabs, it can take an unreasonable amount of time to get the computer to agree to, and accept the margins that you do want. (In the "old" days, you could have set the margins and tabs on a typewriter in about two seconds.) Or, you fiddle around with the fonts ad nauseam. You pick one for the title, one for the subtitles, one for the text, one for words requiring emphasis, and so on. Adjusting formats on a computer can eat up hours if you don't watch your step.

For some people, a computer is an invitation to futz around. The *Chicago Tribune* reported on a survey called the "PC Futz Factor" that was taken to see how people were really using the computer and the software. Sponsored by SBT Accounting Systems in Sausalito, California, the survey results included these eye-opening futz facts:

The average office worker spends 5.1 hours per week futzing with the computer. Assuming there are 25 million office computer users in America, that means 5 billion hours yearly, representing wages worth $100 billion, or 2 percent of the gross national product.

Of that time, 19 percent was spent waiting for the computer or a co-worker to do something, 16 percent was spent helping co-workers, 17 percent was on checking or formatting output, 12 percent was on learning new software, 14 percent was on erasing files, 5 percent was installing software and 17 percent was "other." According to the *Tribune*, "suspicions that the 'other' category represented time spent playing games could not be confirmed in follow-up interviews because the respondents were reluctant to discuss the issue."

You can kill days tinkering with software to make it do this and that, or to explore exactly how a particular function works, even though you know you won't need that function to do your job successfully. When the software doesn't meet your needs—an assessment usually arrived at only because you just heard about a new program that you just have to have—you buy new software. This means that you start all over again, taking up more time to learn the new software (tinkering as you go, of course). Most of the time, the old software was perfectly adequate; you just couldn't resist having the latest package of technological bells and whistles to hit the computer market.

When you can't figure out the software, you spend endless amounts of time tinkering with it to try to determine what's wrong. According to the SBT Accounting Systems survey, men tend to tinker more than women. Women, the survey found, prefer to get help rather than to keep going at the machine until they get it to work. I say that when it comes to making the best use of your time the score is Women 1, Tinkerers (Men) 0.

COMPUTER DOS AND DON'TS

On balance, it is probably not the best use of your time to embrace the computer world with so much unbridled enthusiasm that good sense gets lost in the shuffle. If you really want to make the best use of computers as a timesaving tool, follow these dos and don'ts.

Do:

- Use a computer to organize and store vital business information.
- Use a computer to organize, store and update address lists.
- Use a computer to generate labels for large mailings.
- Use a computer to edit and rewrite lengthy documents or reports.
- Use a computer to organize, store and update important accounting and inventory records.
- Use the computer for E-mail if it facilitates your business.
- Use the computer to create and store large amounts of data in an organized way.
- Use the computer to generate multiple copies of documents that need to be slightly customized (such as a different address on fifty copies of the same letter).
- Use the computer for desktop publishing if it is necessary to your business or if it contributes to your hobbies.
- Use the computer to access reference information.

Don't:

- Underestimate the amount of time it will take you to get all of your papers and files computerized.
- Give into information anxiety by calling up and printing more information than you really need.
- Waste time entering trivia onto the computer.
- Buy games for the computer unless that's how you want to spend your leisure time.
- Overdo by spending far more time than necessary formatting and fiddling with various fonts.
- Use the computer to compulsively edit and rewrite documents.
- Allow yourself to waste more time than necessary futzing and tinkering with the computer and the software.
- Automatically waste time (and money) buying and learning every new software package or computer component that comes down the pike unless you really need it.
- Get addicted to communicating by computer, particularly where your social life is concerned.

E-MAIL

Communicating through E-mail (electronic mail) via a computer network can be a terrific time-saver. The messages are transferred immediately, bypassing the postal system altogether. E-mail makes especially good sense for telecommuters—people who work out of their homes but need to stay in touch with colleagues at the main office. It is also a good tool for communicating with, say, branch managers (and it certainly replaces those slow-moving, oversized brown interoffice envelopes that carried information back and forth via the mail room). And E-mail doesn't take up the space or create the eyesore that piles of mail do.

Downside. Most people dive right in to E-mail, positive that it is a brilliant way to speed up communication and save time. But E-mail has a definite downside. Dazzled by the speed of E-mail, people hastily tap out comments, letters, even tomes, often without benefit of forethought. Mad at someone? Tell them off, right now, this minute, through E-mail. Don't bother to think it through as you develop a written response; E-mail will transmit your fury in all its glory. Regrets can come later. Volume is another problem. The techno-ease of sending E-mail prompts people to run off at the computer even more than they would have run off at the mouth normally. As volume increases, credibility and priority wanes, and the tendency to ignore E-mail for days at a time takes over. E-mail is hardly a prospect for historical documentation. Once consigned to the techno trash basket, E-mail is lost forever. Finally, there are the Bozo Filters. You may think your words are packing a real punch via E-mail, but anybody can be screened out with a Bozo Filter. Michael Schrage addressed the Bozo Filter problem in an article for *The Wall Street Journal*:

> Participants have the option of slapping on a Bozo Filter to block out the comments made by anyone they consider trite, boring, or a network nuisance. Whenever they log on to the on-line conversation, their Bozo Filter flashes to let them know when they're screening out the undesirables. . . . When the rumor circulates that—whisper, whisper—the boss now Bozo Filters the marketing vice president, the politics of that company will change. When managers choose to Bozo Filter their colleagues (but not, to be sure, their bosses), the role of the network for coordination and collaboration is radically transformed. Am I being Bozo Filtered? Or am I just being paranoid?

To balance the downside. Think before you speak via E-mail; don't dash off communication that isn't well thought out. More important, don't send E-mail unless it's absolutely necessary or is specifically beneficial to what you are doing. Encourage others to think the same way so that volume can be reduced and importance can be enhanced. And, when something especially profound or otherwise important is uttered over E-mail—either by yourself or by someone else—print it out and keep it for history's amusement or edification.

TAKING AN HONEST LOOK AT OTHER ELECTRONIC WONDERS

Besides the computer, there are a number of electronic wonders that can conceivably help you streamline your life. Those electronics really can give you an edge in the quest to find more time for yourself as long as you understand the benefits but aren't so blinded by them that you ignore the downside that could waste more time than you save. For the most effective use of electronics, balance the pros and cons by buying and using each item wisely. With that in mind, these are some of the high tech tools that can help you save time.

Fax

A fax machine can send a document from coast to coast in less than a minute per page. Send it by mail and it can take more than three days. Using an overnight mail service still takes about twelve to twenty-four hours. And, if you need to transfer information to an international location—such as Tokyo, for example—a fax makes it possible to do so in only the time it takes to make a phone call. If you need to bypass the time mail or courier service takes, or if you need input based on the documents and you need that input immediately, a fax is the way to go. Most medium to large businesses have them, and even small businesses are installing fax machines. People working at home can find them an indispensable tool in transferring documents to clients or the home office. There is no question this machine saves time.

Downside. People tend to view faxed documents as evidence that an immediate stop-the-press reply is required. This can be very disruptive to your schedule, particularly if you send or receive more than a few every day. The owner of a fax can also be subject to solicitations that are sent over the machine. These solicitations take up time (to read it) and money (to pay for the paper in the machine).

To balance the downside. Don't automatically assume that a document received via fax requires your immediate attention, and conversely, don't expect the recipient of your faxed paperwork to drop everything the minute he receives it. Don't waste time reading solicitations that you didn't request, and let the sender know that you do *not* want any more material sent over your fax line.

Electronic Organizers

These handheld wonders can be small enough to fit in a pocket or purse, and take up much less space than some of the traditional appointment/ address books require. Used mostly for storing phone numbers and keeping track of schedules, many have tremendous capacity for holding information.

Downside. If there was ever a contest to see who could access information faster — someone with an electronic organizer or someone with a traditional planner book — the person with the planner book would win every time. I once ate almost an entire bowl of soup while my companion awkwardly pecked out the letters necessary to get her organizer to call up the information. The compact size of these gadgets makes it difficult to type your entry, and turning a couple of pages in a book can be done in one-tenth the time.

To balance the downside. Be aware of the difficulty in accessing information when you purchase an electronic organizer. Look for new innovations to come onto the market that will make this function as simple as typing only one or two commands. Until that happens, you may want to carry the electronic organizer (especially on trips) to hold large quantities of information, such as addresses and phone numbers or complicated itinerary or client information. You can use the standard appointment/address planner book for immediate daily priorities. When you need extra information you can look to the electronic organizer. This means you don't have to carry a planner book that has hundreds of pages and reams of information that you need only occasionally.

Dictating Machines

If you have a secretary or assistant who types your correspondence, the most efficient way to dictate those letters is with dictating equipment. According to Alec Mackenzie, author of *The Time Trap*, the pace of handwriting equals twenty to thirty words per minute at best and the speed of the spoken word is 150 words per minute. Therefore, Mackenzie concludes, "one hour of dictating machine use is equal to at least five hours of the executive's time handwriting memos and letters or two hours of his (or her) time plus two of the secretary's giving and taking dictation." An additional statistic clinches the case; the U.S. Navy Management Office found that a secretary can transcribe from a machine 33 percent faster than from longhand or shorthand.

Downside. Many managers seem reluctant to master the use of the equipment, and even those who do make regular use of dictating equipment don't always do it correctly. It can be easier to ramble on endlessly with a machine, which means unnecessarily longer letters — and takes time all the way around. Also, unless the equipment is used properly, the typist will have to back up and reenter the information over and over. For example, the dictator needs to end a sentence by saying "period." Without that verbal note, the typist keeps typing until it becomes apparent that a new sentence has begun, at which point the typist has to back up and make corrections.

To balance the downside. Learn how to use the equipment effectively, and resist the temptation to blather. Outline what you plan to say, and then say it as briefly as possible, stating punctuation where it occurs. Ask your transcriber to provide feedback on where you can improve your dictating technique. Then use those suggestions when you dictate. Eventually you'll be able to dictate quickly, and the transcriber will be able to convert the material with significant speed, saving everyone a great deal of time.

Telephone Equipment

Phone equipment is constantly changing, and as it changes, it makes it possible to stay in touch from virtually anywhere at anytime by simply pushing a few buttons. If you want to talk to the boss while you're goofing off at the pool, get a *cordless phone*. If you're in sales, a *car phone* can make it possible for you to move from one appointment to another without ever stopping to find a phone booth. Or, you can phone instructions to your assistant while you are en route to the airport. A *cellular phone* can go wherever you go. You can put it in the glove compartment in your car to use in emergencies or to call ahead, or you can put it in your briefcase to carry when you travel. When there are long lines at all the telephones at the airport, you can use your cellular phone to conduct business on the road. If your phone has a *speaker phone* feature you can have a conversation while you are doing something else with your hands. *Conference call* features mean that you can talk to more than one person at a time, just as you would if you were "in conference." Those other people on the line can be located in other states, saving all the travel time required for person-to-person meetings.

Beepers mean you can be called anywhere, any time; the beeper will go off to notify you of a call whether you are at the ballet or in the bathroom. All you have to do is have the beeper with you wherever you go. *Answering machines, voice mail*, and other message systems make it possible for you to never miss a call, and also make it possible for you to not answer the phone, yet know who is calling. This can be critical when you need uninterrupted time to complete a project, but don't want to miss hearing that someone tried to reach you. (You can return the calls later.)

Automatic dial features on a telephone will allow you to store several numbers and then, rather than punching in the entire phone number, you need to hit only one designated button, and the number is automatically dialed. This saves the time required for dialing and looking up the number in the first place, and is great for numbers that you call frequently. An *automatic redial* feature means that if you call a number and the line is busy, you can push a button, and the phone will continue to redial the number until it rings through. In the meantime, you can be doing something else.

Telephone calling cards are similar to credit cards (and sometimes double as bank credit cards, in fact) and make it easy to place calls from any phone (including pay phones) anywhere. Simply slide the card into the slot in the pay phone, or dial a series of code numbers, and your call goes through; the bill is automatically applied to your own home or business telephone. *Airphones* are telephones on airplanes that enable you to make calls (with a credit or calling card) even while you are flying. This can mean that you can conduct business as usual even though you are, at the moment, flying over Kansas City. It can also make it possible to call and let your relatives know that the plane is three hours late so that they can avoid cooling their heels at the airport for three extra hours. *Call-forwarding* lets you key in some numbers, and have all your calls forwarded to the number where you'll be, and *call-waiting* gives you what amounts to a two-line phone on one line. When you are on the phone, and a second call comes in, a click is heard, and you can pick up the second call while you put the first party on hold. Here again, you can put yourself in the position of never missing a call, whether you are on the phone or at another location altogether.

Downside. The communications revolution is being fueled by consumer demand, and so it would appear that there is no downside to the constantly advancing technology of telephone equipment. After all, it wasn't that long ago that people shared a party line with one or two other families, and had to listen to the rings before they answered the phone. One long ring meant the call was for the Joneses. Two short rings meant it was for your household. And of course, you could listen in on the Joneses, and vice versa, although of course nice people didn't do such things. . . . So we've definitely come a long way. But it is possible to carry a good thing too far. We used to complain about incompetent switchboard operators who answered the phones, now intense frustration sets in as call after call reaches no humans whatsoever, and we are faced with automated voices that make you sit through a menu of choices: "If you want this, push one, if you want that, push two, if you want. . . ." It can be maddening. Car phones and other portable phones can also push the limit of current acceptability. While they can be great time-savers, it can be annoying to see a driver weaving in and out of traffic, obviously paying more attention to the conversation on her mobile phone than to traffic conditions. Portable phones can move from the timesaving realm to the ridiculous. The creative types in Hollywood often seem welded to their phones—even taking them along on a date so that they can get in a quick phone call as they walk from the movie theater to the restaurant down the block. Speaker phones are nice for the person who's using them because of the hands-free aspect (though there is only so much you can do with your hands before your attention starts to wander from the conversation and on to what those hands are doing). But most speaker phones today have an echo, so the other person knows you have put them on speaker, which means: a) someone else is in the room, listening in on, or participating in the conversation; or b) you aren't paying full attention, since you are doing something else with your hands. The party you are calling knows these things about being on the speaker phone, and they usually don't like it.

Many of the other telephone technologies are great for communication access: beepers (although these tend to be labeled as belonging either to doctors or drug dealers these days), call-waiting and -forwarding, airphones, and the like. But the question that all of this instant access telephone technology brings up focuses on the dilemma posed by having it all. How on earth can you ever get away from it all and have some time for yourself if the world of communications—via telephone technology—follows you everywhere you go?

To balance the downside. Don't become addicted to the status and possibilities of telephone technology. Make it a point to regularly turn your back on the telephone altogether, so that you really can have time for yourself, but don't get carried away with that concept. Voice mail should not be used to take over your communications tasks entirely. If you use voice mail, make it as simple as possible, with an easy exit immediately apparent. And if you are a business owner who is ready to install voice mail, take time to explore all of your options before you fire all the receptionists and replace them with the system. Sometimes the best solution is to have a real person answer the phone initially, and offer to transfer the caller to their party's voice mail if there is no answer on that extension. Nearly everyone uses the telephone; how you integrate the new equipment into your life—at home or at work— affects not only your time but how you communicate with others.

As you read this, there are doubtless many more electronic wonders on the market that are not mentioned here. And you may be tempted to run out and avail yourself of the latest in technology, telling yourself that it will help you save time. And it might. But the key to making electronic technology save time for you is to be selective about how much time you devote to that technology. And don't use any time saved to then immerse yourself compulsively in even more technology that you don't really have to integrate into your life. Use that time for yourself instead.

PART FOUR

Finding Time
in Bits and Pieces

We cannot do everything at once, but we can do something at once.
— Calvin Coolidge

If you have started to put the principles of this book to work for you, and find yourself still looking for some immediate time savers that you can apply to everything from travel to telephone to housework, incorporate the final timesaving step into your life: Step 7: "Look for Ways to Save Time in Bits and Pieces." If you think that making small changes every day to save a few minutes here and there doesn't matter, consider this:

Saving	Adds Up To
Thirty minutes a day	More than seven days each year
One hour a day	More than fifteen days each year
Ninety minutes a day	More than twenty-two days each year
Two hours a day	More than thirty days each year

If saving anywhere from seven to thirty days' worth of time each year sounds like something you'd like to do, the dozens of quick time-savers in Part Four will help you do just that. As you read through the tips and begin to apply them to your life, keep one very important thought in mind. Saving time in bits and pieces is important because all time saved equals time you can spend for yourself! So be on the lookout for ways to save time in bits and pieces and you'll discover that with a little thought and creativity, you can find more time for yourself than you ever dreamed possible.

LOOK FOR WAYS

TO SAVE TIME

IN BITS AND PIECES

TIME SAVED IN SMALL INCREMENTS ADDS UP TO
MORE TIME FOR YOURSELF. TAKE A LOOK AT HOW
YOU DO THINGS EVERY DAY AND STREAMLINE HOW
YOU GET THINGS DONE BY SAVING TIME IN BITS AND
PIECES. THEN SPEND THAT TIME ON YOURSELF.

14 Telephone Time-Savers

The telephone is a good way to talk to people
without having to buy them a drink.

—Fran Lebowitz

If not handled properly, the constant interruption of a ringing telephone can be a definite time waster. (To combat the interruptive nature of the telephone, refer to chapter ten.) The telephone is one of those modern conveniences that gives you the opportunity to save more time than you waste on it. Using the telephone to find more time for yourself begins with thinking about how you are using it, and then using the equipment and the time you spend well. These strategies can help you turn the telephone into a tool for saving time.

Speed dial. If there are certain phone numbers that you call all of the time, you may want a phone with speed-dialing features. All you have to do is push one button and your call goes through.

Call rather than write. If you find yourself getting behind in your personal correspondence, use the telephone. You'll be able to say more in less time than it would have taken to put it all in a letter.

Do two things at once. If you spend a significant amount of time visiting friends on the phone, use that time to get other things done while you talk. A portable phone, long cord or speaker phone all make it easy to do two things at once, but even without those things, you can still talk on the phone and probably do some or all of these things at the same time:

- straighten out a junk or pencil drawer
- clean out your wallet, purse or briefcase
- fold some laundry
- do your nails
- prepare food
- do the dishes
- paint
- sunbathe
- do some mending

- crochet or knit
- iron

Use the phone to locate what you need. Before you go out looking for a particular tool you have to buy, for instance, call around and see who has it for the best price. Then make one trip to one store rather than three trips to three stores.

Shop by phone. Order from catalogs or telephone order services rather than taking the time to buy things in person. These are but some of the things that can be ordered by phone:

- stamps from the post office
- concert and theater tickets
- gift certificates to department stores
- food and specialty coffees
- clothes, shoes and jewelry
- gardening equipment
- flowers and other gifts
- gift certificates to restaurants
- airline tickets
- books
- housewares and linens

Keep a reminder list. If you make long-distance phone calls to friends or relatives and tend to forget things you meant to tell them, keep a brief list of things you want to talk about as you think of them. Then when you call (or when they call you) you won't forget anything and can cover everything in one phone call.

Organize the information. Likewise, if you're going to discuss business on the phone, make sure you have all the necessary information close at hand when you make the call so that you don't have to stop to find that information after your party is on the line. If you have everything you need at hand, you might also get your business taken care of in one phone call instead of two or three.

Conduct meetings by conference call. You'll save travel time for all of the parties involved, as well as money and paperwork that invariably goes with traveling to meetings.

Call people during lunch hour. Chances are they won't be in, and you can usually just leave a message, hopefully with all the information you wanted to convey. This eliminates a lengthy conversation punctuated by social niceties that would have otherwise ensued had your party been there.

Leave a complete message. When you leave a message, make sure you tell the person taking the message exactly what your call is about. That way, when your party returns the call, they can have the information you need ready to give to you.

Avoid telephone tag. Leave a message that includes the best time for your party to return the call. Give broad guidelines rather than overly specific times. Saying "early morning or late in the day" is much more reasonable than instructing someone to return your call between 8:15 and 9:00 A.M. or between 4:30 and 5:00 P.M. Similarly, ask others when the best time to reach them might be.

Group your return calls. Rather than stopping several times during the day to make one or two calls, make a half-dozen callbacks during an hour in the morning, and another half-dozen during an hour later in the day. You'll give yourself much needed time to concentrate fully on other projects.

Return phone calls toward the end of the day. People are more likely to keep the conversation short when they are looking forward to going home.

Limit your callbacks to two calls. Don't waste too much time attempting to return someone else's call. If you return the call twice and can't reach them, leave a message, and forget about it. If they want to talk to you, they'll call again.

11 TV Time-Savers

The average American watches ten years of TV in a lifetime,
including two years of commercials.

— TV Guide

Television may be eating up too much of your time. While you're zonked out in front of the tube, life is passing you by. Television has a great deal of merit; it is entertaining and, at times, educational. But it should not serve as the constant backdrop or primary focus of most of your spare time. While you may think that watching TV represents time for yourself, it's more likely it's just a habit that keeps you from doing other more important or fulfilling things. So, if you don't want to devote ten years of your life to the TV, try some of these tactics to help you become more selective about how you spend your TV time.

Don't let TV be a priority in your life. Make plans to do things, have undisturbed family time and meals, and go places first. Watch TV only after all of those activities are finished. Unless there is something truly special on (such as *The Wizard of Oz*, which the children have never seen), plan other activities in your life before you even consult the TV schedule.

Don't automatically turn the TV on the minute you get home. If you do, you'll eventually find yourself addicted to it — even if only to the background noise.

If you're not watching the TV, turn it off. The background drone can be just enough to dull your senses, and keep you from doing something that might be more important and productive.

Decide in advance what you are going to watch. Channel surfing (constantly clicking the remote through the channels to see what's on) usually means you never turn the TV off, and often watch bits and pieces of programs without ever seeing one all the way through. This is, at best, a mindless way to use your time, particularly when other priorities await.

Watch only programs that are really good or that you always enjoy. Turn the TV off the rest of the time. If you think a program will be good, but after the first fifteen minutes you find yourself uninterested in the show, turn the TV off immediately.

Don't get addicted to soap operas. If you must watch them, select only one or two, then only watch them two or three times a week at the most. The plots move so slowly that you won't miss anything at all by skipping a couple of days each week.

Record programs you want to see on a VCR, then watch them later. When you do watch the show, fast-forward through the commercials. In a one-hour program, this can save nearly twenty minutes' time. During football games, you can save even more time by fast-forwarding through the commercials, time-outs and half-time activities. Viewed this way, a game could easily be seen in an hour or less rather than taking up the entire afternoon.

Use TV viewing time to do something else. Just as you can do something else while talking on the phone (such as clean out your wallet or briefcase, fold laundry, do your nails, knit, crochet or iron, etc.), you can also do something else while watching TV. These are some of the additional things you can do while you watch TV.

- Write thank-you notes or address holiday cards
- Organize photos into an album
- Sort and organize coupons by category
- Sort and organize tax receipts by category
- Exercise
- Thumb through catalogs

Use time during the commercials to get things done. These are some of the things you can accomplish during a commercial.

- Water the plants
- Load or unload the dishwasher
- Vacuum or dust one room
- Get the laundry out of the dryer and put another load in
- Read a short article
- Write a card or note to someone
- Take out the trash
- Clean the cat box
- Make a quick phone call

Listen to the TV and do something else. There are a lot of programs you can keep up with without giving the TV screen your undivided attention. Talk shows, some game shows, and slow-moving soap operas, for example, can all be followed simply by hearing the set from another room. Make the bed, cook dinner, dust the furniture, and do other chores with the TV within earshot, and you will probably miss very little.

Pick certain times when the TV won't be turned on, no matter what. For example, the TV never gets turned on during meals, or on Sunday before one o'clock in the afternoon. And Saturday night is family night, so the TV stays off then as well. You'll find that these times spent without the TV will give you an opportunity to tackle things you've been putting off, or to give more attention to your real priorities in life.

10 Commuting Time-Savers

If you commute an hour a day to work and an hour back, you are spending 500 hours a year in the car. That is the equivalent of 62.5 work days or 12.5 work weeks.

—*The Wilson Quarterly*

Time spent commuting is often accepted without question. We adjust to it numbly, as if it is a nasty, time-wasting fact of life that can't be changed or controlled. Sometimes that's true. The commute—for whatever reason—will always be nothing more than a daily endurance test. But often changes can be made to either shorten the time spent commuting or make better use of that time. Here are some ideas you can use to make better use of that commute time.

Get up earlier. Get up thirty minutes to an hour earlier so that you can get on the road before most of the rest of the world does. You'll save time by getting to work sooner because the traffic will be lighter. Once at work, you'll get a bonus of some quiet time to work before phones start ringing and other interruptions arise.

Listen to tapes in the car. According to an article in *Family Circle* magazine, the average American spends twenty-seven hours a year at red lights. Whether you're doing this on the way to work or to the mall, the time needn't be wasted or spent looking at your latest facial wrinkle or gray hairs in the rearview mirror. Instead, use the time to listen to education tapes or a book on tape. The tapes can helpful (you can even learn a new language this way), and while they don't save time, driving is the perfect time to listen to them since you'd probably be hard-pressed to find any other spare time to hear the tapes.

Take a memo for yourself. If you tend to generate ideas while you drive, keep a small tape recorder in the car, so you can verbally make note of them while you drive. You can also give yourself verbal reminders with the recorder. When you get to your destination, simply play the tape and act on it accordingly.

Use a cellular phone. If you have a particularly long commute, or your job requires you to be on the road a great deal, you may want to get a cellular phone. They are expensive to operate, but great time-savers; you can call ahead to your next appointment, and check with the office for messages without driving around trying to locate a public phone. And they can be invaluable in the event of an accident or a break down.

Carpool. You'll still spend time on the road, but you can rotate drivers. When you aren't driving, you can use the commuting time for other things. For example, while you are riding in a carpool (or for that matter, bus or train) you can do the following:

- Read a book, magazine, trade journal, business report or newspaper
- Use dictating equipment to dictate letters, instructions or other ideas
- Revise and organize your to-do list
- Go through some catalogs; mark pages of possible purchases and toss the rest
- Balance your checkbook
- Draft outlines and ideas for new proposals and projects
- Play cards or socialize with another commuter
- Go over business ideas and plans with a co-worker who commutes with you
- Practice your stand-up comedy routine (you've got a captive audience)

Know all the alternative routes. Become well versed in all the possible alternative routes that you can take. Then when there's a massive traffic tie-up, you can take that route, saving time. Also, make sure that your normal route is the best route in terms of not only time saved, but traffic encountered.

Combine commuting with exercising. If you don't have to commute too far, consider walking or riding a bike instead of driving or taking public transportation. Or, you can get off of the bus a few stops earlier and walk the rest of the way. You will have fit daily exercise into your schedule without any apparent effort, and you'll feel better and won't have to try to constantly rearrange your schedule to fit in some kind of organized exercise.

Move closer to your workplace. The amount of commuting time you save will be proportionate to the proximity of your workplace.

See if you can work on a job sharing or flextime basis. If you can get your employer to agree to job sharing, you would either work fewer hours each day and encounter better traffic patterns or work fewer days each week and eliminate commuting time on days off. If you can't afford the pay cut that job sharing involves, see if you can arrange flextime, where perhaps you work four 10-hour days instead of five 8-hour days. You'd leave earlier and come home later, and hopefully, miss the traditional rush hour altogether.

And one day during the work week, you wouldn't have to commute at all. Another flextime arrangement would alternate weekly arrangements so perhaps one week you would work traditional hours that would mean you would spend commuting time in rush hour traffic; the next week you would work a different set of hours which would put you in light traffic and get you back and forth quicker. This type of flextime is rotated spreading the commuting rush hour burden around evenly.

Don't commute, telecommute. Telecommuting may well be the wave of the future. Instead of commuting into an office, see if you can work from home, hooked up to your office or clients by computer and fax. For really long-distance commuting on a regular basis, the video phone (a telephone with a small video monitor that allows you to see who you are speaking to) is gaining popularity. Telecommuting means the complete elimination of the time and aggravation that goes into traditional modes of traveling to and from the office. Employers benefit from telecommuting as well. There's less outlay for expensive office space and furniture, and according to a report in *Your Company* magazine, a 1992 study by Link Resources found that productivity increased by 15 percent when employees worked at home.

41 Travel Time-Savers

From the moment you step out of your door to the moment you arrive at your destination, it's a constant battle. You've got to be on full alert every inch of the way — as though each encounter bears the printed label:
Warning: The Surgeon General has determined that this experience may be hazardous to your mental health.

— George Albert Brown

I deally, the technicalities of travel — making the arrangements and getting there and back — should be uncomplicated both for the frequent business traveler as well as for the vacation traveler. But the truth is that the glitches all too often outweigh the glitter of travel, and the experience gradually leaves more and more to be desired. Yet, if you want or need to travel, it is possible to spend less time with the fuss and aggravation that invariably accompanies traveling, and more time on the reason for the trip, whether business or pleasure. These tips can help you save time and streamline trips.

Plan ahead. You'll save time (and money) by scheduling trips in advance, so plan ahead whenever possible. By avoiding peak travel times, you will increase your chances of being able to travel without being hit with unexpected delays that can play havoc with your schedule.

When you book your flight, for instance, it's helpful to keep certain things in mind. Try not to depart or arrive during rush hour when your chances of being late due to traffic increase. If you travel early in the day, and there is a problem with the flight, you'll have a better chance of booking another flight than if you started late in the day. And make sure you know the difference between "nonstop" and "direct" flights. A nonstop is a flight that makes no stops, and is always the best option if you want to streamline and save travel time. A direct flight, on the other hand, does stop over in an intermediary city, but you don't have to change planes. You can cool your heels during the layover on the plane or in the terminal, but make no mistake, this is not a nonstop flight.

If your trip is by car, one of the best things you can do is to join an auto club so that you get detailed maps for the areas you are traveling to. A good auto club can also provide you with books loaded with hotel and motel information to plan your stopovers. And, perhaps most important, an auto club can provide you with emergency road service—a must for the car traveler, both for frequent short trips and for that occasional long vacation trip.

Don't go unless it's necessary. Don't travel for business reasons unless it really is absolutely necessary. You'll save lots of time, money and energy if the business objective can be accomplished through conference calls or meetings at a more centralized location. If that's not possible, consider sending someone else in your place so that you can continue to maximize the use of your time by being productive in the office.

Let them come to you. Ask the other party to travel to you, instead of you going to them; they can put in the travel time rather than you.

Consider postponing the trip. If the trip is for business reasons, and you really don't have the time to go, see if it can be postponed. You may eventually discover that the trip isn't necessary after all, and you won't have to reschedule the postponed plans.

Always use a travel agent. A travel agent can save you enormous amounts of time, so it pays to shop around until you find one that gives you good service. Let the agent know all of your preferences for airlines, hotels and car rental companies, as well as your frequent flyer numbers and seat preference. That agent can then take care of everything for you—from booking the flight and securing a boarding pass to getting a reservation for a hotel and rental car. You'll get a detailed itinerary along with the tickets and boarding pass in the mail, so you won't have to wait in line at the ticket counter at the airport. All you have to do is make the one phone call to the agent. You may even find that the best agent is located in another state. Many agents are available through an 800-number, so don't let the location of the agency's office be the criteria in selecting who will serve your travel needs. (I live in Wisconsin now, but I have a super travel agent in Mississippi.)

Get your seat assignment in advance. Ask your travel agent or the airline agent for your seat when you buy the ticket. Also ask to receive a boarding pass with your ticket so you can proceed directly to the boarding area without waiting in any lines at the airport. If you request an aisle seat it will be easier for you to deplane at the end of the trip. Window seats often mean that you get stuck under the luggage compartment, hunched over, waiting for someone with enough manners to let you out from under the rack and into the line of people moving toward the exit doors. Along with your aisle request, try to get a seat as far forward as possible. Since so many people carry far more than they should onto the plane, it can take forever on a large plane to get everyone organized and off the plane. Being up front means you don't have to wait so long to get off, but front seats do have one drawback. There is a rumor that in the event of a plane crash, you are more likely to survive if you are in the back of the plane. I don't know that there is any validity to this, but if you think it's true, you may want to sit in the back, even though it is more time-consuming. If you sit in the back, don't bother getting up as soon as the plane lands. It will be quite some time before everyone gathers their things, and even more time before the herd of people actually starts to move toward the exit doors. Use those extra minutes to continue reading, comb your hair, freshen your lipstick, or just collect your thoughts.

Build some flexibility into your travel plans. Sooner or later, the chances are you will run into some delays when you travel, so try to allow some time for unexpected glitches. Try not to book connecting flights too closely, and try to avoid traveling to and from airports during the rush hour. Get to the airport early enough to check your bags (if necessary), go through security (you may run into a line there, so allow time for that possibility), and board the plane without running, like a track star, to the plane at the last minute.

Always keep your tickets in the same place. Select a drawer or spot on your desk, and keep each ticket in an envelope there. Mark each envelope with the city (destination) and the date of travel. When you are ready to go, you won't have to spend time frantically looking for the tickets. When the trip is over, put the ticket back in the envelope and keep it in another drawer or box in chronological order to back up your tax expense records.

Take advantage of frequent flyer programs. If you travel a great deal, join frequent flyer clubs and take advantage of their benefits. Make sure your travel agent has all of the numbers so he can automatically enter them every time a ticket is purchased. Benefits include free tickets and hotel and airline upgrades after a specific number of miles have been accumulated in your account. Once you reach a certain level, you can also board the flight early with the first-class passengers and the passengers traveling with children. Boarding early is strongly advised, primarily because far too many passengers carry on far too much luggage. If you get on the plane at the last minute, you may not even have room for your coat and briefcase since the overhead bins tend to get packed to the gills before everyone has boarded.

Consolidate frequent flyer information. If you have a lot of frequent flyer cards for airlines (and hotels), write the numbers down on an index card and carry it in your wallet instead of all the laminated airline and hotel cards. It saves space in your wallet, and you won't have to waste time shuffling through a dozen cards to find the number you need when you are checking in or confirming that the hotel or airline has your number credited. You can also set up a simple frequent flyer log to keep track of trips. Simply enter the date of your trip along with the flight numbers, airlines and destinations. When your frequent flyer mileage statement arrives you can check it against the log. If there is a discrepancy, contact the appropriate hotel or airline and provide copies of your ticket or bill, and you account will usually be credited appropriately.

Assemble things in advance. When you know you are going to take a trip, set up a tote bag or briefcase in advance so that you can toss things in it the week or so before departure. This can include papers and files that you don't want to forget as well as things like cassettes and reading material or special items that you want to remember to take along.

Prepack. If you travel frequently, keep a travel kit packed with toiletries ready to go. When you pack, you'll only have to grab the kit rather than rummage around in the bathroom trying to pull everything together at the last minute. Keep a spare toothbrush, razor, and hair comb or brush in the kit. Women might also want to keep a bag of cosmetics packed. It's also a good idea to keep packed one or two pieces of inexpensive jewelry that can be worn with anything. Keep a simple gold and silver necklace and earring set always ready to go, and you won't have to dig through your jewelry box at the last minute to figure which pieces to take. Just grab the bag and go.

Keep a checklist of things that you need to pack. This can include the toiletry kit, hair dryer, vitamins or medicines, workout clothes, bathing suit, rain gear, and the like. When you pack, check the list to make sure you haven't forgotten something so that when you get to your destination, you won't have to purchase or send for what you forgot to pack.

Always travel light. The more you pack, the more time it takes to pack and unpack. Don't forget that each destination means *four* times packing or unpacking. You pack to go, you unpack when you get there, you repack to leave, and you unpack again when you get home. Plus, the more you pack, the more laundry or pressing you are likely to have to deal with when you get home. Figure out what you need to take, and then take half of that. (If you tend to stay at the more expensive hotels, you may want to call ahead to see what amenities they provide in the bathroom. Sometimes they have literally everything you need—including a robe—which means you won't have to pack toiletries or a robe at all.)

Streamline your luggage. Don't underestimate the value of bags on wheels or a luggage cart. Even the smallest of bags can seem to weigh a ton (and slow you down) after you have hauled it for what seems like miles from your car to the plane. Also, you may want to pack a collapsible nylon travel bag to use in the event you pick up things on your trip—from gifts to clothes to convention materials—that you need to bring back.

Tag your bags. Proper tagging can mean the difference between spending days trying to locate lost luggage and having your luggage delivered to you within a few hours or a day after it is reported missing. Make sure your luggage is tagged with your name, address and phone number, and that a tag of some kind is also placed inside the bag, in case the outer tag gets torn off. You can also tie a bright piece of ribbon or yarn on your suitcase handle so that you can easily identify your luggage from all of the other suitcases on the baggage pick-up carousel.

Always use a travel itinerary. Keep the itinerary in the same place in your briefcase or purse at all times so that you don't waste time looking for it several times each day. Give a copy to your family or office so that they know where to reach you if needed. Carry important phone numbers with you as well, so that you don't have to stop and call your house or office to find someone who can give you the information you need at the last minute.

Get others to take care of things for you during your absence. Let your assistant handle as much as possible while you are gone. It can also be helpful to try to anticipate what might come up in your absence — both at home and at the office — so you can inform others of the possibility and suggest how things should be handled. This planning can significantly reduce the number of interruptions you receive while traveling. If you're away for a long vacation, but someone is at your house, ask them to at least sort the mail for you. When you return, the bills will be in one stack, the catalogs in another, and the magazines in yet another stack. (After all, anyone can tell the difference between these three items.) Junk circulars should be tossed, and newspapers temporarily halted. This leaves only some miscellaneous mail (such as personal correspondence) in another stack. When you return, look at the bills and correspondence, and leave the other two stacks for later. Do the same thing at work; let your assistant handle as much as possible, and sort the rest. You won't be faced with a truckload of mail to sort when you return, and you can tackle the most important things first without wading through all the junk mail and reading material.

Give yourself extra time the day before. Try to give yourself at least a few hours of extra time the day before your departure to gather your thoughts and pack for the trip. You'll get off to a smoother start when you leave, and are less likely to forget something important. The frenzy of getting everything ready and racing out the door at the last minute can be eliminated simply by setting aside this small bit of open time.

Call ahead. These days, it's always a good idea to call the airport before you leave your home or office to see if the flight is due to depart on time. If the weather is bad either at your airport or at the city you are traveling to (check the weather report), you can make sure that your plane is leaving on time. If it is running several hours late (or maybe even cancelled) you can spare yourself the aggravation and time wasted in racing to the airport only to wait there for hours or ultimately returning to your home or hotel. If there is a major delay that is not weather related, you might want to transfer your ticket to another flight. In many cases other airlines will honor your ticket at no extra charge if they have the room on their flight.

Leave early. Don't delude yourself into thinking that you are such a consummate jet-setter that you don't have to get to the airport early. Unless you are traveling at the highest priced, first-class ticket price, the later you arrive, the greater your chances are of getting bumped off a full flight. Give yourself ample time to fight traffic to the airport, stand in line to go through security, and check in at the gate *before* the flight boards.

Take the airport shuttle. Rather than driving to the airport, consider using a taxi or shuttle service to get there. You'll avoid the time it takes to circle the parking structure looking for a spot and the time it takes to get from a remote parking location to the terminal will be eliminated.

Have your car serviced while you are away. Put your car in to be serviced, and when you return, it will be ready for you. This way, you won't be inconvenienced by a car in the repair shop when you are home and need it most.

Check your bags at the curb. Always check your bags with the skycap at curbside. The dollar or so per bag that you pay in tips will more than make up for the time you will save waiting in line to check those bags. If you drive your car to the airport, drive up and check your bags first, then park the car (this way you won't have to haul luggage from the parking structure). With your ticket and boarding pass in hand, you can proceed directly to the gate, bypassing long lines at the ticket counter. You'll save even more time if you don't check your bags at all. If you can, travel with only a carry-on bag. But don't overdo it; carrying a huge overstuffed garment bag along with large shopping bags and a briefcase (for example) only contributes to the congestion in the passenger cabin.

Note your location. When you park your car at the airport, don't forget to write down the area and row number; when you return from your trip you may be too tired or dazed to remember where you parked. There's nothing quite so frustrating as wandering around an airport lot (especially in freezing weather) trying to remember where you parked the car.

Use the phone to solve problems quickly. If your flight is cancelled or delayed for several hours, don't stand in line with a planeload of passengers to try to make alternative arrangements. Instead, go directly to the telephone and call the reservations number for the airline. Most of the time, you can get right through and make the best arrangements in just a few minutes.

Make good use of your travel time. One of the best things about long trips is that you have uninterrupted time. Use this waiting and travel time to catch up on reading or to handle paperwork. Carry some basic supplies, such as paper and envelopes, and draft articles, dictate reports or make lists of things to do. You can also use the time to think through creative ideas and proposals and to rehearse mentally a presentation that you need to make. If you have a laptop computer you may be able to work on that to complete projects that need your attention or to communicate via E-mail with the office. You may want to crochet or knit, or work on some other portable craft. It's a perfect time to do some brainstorming or some catching up.

Handle phone calls on the road. Airport time can be good for catching up on business telephone calls. Although it can be costly to return calls from a long-distance location, it is usually well worth the few extra dollars to keep on top of obligations during this waiting time rather than letting calls to return pile up until you get back to the office. Either carry a cellular phone with you for this purpose, or use a calling card at the public phones in the airport. (If you use a calling card, make sure no one sees you enter your personal code number. Today's telephone fraud includes using those numbers to make international calls. If someone sees your complete number as you punch it in, they could run your bill up wildly.)

Another good time to call is early in the morning from the hotel while you are waiting for room service. This is particularly valuable where there is a significant time difference. If you are in California, for example, and want to call your office in New York, you can check in at 6:30 A.M. which is 9:30 A.M. in New York. You might want to establish certain calling times as well. If your office knows you will call every day at a certain time, they can make sure they have all their questions ready for you then. A standard time for calling home can also be helpful for your family in case they need to go over anything with you.

Use VIP services at car rental agencies. These special services allow you to proceed directly to a van that takes you to your rental car—with the keys and the contract inside. All you have to do is get in and drive. You don't have to fill out paperwork and get keys because you provide information in advance. When you return the car, just fill out the mileage and gas levels on the contract, and either leave it in the drop-off box, or hand it to one of the check-in personnel in the return lot. She will quickly give you a receipt from a handheld computer. Not all VIP services are equal, and some car rental firms don't even offer the service. Needless to say, it costs a bit more (but not much more) to use this service, but particularly if you are a frequent business traveler, this service is a timesaving must.

Eliminate down-time. If you have checked your luggage, while you are waiting for it to come down the carousel, you can pick up your car rental papers (at airports with on-site rental desks), or make a quick call to the office. This is also a perfect time to freshen up if you want to make a good impression at your final destination. Remember, it can sometimes take twenty minutes for your bags to come down to the terminal from the plane.

If you are traveling with a lot of materials (say, for a convention) let skycaps and hotel bell staff load and unload these from the cab and transfer the items to your room. It's worth a few dollars in tips to have this taken care of while you pay the cab driver and check in.

Allow extra time to commute to your destination. It may take longer than you think to travel between appointments in an unfamiliar city.

Stay at a hotel that caters to your needs. If you travel a great deal on business, or if you need to keep in touch with the office even when you are on vacation, try to stay at a hotel that offers a range of business services and equipment, such as a fax, access to a copier, and overnight mail pick-up services. These things facilitate business and communication on the road and can significantly reduce the catch-up work you would have to tend to upon your return.

Stay on a lower floor in a full hotel. If you stay at a large hotel that you know will be filled to capacity (as often happens at conventions), you may want to stay on the first few floors. That way, when all the elevators are tied up and you're faced with long waits, you can quickly take the stairs. (For safety reasons, however, it is not a good idea to stay on the ground floor, particularly if there is parking area just outside the room. A ground-floor room with a window or sliding glass door near the parking lot or other dark areas is an easy target for an intruder.)

Use concierge services at the hotel. Ask them for recommendations, and then let the concierge make reservations for you for things like dinner, the theater, and other outings. This saves you time that would have otherwise been spent calling around to research things and make reservations.

Use room service. It costs more than going out, but you can catch up on paperwork or phone calls right up until the food arrives. Try to stay at a hotel that also provides morning room service that you can order the night before. That way, you don't run the risk of late room service in the morning. Simply hang a tag (the hotel provides this menu tag) on the door with your menu selections along with the time you want the food delivered. The next morning, the food arrives within fifteen minutes of your designated time, and you don't to worry about getting through to room service or waiting an hour for the food to come up.

Use overnight mail. If you conduct business while on the road, carry a few preprinted address labels for Express or courier mail services so you can send things back to the office for action in your absence. Ask the office to send materials that only you can handle to the hotel via overnight mail. This helps reduce that overwhelming pile of work that you would otherwise face when you get back to the office.

Mail it to yourself. You may want to carry some self-addressed, stamped envelopes with you if you will be at meetings where you will be picking up or requesting more information. Simply put the papers in the envelope and mail them to yourself. Or give the envelope to the person you are making the request to, and ask them to forward the material to you. This eliminates the inconvenience of lugging around a ton of papers during your trip.

Pass it on. If you're going to be away for more than a few days, have circulated material, such as magazines and journals, moved on to the next person. Ask someone to cross off your name and rewrite it on the bottom of the routing slip. Then your absence won't create a backlog for others.

Organize the papers in your briefcase. Keep file folders marked to-do, to-pay, to-file, and to-read in your briefcase. As you collect papers and notes during your trip, put them immediately into the appropriate file. When you have waiting time, you can handle some of the work quickly, and when you get back to the office, the remaining papers will be organized so that you won't have to waste time sorting through an untidy pile of papers from the trip, taking the time to remind yourself of the action that needs to be taken. Instead you can tackle each category (or pass it on to the appropriate person for action) immediately.

Keep track of your receipts as you travel. Put the receipts you accumulate in an envelope as you travel (and put the envelope in your pocket or purse). At the end of the trip, simply add up the receipts by category (meals, taxis, etc.), and write the figures and total on the front of the envelope. You'll have a complete record for tax or reimbursement purposes, and you won't have to waste time hunting around for all the papers that get scattered in your pockets, purse, suitcase or briefcase. If you submit a form along with the receipts for reimbursement, the form will be much easier to complete with the envelope recap to guide you. Therefore, there should be no excuse of procrastinating; complete and submit the documentation as soon as you return. Failing to do so only means that you risk losing the envelope, you may forget some of the details (such as who went with you to lunch on that particular Monday), and you'll annoy the accounting people, who in turn, will hold up your check.

Go home a day early if possible. Use this day to catch up on your rest along with anything else that needs your attention before plunging back into your normal daily routine. Whether you use the day to catch up on the laundry at home or the mail at the office, this extra day of transition will make the trip seem more pleasant and productive, and you'll feel less harassed than if you had returned immediately to the fray. Don't tell anyone you are back or schedule appointments for this day. When people want to know when you'll be back, give them the date of your *second* day back.

21 Housework and Kitchen Time-Savers

The main difference between a sand hog and a housewife is that he has a nice, clean tunnel later to show for his efforts, and it stays put, while she has to do it over again the next day. She must simply keep tunneling.

—Peg Bracken

How much time you spend on housework depends on your circumstances. If you live alone, chances are you don't devote nearly as much time to it as someone who has two children. If your budget can accommodate it, maybe you're one of the lucky people who has a housekeeper or a cleaning service. If you're like most people, at least some of your time — and probably far more of your time than you'd like — is devoted to housework. Usually people do housework in their "free" time, which of course means that time isn't free anymore. Unfortunately there is no magic wand that can be waved to make housework disappear; it's one of life's never-ending, but necessary tasks. But it needn't take up most of your free time. To keep housework from becoming a full-time job, try these timesaving tips.

Reduce your expectations. Stop demanding that the place be perfectly clean and spotless. If it ever gets that way, it won't stay that way, and why run like a rat on a treadmill if you don't have to? Train yourself to ignore a little dust. Cut back on your efforts here and there, and start adjusting yourself to a little less spit and polish so long as the basics are taken care of and the place is picked up and organized. You don't want to ignore the housework altogether, but a little bit of "who cares" attitude goes a long way when it comes to housework.

Schedule the housework. Make time to do the basics by putting housework on your schedule. Otherwise you might let it all go just a little too long and wake up one day to the Health Department banging on your front door. If you don't want to spend all day Saturday doing housework, contribute thirty minutes in the morning, and another thirty minutes in the evening each day, or at least a couple of days during the week. Then when Saturday rolls around you've already put in several hours keeping up with the cleaning, and you can take most of the day off. Here's some of the cleaning you can do in thirty minutes:

- Dust the furniture
- Clean the bathroom
- Vacuum
- Clean the kitchen floor
- Iron three shirts
- Clean counters, cabinet fronts, and wipe out the refrigerator
- Change three beds
- Do a load of wash (add thirty more minutes to dry)
- Clean windowsills and sweep porches

Get rid of knickknacks. You won't have to spend so much time dusting if you do.

Keep the laundry up. Don't let the laundry back up on you or not only will you not have enough clothes to wear, you'll find yourself spending practically the entire weekend catching up. If you have a large family, do a load a day and get family members to help get the clothes to the laundry area, sort them and fold them. If you live in an apartment and have to go out to do the wash, schedule going to the Laundromat at least once a week. But instead of going on the busiest day (Saturday), go during off hours. There will be more machines available and you'll get through much quicker. Early mornings are the best time at Laundromats (Sunday morning, for example) to get in and out quickly.

Send clothes out to a professional service. If you can afford it, send at least some of the laundry out to a professional laundry service. Sheets and shirts in particular will come back looking fabulous, and you'll save wads of time by not having to wash and iron those items.

Clean as you go. If you clean as you go—particularly in the kitchen and bathroom—you won't have to spend so much time scrubbing later. In the bathroom, make everyone in the family take an extra couple of minutes to clean out the tub as they get out. Keep a cleaning sponge and some cleanser handy. As the water runs out, add cleanser and clean sides of the tub. Run some clean water to rinse and do the bottom, and the tub will always be clean. Keep a roll of paper towels mounted in the bathroom (you can use a decorative holder) so that people can wipe the mirror when it is steamed up, or clean up extra water and wipe around the sink.

In the kitchen, clean up as you cook, and put the pans into a sink of hot soapy water to soak before you sit down to eat. You'll save time scrubbing after dinner. If you spill something in the refrigerator or on the floor, take four minutes right then to clean it. Once it has time to set, it could take forty minutes to scrape off. Clean now, and you won't have to scrub later.

Pick up every day. Make it a habit to give the house a quick pickup every day. Getting rid of the clutter will make you think it is cleaner than it really is, and there are always a few minutes here and there to straighten the living room or the bedroom. Make sure the family picks up their stuff as well. Children need to gather toys and papers and put them away in their room. Everyone needs to pick up dropped clothing and either put the clothes away or in the laundry hampers (an attractive hamper in each bedroom can be very helpful here).

Hire someone else to do at least some of the housework for you. Between cleaning, laundry, ironing and cleaning the kitchen, it is easy to spend, say, twelve hours per week on housework. By the end of the year, that adds up to 624 unrewarding hours, which comes to about twenty-six days total, or nearly a *month* every year devoted to housework. If you think you can't afford that, look around for creative ideas. Press a cash-starved teen into service, or see if you have a neighbor who is looking for a bit of extra money but can't work outside the home because she has small children. Drop your laundry off at the Laundromat. Get rid of as much of the housework as you can. You won't miss it a bit.

Don't clean anything that isn't dirty. It will get dirty soon enough. Then you can clean it.

Keep like items near their point of use. Keep pots and pans, pot holders, spices, and large cooking utensils near the stove. Knives should be near the cutting board, cups by the coffee pot, dish towels near the sink, and so forth. You'll save many steps, and make cooking as well as cleaning much easier every day.

Replace broken appliances. If it doesn't work, either get it fixed or get rid of it. A blender that is on the fritz is of no use. It only takes up counter space and wastes your time, because now that it's broken you have to do things by hand.

Plan the menu every week. Once a week, sit down and plan the menu for the next week. This works well for someone cooking for a big family as well as for a single person who is on a diet. Then do all of your grocery shopping in one visit—preferably during slow supermarket hours (early in the morning or late at night are always good; the stores are nearly deserted then). Make sure you take a list of needed items with you and stick to your list so that you won't have to make last-minute runs to the market during the week for things you forgot.

Replace things before you run out of them. Keep a pad of paper and a pencil in the kitchen and jot down items you need when you see you are *running out* of the item. Don't wait until you are *totally out* to make a note of it. By that time, it's too late, and you're off to the store on yet another emergency time-wasting trip for only one item.

Have things delivered. Have whatever you can delivered. If the store doesn't offer delivery, find a service, even if it's only the kid next door who can pick things up for you.

Buy ready-made foods. Although it costs a bit more, you can save significant chunks of time in the kitchen by purchasing prepared items at the grocery store. Bags of precut and washed lettuce and vegetables, for example, can make salad preparation a five-minute, rather than a fifteen-minute affair. Chicken that has been precut for stir-fry can mean the difference between thirty to forty minutes spent deboning and chopping and less than one minute tossing the already cut chicken pieces into the skillet. You may spend a couple of dollars more but isn't an hour of your time worth more than two dollars?

Prepare foods in advance. When you shop, as soon as you bring the food home, do some of the prep work *before* you put it away. Clean all the vegetables, and cut and slice some of them and put them in sealed food-storage bags. Then it's easy to throw them into a salad or stir-fry without having to chop everything first. This is also a must for people on a diet. Having nutritious foods ready to grab and snack on can keep you on the diet much longer than if you are faced with fifteen minutes of cleaning and chopping vegetables versus a candy bar.

Traditional meal preparation time—late afternoon or early evening—is usually the most hectic time of day, so the more you can do in advance for dinner, the better. Crock-Pot meals, spaghetti sauce prepared and frozen, and other foods made in advance can make a difference in your energy and temperament at the end of the day, not to mention the time you can have for yourself. You may want to take one or two days a month to shop in bulk and prepare and freeze meals for the next week or two. You can make it a family affair. One person can do all the shopping, another does the washing and chopping, and another cooks and freezes the food. Everyone helps clean up the mess. The result is freezer-to-table home-cooked meals that will make it possible for you to *enjoy* that part of the day rather than dread it.

Use a Crock-Pot. You can put a meal in the pot in the morning before you leave for work, and your dinner will be waiting for you when you come home.

Make two things at once. If you're cooking or baking, double up and freeze one portion to eat later. It's just as easy to cook two meat loaves as one, and it's not extra work to make a double batch of spaghetti sauce. Freeze the second portion, and it will give you an evening when all you need to do for the main dish is to thaw it and heat it up.

Make your own TV dinners. You can make up several portions of, say chicken, and three vegetables and divide the food into divided food trays. Wrap them or cover with a lid and freeze. When you need a meal in a hurry, pull out a tray and heat it in the microwave.

Delegate and rotate K.P. If you have a family, delegate kitchen patrol, and rotate the duty according to schedules and ability. Dad can certainly cook one night each week (minimum), and the kids can help out with everything from setting and clearing the table to washing the pots and loading and unloading the dishwasher. Older kids can help cook as well, by making the salad, or coming up with a simple dessert.

Order in or eat out. Try to make it a regular habit (say, twice a month, for example) to order in or eat out. Even fast food can be nutritious. You can get a salad at a drive-through burger stand, and put your own dressing on it, and you can order beans as the side dish to go with the take-out chicken (rather than the fried potatoes, for example). Pizza, Chinese food and ribs are all quick things that can be picked up already prepared and served on paper plates. Every time you do this you will save yourself at least one to two hours in the kitchen cooking and cleaning. At a savings of two hours, if you only do it twice a month, by the end of the year you will have saved almost *two full days* in the kitchen cooking and cleaning!

16 Shopping Time-Savers

Buying does stimulate our emotions and to strike a happy balance
between mind and desire takes discipline, determination, and a plan.
— Judith Keith

Shopping is one task that must be done on a regular basis whether there's time for it or not. Some shopping can be eliminated altogether with proper planning, but you'll still have to go to the grocery store regularly and make periodic forays to shops and department stores for gifts, new clothes for work or special occasions, school clothes and supplies for the children, and household goods. Streamlining how you approach your shopping can give you more time to do what you really want to do. Use these shopping tips to save time.

Always shop with a list. Keep a grocery list in the kitchen and note items that you need before you run out. You'll always be fully stocked, and you won't have to waste time running to the store at the last minute. At the store, the list will help you focus so you don't buy things you don't need. Use lists for other shopping needs as well, from gifts to clothes. When you shop take the list; if it's not on the list, don't buy it!

Shop during off hours. Take advantage of off hours, if you can, at restaurants, banks, department stores, the supermarket and the post office. You'll spend less time waiting in line, and receive better service. Avoid shopping when everyone else does (noon, after work and weekends) if at all possible, and you'll save yourself lots of shopping aggravation along with the time. If you go to the supermarket on Saturday night after 8:00 P.M. instead of Saturday afternoon, you'll probably get done in half the time.

Shop at organized stores. Shop only in stores that are organized and make sense to you. Otherwise you'll waste time wandering around trying to find things.

Limit comparison shopping. Don't allow yourself to be consumed by cost-comparison shopping. Before you set out, gather information from ads and consumer reports along with recommendations from friends. Call ahead to confirm the item's availability and price, and then limit your comparison shopping to three or four choices. Otherwise you can spend unlimited amounts of time comparing prices and quality. In the end you might get the best deal, but you will have spent untold hours of your time to get it. After all, if you spend a total of only three Saturdays and two evenings comparison shopping for a particular item (such as a washing machine, for example), you will have lost approximately thirty hours to the effort. That's more than one day of your life—gone. Is the extra few bucks' savings worth it?

Buy in bulk. Shop for certain clothing staples only once or twice a year, and then buy plenty so that you don't have to shop for those items again for quite some time. Buy two or three dozen pairs of nylons or socks, for example, in January at sale time, and you won't have to think about buying those items again for quite some time.

Consolidate your shopping trips. Don't waste time making several trips when one will do. If you're going to be on the south side of town, figure out what needs to be done in that part of town and get it all done at once. Try to organize your list so that when you set out to buy the items you can pick up several in one area or store. For example, maybe you can get all of the toys at one time at one toy store. Perhaps all jewelry items can be purchased at another, and all clothing at still another store. There's no need to waste time going from one store to another, and then back again to the first store, just because you didn't think ahead to organize the list so that you could consolidate the trips made for shopping purposes.

Keep a spare car key. Always carry an extra car and house key in your wallet. The next time you lock yourself out with your keys inside the house or car, you'll be able to solve the problem immediately. This can make or break your day, as a woman I know named Ann can testify. She once locked her dog and toddler in the car (the toddler was securely strapped into the child car seat) while she dashed into a convenience store to pick up a quart of milk. When she returned, she discovered she had locked keys, kid and dog inside the car. The dog went wild, woofing himself silly, and the child alternately grinned, cried, and slept through the ordeal that followed while Ann desperately spent the next hour and a half rounding up a locksmith who could get her back into her car. Time was of the essence since, among other frustrations, Ann had left the motor running. While you're putting an extra key in your wallet, you might want to also consider leaving a spare set with a trusted neighbor for extra security as well.

Eliminate unnecessary returns. If you need to shop for a garment to go with something you already have, take the item with you or wear it when you go shopping. This way, you won't make a mistake with your purchase and have to spend time returning it and looking all over again for what you need.

Don't buy things that are too complicated. Don't buy anything that has assembly or operational instructions that you can't understand. It will take twice as long to figure it all out, and chances are you'll be mad enough to spit nails by the time you make sense of it as well.

Don't buy things you have to assemble. Unless you have a real aptitude for assembly and don't mind doing it, it can be worth it to pay the extra money to have the item assembled and delivered. The words, "simple assembly required" are very misleading. The assembly is almost never truly simple, and it definitely takes up time that you could be using to do something else.

Buy gifts throughout the year. When you are shopping for yourself, you can pick up a gift as well. If you have children, keep children's gifts on hand for those invitations to parties that come up through the year for the kids (always at the last minute, it seems). You can also keep some generic gifts on hand (such as something to take when invited to dinner) so that all you have to do is grab the gift and go. By buying gifts throughout the year, you'll either have what you need (in advance) when you need it, or you'll be way ahead of the shopping game when holiday time rolls around. And you will have done it without taking the time to make a special trip out to shop for gifts.

Shop by phone. Shop with catalogs and order by phone. You can get a lot of shopping done in a fraction of the time it would take if you went out shopping personally. This timesaving shopping tip is especially helpful at holiday time.

Stock up on greeting cards. Make one trip to the card shop and lay in a supply of a variety of greeting cards including thank-you cards, birthday cards, anniversary cards, sympathy cards, and love and other types of cards. Then when you have to send a card (usually at the last minute, because you forgot all about the occasion), you won't have to drop everything and take the time to run out and find a card.

Hire an errand service. Personalized errand services can do everything for you, from picking up your cleaning to purchasing gifts and doing your grocery shopping. If you don't have time to do it yourself, hire someone. There are much better ways to spend your time than doing errands.

Use a personal shopper. Many shops and department stores have personal shoppers who will help you shop by obtaining the information from you on your preferences and then putting things together for you to look at. They will also call you when new things that they think would suit you come into the store. And you can call your personal shopper and ask them to recommend and select a gift that you need to purchase. They'll make their recommendation, put the purchase on your credit card, wrap it and mail it for you. The only time you have to spend is the times it takes to make the phone call.

Don't waste your time shopping for things you don't need. Period.

22 Holiday Time-Savers

If ever there was a time for planning, writing things down, making lists, and accepting our limitations, this is it.

—Bonnie Runyan McCullough

Before you can experience the joy of the winter holidays, chances are you will run yourself ragged trying to do what needs to be done to make the holidays happen according to tradition. You can streamline how you spend your time during this stressful time, and have enough time left over for yourself so you can sit back and enjoy the season yourself.

Set a shopping deadline, and start early. Plan to complete your shopping early so you can get it all done before the last-minute rush of shoppers. You'll get it done in half the time it would have taken had you waited until the last minute.

Use a list. Think your gift list through, and write down exactly what you intend to buy. Then consolidate shopping trips so that you pick up as many in one trip as possible (get all the clothes when you go to the mall, and all the toys when you go to the toy store outlet). Deciding in advance and sticking to your list saves time you would have wasted wandering aimlessly up and down department store aisles looking for a perfect gift or two to jump out and grab you.

Shop by phone at home. Use your credit cards and shop by catalog or order by phone, and avoid the time it takes to fight the crowds altogether. You can order all kinds of things over the phone—from concert tickets to gift certificates, toys, clothes, furnishings, electronics, jewelry, food, and any other type of gift item you can think of.

Give money as a gift. While it used to be considered gauche, today, sometimes money is the best gift of all. Children, teenagers and newlyweds in particular like money. The best part is, if you give money, you won't have to spend any time at all shopping.

Use personal shopping services. Shop at department stores with personal shopping services; they will preselect gifts for you, saving you lots of time searching in different departments. Or shop at small stores where the personal attention and service can cut your shopping time significantly.

Wrap gifts as you go. Don't wait until the last minute to wrap gifts; do it as you buy them. You can set up a wrapping table at home with all of the supplies neatly laid out so that you can wrap the gift as soon as you pull it out of the bag. Better yet, have the store wrap the package. If you don't like to wait in the gift wrap area, buy two gifts, drop them off for wrapping, and continue shopping or stop for a snack. When you're finished, your packages should be ready. If you've purchased another gift or two, take them home to wrap, along with your already wrapped gift.

Keep some gourmet food specialties on hand for last-minute gifts. Gourmet specialties or foods from a special bakery make excellent gifts and don't require a lot of shopping time. If you keep some small gourmet food treats on hand (special jellies, teas or nuts, for instance), you can take them as last-minute hostess gifts when you go to parties, or give them as gifts if someone drops by and unexpectedly gives you a gift.

Cut your shopping list by drawing names. Why not ask family members or people at the office to draw names and buy only one or two gifts this year? It will save you time and money, and will make things easier on everybody else too.

Reverse tradition altogether if you need to. The tradition of buying gifts may be one that you can't keep up with for financial or other reasons. If so, this holiday, try to reverse tradition by not giving into the pressure to purchase so many things. Tell others of your pared down gift list, and ask them not to buy for you either. You'll save all kinds of financial worry and shopping time, and chances are others will be relieved to be able to cross you off their list as well.

Order gifts shipped. To simplify the gift-giving process for friends and family who live out of the area, buy the gifts from a catalog or from a store that will handle the wrapping and shipping of the gift. All you have to do is pick the item and pay for it; you won't have to spend time wrapping it and standing in line at the post office. Take your address book with you so you can provide the necessary information to store personnel.

Wait a few days before you return gifts. If you need to return a gift that you received, first check to see if it is something the store will have on hand after the first of the year, and if so, wait until then to exchange the item. Resist the temptation to return or exchange items the day after Christmas, which is one of the department stores' busiest and most crowded days of the year.

Address a few cards each day. Cut your card list by at least 20 percent this year; if you still are faced with sending out a lot of cards at holiday time, but never have the time to get them out, spend twenty minutes every day on the project, and before you know it, they'll be in the mail. Or, you can pay a senior citizen to do the addressing for you (they usually have terrific penmanship and a little extra time on their hands). If you don't have a relative who would like to do it, check with your church group or local senior citizen or community center to find someone to do your cards.

Order stamps by mail. You'll save yourself the agony of spending your time in a long line at the post office.

Delegate holiday chores to family members. Make the entire family pitch in to help with the holiday chores (nearly everyone can do something). You can assign three or more chores to each family member, which adds up to three less things per family member that you have to do.

Hire others. If you can, hire others to do some of the work of the holidays. You can pay others to run errands, shop, and cater your parties or holiday meals. You can pick up baked goods and holiday platters, saving yourself hours of prep time. And you can hire people to clean—both before guests arrive, and after the holiday festivities. Look for teenagers, senior citizens, caterers, specialty shops and personal service firms. If you can afford it, do it. Your time is better spent doing the other things that make the holidays special for your family and friends (such as spending joyful time with them).

Reconsider what and how you host. Rather than spending days getting ready for a major dinner at your house, you might want to host a brunch, open house or a dessert and tea get-together. Those types of events are very nice, and are less expensive and time-consuming than an all-out dinner. If you must have a major holiday meal at your house, consider starting a pot-luck tradition. When guests offer to bring something, let them! And if they don't offer, ask them to bring something, letting them know how wonderful you know it would be—coming from them and all. Most people are flattered and will happily contribute.

Accept offers of help. When dinner guests come into the kitchen to help with the cleanup, don't turn them down. The cleanup will get done in half the time, and the kitchen is usually the best place in the house for people to congregate and talk while the work—whether it's food preparation or after-dinner cleanup—is being done.

Resist the urge to overcommit yourself. You don't have to say yes to every party invitation or request for holiday help that comes your way. Nor do you have to spend all of your free time shopping and cooking for others. Start the holiday season out by making a list of what is important to you; then see to nurturing that list, and politely decline everything else.

Leave town. If you don't want to get caught up in a lot of time-consuming activities this year, give yourself a trip out of town for Christmas. Then spend all of your holiday time relaxing and enjoying yourself.

Use the holiday time to spend your time where it counts. The period between Christmas and the New Year is a good time to call and visit friends and relatives that you haven't had time to see or talk to during the year. Many people have extra time off from work during this time, so it's a good time to take in a movie with someone, make a few calls to friends that you have started to lose touch with, and to take some time to sit down and send out your personal thoughts and thank-yous to the people who mean the most to you.

Take time to reflect on the meaning of the holidays. If you find yourself getting caught up in the holiday rat race in spite of yourself, take a few minutes each day during the season to reflect on the true joys and meaning of the holiday season. Often that is enough to get you back on track so that you can stop spinning your wheels and make the time you spend on the holidays a time of peace and joy.

Don't forget to make your New Year's resolution. Vow to find more time for yourself every day, so that you really can do what you want to do and make the most of the rest of your life.

Congratulations . . .

Now that you have finished this book, your success in finding more time for yourself should be obvious. Take that extra time and revel in it. If you occasionally find yourself slipping back into old time-consuming ways from time to time, don't worry. Simply review your Seven-Step Plan and get back on track as soon as possible. Today is the first day of the rest of your life. Have a good one.

ABOUT THE AUTHOR

Stephanie Culp is the owner of the productivity consulting firm The Organization. She is also a national speaker and trainer who specializes in topics that help people and businesses get organized, save time and manage paper more effectively. For more information, contact:

Stephanie Culp
The Organization
P.O. Box 108
Oconomowoc, WI 53066

(414) 567-9035
Fax: (414) 567-0736

INDEX

A

Addresses, 51
Alarm clock, 55
Answering machines, 112, 170
Appointments
  maintenance, 54
  making and keeping, 63-65
  and reducing waiting time, 66

B

Bad habits
  changing, 3-4, 50
  excuses for, 2-3
  and paper pile-up, 145-146
  in scheduling, others', 58-59
Balance
  in life, 16-18, 41
  in scheduling, 56-61
Bathroom scheduling, 55
Bill paying, 54

C

Calendar
  for special events, 58
  types of, 50
  using a, 51-54
Children
  interruptions by, 114-115
  and morning organization, 55
  spending time with, 17, 59-60
Clutter, conquering, 133-144
  eight-weekend plan for, 140-141
  guidelines for, 137-139
  and letting go of, 138
  and passing down to heirs, 143-144
  tips for, 137-139
  where to start, 136-137
Commuting time-savers, 181-183
Computers, 162-167
  as time-savers, 162-163
  as time-wasters, 163-165
Conquering the Paper Pile-Up, 131
Correspondence, 161
Crisis management, 61-63

D

Deadlines, setting, 53
Deciding what you want, 21-30
Decision-making, 84-86
Delegating, 90-102
  and scheduling, 57
  where to find help in, 102
  vs. working too much, 125
Desk, organizing, 154-158

Dictating machines, 169-170
Disorganization, 125, 126
Doing too much, 57-58

E

Early risers benefit, 56
Effective Executive, The, 41, 116
Efficiency vs. effectiveness, 41
Electronic mail, 166-167
Electronic organizers, 168-169
Electronic technology as time saver/waster,
  162-172
Energy level, 53
Errands, 46, 200

F

Family
  balancing time with, 17
  planning calendar for, 52
  prioritizing relationships with, 34-35
  quality time with, 59-60
Fax machines, 168
Filing
  in conquering clutter, 141
  in controlling paper, 159-160
  paper sorting and, 151-153
Filing systems, 152-153
Finding more time
  and balancing life, 16-18
  in bits and pieces, 173-205
  for family, 17, 35, 59-60
  for friends, 17
  obstacles to, 43
  plan for, 9
  seven steps to, 6-7
  for spiritual life, 17
  See also Time; Time-savers; Time-
    wasters
Friends
  finding time for, 17
  prioritizing relationships with, 34-35
  reevaluating, 34-35
  selecting, 35

G

Goals
  achieving, plan for, 25-28
  long-range, scheduling, 53
  mission statement and, 22
  setting, 24-25
  short-range segments for, 53
Grocery shopping, 54

H

Happenings, 39-40
Health and fitness, time for, 17
Holiday time-savers, 201-204
Home
  and balanced lifestyle, 17
  paperwork, 57, 141
Household
  chore list, 100-102
  paperwork, organizing, 141
Housework
  delegating, 98-102
  finding help for, 102
  household chore list for, 100-102
  and morning organization, 55
  schedule, 57
  time-savers, 193-198
How to Conquer Clutter, 131
*How to Get Control of Your Time and Your
  Life*, 74

I

Indecision, 84-86
  and working too much, 126
Insecurity and doing too much, 57
Interruptions
  eliminating, 103-115
  and interruption circle, 114
  and telephone screening, 109
  as time-wasters, 53
Invitations to social functions, 38, 54

K

Keys, 56, 99
Kids' gear, organizing, for morning, 55
Kitchen time-savers, 193-198

L

Laundry, scheduling, 54, 57
Letters, writing, 160
Lifestyle, balanced, 16-18
  changes for, 16-18
  planning for, 41
  scheduling for, 56-61
  six key areas in, 17-18

M

Mail, 161
Maintenance appointments, 54
Management crisis, 61-63
  See also Scheduling
Managing schedule. *See* Scheduling
Meetings
  arranging, 118-121
  attending, 121-124

  going out for, 123
  making most of, 118-124
  purpose of, 116-117
  useless, 117-118
Memos
  posting, 161
  writing, 160
Mission statement, 22-24
Morning
  as best time for work, 53
  organizing, 54-56

N

Need to achieve, 57
No, saying,
  in prioritizing, 35-39
  specific ways of, 37-39
  vs. doing too much, 57
Notepad for calendar/planner, 51-52

O

Obligations and prioritizing, 32
Office equipment and supplies, 156-157
Office furniture, 157-158
Organizing
  clutter, 136-144
  desk, 154-158
  morning, 54-56
  paper pile-up, 145-161
  projects, 45-49
  to-do list, 48-49
  unfinished business, 43-44

P

Paper
  clutter, 141
  controlling, 158-160
  dumping, 154
  filing, 141, 151-153
  four-step sorting of, 149-153
  letting go of, 155
  organizing, 148-158
  personalities, 146-147
  reading and keeping up with, 150-151
  streamlining, 160-161
  valuable, 161
Paper pile-up, 145-161
Paperwork
  organizing household, 141
  scheduling home, 57
Peak Performers, 22
Perfectionism, 80-83
  and doing too much, 58
  as habit of workaholic, 127

and working too much, 125
Plan for finding more time, 9-68
 seven-step, 6-7
Planner book, using, 51-54
Planning, 31-41
 in advance, 50
 calendar for, 51-52
 efficient, vs. effective, 41
 planner book for, 51-54
 projects for unfinished business, 47-49
 secrets of successful, 40-41
 techniques, 40-41
 vs. working too much, 126
 See also Scheduling
Pressure, working best under, 58, 62
Priorities
 clarifying, 34
 energy level and, 53
 establishing, 31-34
 and relationships, 34-35
 techniques for deciding, 32-34
Prioritizing, 31-41
 and ability to say no, 35-39
 assessing skill for, 32
 efficient, vs. effective, 41
 relationships, 34-35
 techniques for, 32-34
 vs. working too much, 126
 See also Planning; Scheduling
Procrastination, 71-79
 escapes, 74
 forms of, 71-72
 overcoming, 75-79
 and paper pile-up, 159
 price of, 78
 reasons for, 73
 and working too much, 125-126
Profession/career time, changing, 17
Projects
 long, deadlines for, 53
 organizing, 45-49
 planning, 47-49
 scheduling important, 53
 for unfinished business, 43-49
Purpose in life, 21-30
 mission statement of, 22-24

R

Reading
 and controlling paper, 158
 eliminating clutter and, 141
 keeping up with, 150-151
 and paper sorting system, 151

Relationships
 prioritizing, 34-35
 selecting, 35
Reports, writing, 160
Romance
 finding time for, 60-61

S

Saying no
 vs. doing too much, 57
 specific ways of, 37-39
 as tool in prioritizing, 35-39
Scheduling
 appointments, 63-65
 balance in, 56-61
 calendar, 51-54
 catch-up day, 57
 and coping with day that gets away,
  65-68
 and crisis management, 61-63
 day off, 67-68
 and doing too much, 57-58
 and early rising, 56
 expectations, adjusting, 58-59
 housework, 57
 and morning organization, 54-56
 in off-peak hours, 54
 paperwork at home, 57
 planner, 51-54
 and planning in advance, 50
 quality time with family, 59-60
 and reducing waiting time, 66
 romance, time for, 60-61
 special situations, 58-59
 time for yourself, 56
Self-development, time for, 17
Shopping
 grocery, 54
 holiday, 201, 202
 by phone, 176, 200, 201
 time-savers, 198-200
Social events
 calendar for, 54
 invitations to, 38
Spiritual time, 17

T

Tax records
 and calendar, 52
 and eliminating clutter, 141
Telecommuting, 183
Telephone
 answering machine, 108, 112, 170
 conference calls, 123, 170

grouping calls by, 46
interruptions, 108-113
messages, 108, 111-112
numbers, 51, 64, 111, 112
returning, calls 53-54
screening, 108, 109
shopping by, 176, 200, 201
time-savers, 175-178, 200, 201
voice mail, 108, 111, 112, 170
Telephone equipment, 170-172
answering machine, 108, 112, 170
downside of, 171-172
for home-based business, 112
voice mail, 108, 111, 112, 170
Telephone solicitors, 112-113
Television
time-savers, 178-180
as time-waster, 53
Time
analyzing value of, 16-18
best, to get things done, 53
cost of clutter, 135-136
estimating, 53, 57
excuses for not having, 2-3
reasons for not having enough, 1-2
spending, changing habits of, 3-4
underestimating, for projects, 53
value of, 11-19
worth per hour, 15-16
See also Finding more time; Time-savers;
    Time-Wasters
Time log, 13-15, 16-18
Time Trap, The, 11, 57-58, 95, 169
Time Worp, 750 of the World's Greatest
    Time Saving Ideas, 160
Time-savers:
electronic technology, 162-172
holiday, 201-204
housework and kitchen, 193-198
shopping, 198-200, 201, 202
telephone, 170-172, 175-178
television, 178-180

travel, 184-192
Time-wasters:
clutter, 133, 135-136
electronic technology, 162-172
interruptions, 53
television, 53
time log and, 14-15
To-do list
master, 43-44
organizing, 48-49
projects for, 45-47
Travel
itinerary, 58
for meetings, 123,
plans, 58
time-savers, 184-192

U
Unfinished business
master list, 43-44
turning, into projects, 45-49

V
Value of time, 11-18
dollar, 12-13
Visitors, drop-in, 105-108
Voice mail, 11, 112, 170
Volunteer work, 36, 57

W
Workaholic, 126-127
overcoming tendencies of, 128-129
reasons for being a, 127-128
time-wasting habits of, 126-127
Working
under pressure, 58, 62
procedures, improving, 128-129
too much, reasons for, 125-126
wisely, 125-129
workaholics and, 126-129
Working Smart, 78-79, 89

Y
Yard work, scheduling, 57